Living with Magic

DAVID FARREN

Simon and Schuster : New York

PUBLISHED BY SIMON AND SCHUSTER
ROCKEFELLER CENTER, 630 FIFTH AVENUE
NEW YORK, NEW YORK 10020

DESIGNED BY IRVING PERKINS
MANUFACTURED IN THE UNITED STATES OF AMERICA
BY THE BOOK PRESS, BRATTLEBORO, VT.

1   2   3   4   5   6   7   8   9   10

LIBRARY OF CONGRESS CATALOGING IN PUBLICATION DATA

FARREN, DAVID.
    LIVING WITH MAGIC.

    BIBLIOGRAPHY: P. 299
    1. MAGIC.   2. WITCHCRAFT.   I. TITLE.
BF1611.F29   133.4   74-4359
ISBN 0-671-21805-0

For Terri and for Michael,
and for all the other children
   who have not yet forgotten what it means
to live with magic

Contents

8 : Contents

Preface

LET ME BEGIN by saying that I take magic quite seriously even though everything in my temperament and training argues against it. When I met the woman I call Tanya, who later became my wife, I was an ex-Jesuit seminarian who had spent four years teaching philosophy at a community college in Southern California. I did not think then that a golden-eyed girl half my age would be able to shake my confidence in an entirely rational approach to the world, much less remake my life. Yet this is just what happened.

Tanya, in common with many other persons of her age, called herself a witch and claimed that witchcraft was a family tradition reaching back more than a dozen generations. Only gradually did I come to take seriously the possibility that this self-definition involved quite genuine capabilities for paranormal phenomena. I had already developed a strictly intellectual interest in the background of the group of Victorian magicians who called themselves the Hermetic Order of the Golden Dawn, and I was curious about the connection between this unusual fraternity and the lore represented by Tanya and her family. I continued my research, but at the same time I found myself being drawn through Tanya into a set of experiences that could not be explained through any of the physical or psychological categories I held after my final break with the supernatural outlook of my Catholic past.

This book is the story of my efforts to come to grips with magic as a fact. I have included in it both historical scholarship and personal experience with the hope that the one illumines the other. An ambitious reader is able, if he chooses, to re-create the scholarship by consulting the materials listed in my bibliography, but he will simply have to take my word that the stories I have to tell about my own or others' encounters with the world of magic are either true or definitely believed to be so by the teller. I would, however, strongly advise against the reader's attempting to duplicate such experiences without proper guidance. Sorcery, as I will explain, is not to be approached on a do-it-yourself basis.

Living with Magic

1.

Beyond Revolution

In the spring of 1970 most of us caught up in what we called the "Movement" expected the campuses to become more rather than less explosive. I was then teaching at a community college near Los Angeles, and I had a somewhat overblown reputation as a bearded, longhaired firebrand. The year before, I had worked with students organizing a chapter of the S.D.S., I had agreed to sponsor a local version of the Black Students' Union, and I had taken a group of students to San Francisco to participate in the November Moratorium. In addition I was speaking both on campus and on a local radio station about the idea of revolution that was then so much part of the rhetoric of protest.

None of this was particularly unusual or significant for the period when I compared it with the commitments of men like Daniel Berrigan, Benjamin Spock, or any of the other New Left heroes. Nor, given the prevailing calm on my own campus, was it even particularly risky. I mention my involvement only to show how unlikely I would have thought it then that two years later I would be married to a witch and writing not about politics but about the occult.

Ironically, it was my concern with politics that made me so curious when one of my students told me she was, as she put it, "into witchcraft." Allen Ginsberg, I knew, had led a horde of protesters in an attempt to levitate the Pentagon with a mantra during the 1968 demonstrations. In the confusion of the late 1960s the ancient lore of astrology, the tarot, and spell-casting seemed as much part of the scene dubbed "the counterculture" as were drugs, draft resistance, and student strikes. Was magic a cop-out on activism, or might it—or at least the belief in it—be one of the most potent weapons "we" had in the assault on "the system." I felt I had to know, and Tanya, my witch student, might hold part of the answer.

Tanya in her turn was becoming involved in politics in the wake of Cambodia and Kent State. Her father, a conservative Republican businessman, disapproved; and my first meeting with Tanya's mother came about in an effort to reduce the family tensions. Over cocktails we talked about demonstrations—and about spells. I had, at Tanya's urging, decided against bringing up the topic of witchcraft, but her mother mentioned it within a few minutes of our first meeting. Later Tanya told me that this was unprecedented; her mother, she explained, was from a generation in which any talk of the occult was kept strictly within the family. I was the first outsider to whom she had ever acknowledged her own practice of witchcraft.

There were many of my college students who, like Tanya, were not at all reticent about their involvement in the world of magic. Most of this dated from 1968, the year when the fallout from the Haight-Ashbury was settling over the entire country. During the summer Louise Huebner, who for the occasion had been ceremonially designated "Official Witch of Los Angeles" by the County Board of Supervisors, appeared in the Hollywood Bowl leading a throng of Angelenos in a ritual incantation to increase the sexual vitality of their city. And in the bookstores one could find stacks of Sybil Leek's *Diary of a Witch*, an autobiography in which a lady already well known from her appearances on radio and television candidly discussed what it meant to be a covenist in the twentieth century.

Louise Huebner and Sybil Leek were not the first to talk about witchcraft as a living tradition—they had been preceded by Gerald B. Gardner in the early 1950s—but they gained public attention shortly after the film *Rosemary's Baby* had sensitized millions of Americans to the possibility that a classical devil worship just might have survived into the age of nuclear technology. For those who saw Mia Farrow "bewitched" in the superbly produced version of Ira Levin's novel, there was also the suggestion, conveyed in one scene by having Miss Farrow pick up the issue of *Time* with the black and red cover questioning the death of God, that the "brave new world" of the late twentieth century *did* belong to the Prince of Darkness. This suggestion was strengthened for many by the fact that the actor who portrayed the Devil in the scene in which Rosemary is impregnated with his child was none other than Anton LaVey, a colorful promotionist who in 1966 had organized the First Church of Satan in San Francisco.

Both Mrs. Huebner and Mrs. Leek were emphatic that their idea of witchcraft was far removed from the lore of Black Masses and death-dealing covens. Theirs was the "Old Religion," and it was only through ecclesiastical hostility that their symbol for the power of nature, the Horned God of antiquity, was equated with the Satan of the Bible. Television might attempt to portray witches as impossible beings—the Samantha played by Elizabeth Montgomery or the Sabrina of the Saturday morning cartoon series—but witchcraft was quite real both as a religion and as a manipulation of the psychic capacities which all of us might have in a greater or a lesser degree.

For most of my would-be witches, I found, magic was primarily a matter of burning candles and reciting rhyming incantations (such as "Light the flame / bright the fire / red is the color / of desire") with the hope of making things happen through non-physical means. They did not regard their actions as worship of any kind, much less as a ritual worship of the Devil. The occult for them was a fun thing, a fanciful manner of escaping the overly mechanized world of the late twentieth century. They followed Sybil Leek and Louise Huebner only to a point.

Tanya, however, had told me that she represented a family tradition reaching back thirteen generations into the native Russia of her grandmother. After coming to the United States, both her grandmother and her Cuban-born mother had belonged to covens in Southern California, and she herself had once attended a coven in which Satan was most definitely and dramatically invoked. All of this argued an underground set of beliefs and practices much more impressive and possibly much more disturbing than the flower child rituals then being popularized in the national media.

In the fall of 1970 Tanya, who by now meant far more to me than just an interesting student, left my classes in order to continue her training in the theater arts department of another local college. At the time I was working on a book, never finished, in which I attempted to compare the "mystical" outlooks of the first Christians, the late Greek philosophers known as the Neoplatonists, and the nineteenth-century occultists who followed the path set by the French magus calling himself Eliphas Levi. All three, it seemed to me, represented variants of a state of mind that sought to escape the dilemmas of what the existentialist philosopher Merleau-Ponty has called the "vulgar immorality" of historical involvement. That did not mean, however, that mysticism might be entirely a cop-out, to use the overworked term of a late 1960s activism.

The young Catholic philosopher Michael Novak, whose work I greatly admired, had spoken at the Center for the Study of Democratic Institutions about the idea of "secular saints." The phrase came from the French existentialist Albert Camus, but in the years following the appearance of theologian Harvey Cox's controversial *The Secular City* it seemed to hold a new meaning. What, I asked myself, might be the value of a secular mysticism, a non-religious effort to transcend contemporary issues in order to find other directions for the self and society alike?

My activist sympathies were obvious in this manuscript, as was my distaste for the classical occultism of the Victorian magicians. Despite my feelings for Tanya, magic at that time still appeared to be nothing more than a peculiar manner of interpreting existence. I was willing to accept the phenomenon of ESP, unable as I was to explain it, but the lore of spells and incantations seemed entirely absurd except in so far as it involved the suggestibility of the sorcerer—or of his object.

Nevertheless, there were puzzling breaks in the flow of my rationalizations, some of which arose out of the close relationship that had developed between Tanya and a somewhat older woman whom I had also come to know through my classes. Pat in many respects resembled Tanya's mother, and there seemed to be a basis for a strong bond between the two even in the furnishings of Pat's home. A coffee table similar to one which Tanya recalled that as a little girl she used to polish for her grandmother stood in a corner of the living room. Examining it more closely, Tanya saw nicks along the edge which led her to think it was the same table, but that seemed impossible. Her grandmother, when asked about the table, could recall only that she had once put it in storage and then forgotten about it. Pat, we learned, had bought the table at an auction of unclaimed goods. As far as we knew, it was the same table, a link between one witch and another.

Pat, unlike Tanya, did not come from a family in which the idea of witchcraft was taken seriously, yet from childhood she had heard voices directing her to act in a manner which approximated the forms of a so-called low magic, the folk practices which make up most of the lore of witchcraft. She had never talked about these voices but felt that to have done so would have marked her as insane.

As an example of the directions she had been given, Pat showed us a black candle she had bought and mounted in a bottle given her by her fiancé. Originally, she said, she had been told to buy three such candles from an occult shop and place them in the window facing on the home of a woman she regarded as someone who threatened her interests. She had resisted completing the performance and had instead placed the candles on a shelf. The candles kept bending in the direction of the window until Pat had disposed of two of them and placed the stub of the third in the bottle—something she felt would ground its power.

As Tanya took the bottle in one hand and passed the other over the top of the unlit candle, she winced and told us that her hand had been burned by an unseen flame. It was, she explained, a candle made with the attar of the black narcissus, a flower regarded as particularly significant for some practitioners of a black or harmful magic. Pat had been directed, it would seem, to carry out an especially potent piece of witchcraft and at the last minute had held back.

The atmosphere in Pat's home seemed particularly oppressive that afternoon. We had gone from the two women discussing their experiences with what is called astral projection (the movement of the self outside the body) and my aura (the colored emanations said to encircle a person's head or body) to this talk of black narcissus candles. Shortly afterward we took out a Ouija board and Pat attempted to achieve contact with her mentor, the spirit that some occultists claim each of us has as a kind of other-worldly tutor. How much of all this, I wondered, was more than just coincidence, hysterical imagination, or wishful thinking? Were there powers at work here that lay outside the categories of completely natural phenomena? Tanya did not doubt it, Pat was now accepting it, and I was badly shaken in my skepticism.

Before this I had found little to go on that would be proof that witchcraft was for real. Once, in talking with Tanya about the boarding school she had attended in New Hampshire, I had formed a remarkably clear mental image of what she had looked like coming in from the snow one afternoon. In particular I thought I saw the type of material used in the plaid skirt she was wearing. Tanya, surprised, assured me that I was entirely correct in my description. At another time I had suggested that Tanya should have been called by a different name; later her mother confirmed to Tanya that she had originally planned on giving her just that name but had been dissuaded by Tanya's father. By this point both mother and daughter were willing to call me a warlock (a male witch) in my own right, but I was not yet sure of whether there was anything involved beyond a kind of ESP. Even this, however, was more than I had previously acknowledged as within my range of abilities.

There had been one other incident that went unexplained. At the Renaissance Faire, an annual event staged in the hills above Malibu, I had bought Tanya a copper amulet from a self-described warlock. She had been reluctant to accept it, but the merchant, who was operating a booth in the occult section of the fair, had been remarkably eager for me to obtain it for her. A few days later Tanya received a startling phone call from the man, who presumably could not have known her name or her unlisted phone number. She was invited to accept membership in his coven and was placed in trance when she refused. Her mother, sensing something was wrong, rushed to Tanya's room and broke the warlock's hold on her daughter.

Tanya buried the amulet that was her link to the man, yet the next morning her father awoke with it around his neck. Her mother, whom I accused of a bit of sleight of hand, laughed about what it took to convince nonbelievers. I was able to accept the reality of the phone call (ESP would explain that), but I did not believe that amulets could unbury themselves and find their own way around someone's neck. Nor did I believe that anyone, even a self-styled witch, would be able to get an object out of the ground without taking the steps to dig it up. Yet, skeptical as I remained, I discovered myself increasingly prepared to acknowledge that weird things like this could and did happen.

Since I was so ready to explain many of the events to which I was being exposed as results of the power of suggestion, it seemed time to take up a long-standing invitation from my father to examine the subject of hypnosis more carefully. Despite the fact that I knew him to be an experienced practitioner, I had never before felt the slightest desire to learn more about what could be done with a trance. Some of this lack of interest may have been the result of my Catholic education, but I think it owed mostly to an excessive concern with the rational, conscious side of the human mind. Hypnosis, like occultism, seemed to belong to a dream world with which I had very little patience.

Another student, one of Tanya's friends who similarly was "into witchcraft," agreed to act as my first subject, and Tanya herself was my second. I found that, with these two at least, inducing a hypnotic trance was surprisingly easy. They were able, for instance, to enter into scenes that I described for them. I could have them experience sensations for which there were no physical stimuli, just as I was able to turn off sensations for which such stimuli were present, and I was able to leave them with posthypnotic suggestions. None of this was especially dramatic, but at least I was convinced that the hypnotic state did occur and that it could be induced with little effort.

This increased knowledge quickly came in handy. I was at that time in the last months of a failing marriage, and Tanya's mother was uneasy about her daughter's interest in me, especially since Tanya seemed to be slighting her theater arts program in order to visit my campus. One day Tanya appeared at my office showing the signs of what I had come to recognize as posthypnotic suggestion, a direction placed in the mind which the subject feels compelled to follow without consciously understanding why. By placing her in trance I learned that through hypnosis her mother had directed Tanya to feel a certain amount of physical pain whenever she disobeyed the parental edict against visiting me. Since whatever is suggested through trance can typically be canceled out in the same manner, I removed the force of the suggestion. I could appreciate her mother's feelings, but I was unwilling to see this type of coercion utilized if I could prevent it.

The next time that I saw her Tanya seemed to be in pain again, but I held off on hypnotizing her. I did, however, chance to mention the word "coven," and Tanya fell spontaneously into a deep eyes-open state of trance. Surprised, I asked her where she saw herself and was told that she was inside a large room draped in purple, with mirrors placed so as to create infinite series of reflections. It was the setting that she had previously described of the one coven she had attended as the date of a young actor.

Asked what was happening, she responded with a bizarre story of being threatened with continuing illness unless she promised to add her witchly power to that of the other members of the group. The word "coven," pronounced when she was in pain, was the key for her to fall into a trance state. As she went on, I was told of how she at times had been stopped by coven members on the streets of Hollywood, where she had then been attending school while following out a career as a teenage actress and model, had her arm twisted, and the code word repeated in order to render her unable to resist a trip back to the house where the coven met. There, she said, she would be obscenely tortured and the threats renewed.

Did such things happen, or was I tapping some irrational fear dramatized within Tanya's unconscious? It hardly mattered if I could use my new-found skill to cancel out the effects of this suggestion, whatever its source. I did this, but I was beginning to grow concerned about the kind of underworld I might be challenging. If there was a coven like this, its members might decide to make me their next target. Wonderful.

I was already paranoid enough because of my radicalism; I
hardly needed *Rosemary's Baby* come to life. Witchcraft
might be real after all, but I was beginning to hope almost
frantically that it wasn't.

On Halloween, which in 1970 fell on a Saturday, I tempted
fate. Some time before, I had purchased but never played an
album of hymns to the Devil recorded by an offbeat rock
group. Since one of my neighbors had rigged up his stereo to
project spooky sounds out to the street, I reciprocated by putting on the album, Black Mass and all, while I took my daughter out for trick-or-treat. When I returned I found my wife
ashen; the house, she told me, had begun to fill with smoke as
the record played. She had been unable to get the controls of
the phonograph to respond when she attempted to turn it off,
and the music had stopped only when she forced the record off
the turntable.

I stared at the album and at the now smoke-free house.
Only a little earlier Tanya had called to wish me a happy
Halloween—and to mention that her mother was levitating
past her bedroom window. Tanya, I still felt, might have an
overactive imagination, but my wife was one of the calmest,
most prosaic persons I knew. If *she* was experiencing these
weird things also . . .

My turn came two nights later. I had an evening class and
returned late to discover in my darkened living room a brood-
ing presence that sent chills up my back. My wife and daughter were already asleep, and I decided it was time to confront
this force on my own. I lit a white candle, curled up cross-
legged on the couch, and softly bade the presence to return to
its source. Then it was gone.

The next morning my wife told me that throughout the
day she had been aware of someone following her as she

moved through the house. She had also been awakened in the early hours of the morning by a woman's voice that had seemed to be chanting in the living room.

Tanya agreed that what we had experienced could have been a psychic attack originating with her mother. If Tanya was no longer following the hypnotic suggestion not to see me, then perhaps stronger measures were being taken. Still, I had responded appropriately in this psychic contest and perhaps now I would not be bothered by future assaults. I was proving myself a fairly adequate warlock after all.

Things did ease. By now I was taking magic very seriously. I was beginning to talk more about witchcraft in my college classes, and I was finding that many of my students already had a great amount of background knowledge. Most had been caught up only in the generally frivolous magic of the counter-culture, but a few had experimented with darker practices, and a few came from families that, like Tanya's, preserved the lore of European folk magic. Without ever intending it, I was being drawn more and more into the world of magic.

My first marriage, long strained by my changing outlooks, ended early in 1971. Tanya, whom I had come to love deeply, became my wife, and our first child was born the next year. Any conflict with Tanya's mother had long since ended; her own wedding present to Tanya was to complete her ritual initiation as an adult witch. Over the phone she laughingly described it as a "White Mass." Tanya, who observes the ritual injunctions not to speak of the more esoteric ceremonials of witchcraft, commented only that her mother's improvisation included the gleeful smashing of a modest amount of crockery.

I should explain at this point that marriage to a witch does not change my status as an outsider for those who maintain a traditional witchcraft. To call someone a witch is to state something about his or her psychic capabilities, but it may also indicate ritual inclusion in a confraternity of practitioners. Tanya, who has otherwise held herself aloof from the contemporary coven tradition, has respected the rule by which certain types of knowledge are to be passed on only to another initiate —or to one's child if that child appears to possess the characteristics of someone born to magic. The lore which she learned through her family, primarily through her grandmother, and from a summer spent visiting the Gypsies of England's New Forest area, the location of the dancing school where she spent several years of her childhood, remains her own secret.

Despite Tanya's silence, I still found myself continually learning about a tradition whose roots, if some enthusiasts were correct, went back to the Stone Age. We had a number of friends who were deeply involved in the world of magic, and I also discovered that my father's career had anticipated my own. He too had remarried a woman who was the daughter of a witch, a man known as a rainmaker from the wild country of northern Italy.

In years past my father had visited a number of covens ranging from solemn groups professing the "Old Religion" to meetings which were little better than pretentious excuses for orgies. He had also spent a dozen years of study with the Rosicrucian Fellowship, an organization headquartered in San Jose which some have unkindly depicted as specializing in "mail order mysticism." There was, however, one principal difference in our attitudes toward the occult. My father remained the perpetual candidate for enlightenment, while my concern was with making some kind of sense of an extraordinarily challenging historical and scientific puzzle.

Most occultists, I soon learned, were, like my father, more than willing to accept the existence of a secret knowledge passed on through countless generations by means of one or another elusive fraternity. The Theosophical Society of Madame Blavatsky, for instance, claimed to be guided by the Mahatmas, enlightened beings who had preserved the secrets of the lost continent of Atlantis. The Rosicrucians, who had included my father in their number, similarly claimed to be the heirs of a teaching as old as the Pyramids. The writer Idries Shah in the same way has popularized the concept of the Sufis, the members of various Islamic mystical sects, as adepts possessing a truth far older than the historical movement begun by Muhammad. The witches who routinely stressed the neolithic origins of their practices were acting no differently than the Theosophists, the Rosicrucians, and the latter-day Sufis.

What, however, was the truth of any of these claims? On the surface the witches seemed to make the best case for having an ancient origin, but the similarity of their beliefs and practices to those of other groups whose origins could be charted quite easily made me rather suspicious. Patterns of initiation, for example, seemed to follow Masonic practice. This had been taken as evidence for the influence of traditional witchcraft on Masonry, but I felt rather certain that the reverse was the case. What, I asked myself, was the actual continuity of witch practices from one era to the next? Were the covens of the twentieth century untarnished links with the past, as they claimed to be, or were they elaborate reconstructions of a tradition that had never existed except in the imagination of those who damned their countrymen to torture and death during the several centuries of the witchcraft trials in Europe and England?

There still remained the issue of whether the phenomena recorded by various proponents of the occult were genuine. I had by now experienced several things that did not quite fit a more scientific conception of how things happened. Was, for instance, my catchall invocation of ESP sufficient to explain reports of the materialization of objects? Either people were habitually deceiving themselves or violations of the known laws of nature proved that magic was something physical as well as psychological. Could this "something physical" eventually be fitted into an expanded conception of nature, or was there some indication that, contrary to the statement that today's magic is only tomorrow's science, the world of magic was not coterminous with that of our more ordinary experience?

Tanya's fidelity to her promises of secrecy was not the only impediment to my understanding of the reality of her witchery. She had long before told me about the months she had spent in UCLA's Neuropsychiatric Institute when, as a child of eleven, she had experienced what was then diagnosed as a schizophrenic breakdown, and there were signs that schizophrenic episodes recurred as a response to unusual stress. I thought of the bizarre story she had told me in trance of her experience with a Hollywood coven, and I thought too of incidents in our home that we tended to attribute to poltergeist activity.

In the experiences of others, we learned, there were parallels to the strange things that Tanya had told me about herself; I took this as indirect confirmation of her basic veracity. But what really were the links between Tanya's magic and a deviant perception of reality? Impossible as it sounded, there seemed to be some evidence that a person *could* affect his environment through his consciousness of it. Was this what was happening with my wife, and was her magic then no more than an outgrowth of the childhood disturbances that had finally brought her to the doctors at UCLA?

I found this possibility even more disturbing than the idea

that I was the object of a prolonged romantic hoax. If I encouraged Tanya in her witchcraft, might I not be pushing her back into the shadows that had enclosed her as a child? Moreover, if anything of Tanya's witchery could be explained in terms of abnormal psychology, what was this saying about magic itself?

By now I had already begun to write and talk somewhat sympathetically about the occultism appearing on college campuses. A first article appeared in *Commonweal*, a respected weekly journal of opinion, in September of 1971. With this as a base I began searching out a publisher willing to take on my idea for a full book. By the end of the year I had completed a manuscript and was on my way to being a published author.

With the appearance of my first book, *The Return of Magic*, I had defined my continuing role as an interpreter of the world of the occultist. Yet I was not myself an occultist. I was concerned with understanding and making sense out of magic, both as a reality and as something affecting the outlook of those accepting it, using my training as a philosopher and as a social scientist. Since I felt that magic had to be understood from the inside, I was also describing the mental journey that had taken me from the firm religious beliefs I had held as a Jesuit seminarian, through an atheist existentialism, to magic as a substitute for belief. One question I was asking was whether my personal odyssey was in some manner a clue to the intellectual history of my era.

But what was meant by "magic"? I could not say for sure. In one sense I was referring to a type of fantasy, a poetic outlook that personalized the world of nature. In another I was referring to a sphere of understanding and action distinct from both religion and science in which paranormal events occurred in response to the forces of human imagination and will. And in yet a third I was referring to an order in which supernatural beings, both benevolent and malicious, responded to human invocation. My own sympathies were clearly with the second as *the* meaning of "magic."

The book did not excite any great amount of comment. Apart from one Pennsylvania Jesuit who took issue with my somewhat cavalier usage of Catholic terminology, the reviewers were kind, yet the type of debate I hoped to provoke did not take place. Was there really any point in continuing to write about magic, particularly when what I took to calling the "costumed occultism" of the counterculture was giving way to newer, more serious discussions of human transcendence?

I perhaps had no choice. The fact that Tanya was a witch meant that magic would keep touching our lives. Our closest friends were individuals who also were touched by it and who could become involved in it with far less caution than both Tanya and I felt necessary. Pat, for instance, broke with her fiancé in order to marry another man who was unreservedly into Satanism, while a young man whom I had originally encouraged to begin the S.D.S. chapter on my campus started dabbling in sorcery and succeeded finally in provoking one of the strongest series of psychic attacks that Tanya and I have ever experienced (a story to which I shall come back later). And there were always the students in my classes who had either a background in magic or a certain irresistible fascination with it. No, I could not ignore the world of magic. There was much I still had to understand, and perhaps if I recorded my findings I might be able to help others who were bewildered by its extravagant claims.

Originally I intended to present a layman's geographic introduction to the different areas of Western occultism that would supplement the interpretations given in *The Return of Magic*. The editors for this new book asked what it was like to be a part of the world of magic. What kind of things happened, and how did people like Tanya and myself feel about them? Gradually, with their assistance, I recognized that what I was involved in was a quite complicated detective story that would attempt to piece together the true origins of the lore of magic and also probe the outer limits of the physics and the psychology of the events to which occultists perhaps too readily attributed other-worldly explanations.

Was there room for this type of study? The remarkable success of the first wave of books dealing with various features of the occult in the wake of *Rosemary's Baby* had led to a saturation of the market. Accounts that stripped away the last vestiges of secrecy from what had long been a covert tradition, as well as skillfully presented recipe books for individual and group sorcery, were available everywhere. Journalists such as Nat Freedland and John Godwin were saying almost all there was to say about the state of contemporary occultism. Louise Huebner, Sybil Leek, Anton LaVey, Paul Huson, and many others were providing manuals that eliminated the need of an earlier generation either to join a coven in order to obtain its Book of Shadows or to consult the old grimoires that had been the source of the ceremonial magic used from the late Middle Ages down through the early twentieth century.

It seemed that anyone with the ambition to plow through even a sampling of this literature would know all that I did about the reality of the world of magic. Or would he? For it seemed that journalists who specialized in the occult had almost a vested interest in avoiding specific details and had to market their wares as curios only.

For what if magic *is* real, not just as an outlook that many persons have because they find they must believe in something. What if it is a way of dealing with the world through powers of the mind as yet barely understood? The knowledge of magic would then be a source of power that, unless circumscribed by a strict code of ethics, could prove incredibly destructive. Far-fetched as it might seem, an unchecked enthusiasm for sorcery, particularly among the young, could lead easily enough to a voodoo version of Anthony Burgess's chilling *Clockwork Orange*—if it were not first taken over for government purposes, as some have suggested is already happening.

Many young people who had previously experienced the transformation of ordinary reality through the use of hallucinogenics could ask reasonably enough why the normal categories of space and time and causality collapsed through LSD or mescaline should be any more "real" than the rival categories of the sorcerer.

The cautionary tale of the sorcerer's apprentice presents one of the first lessons of any magical career: a little bit of successful conjuration whets the appetite for still grander results, and the neophyte who fails to internalize a strong respect for the mysteries of the world of magic is soon overwhelmed by them. Magic, like anything that touches on the deepest parts of the human psyche, is not to be treated casually. Do-it-yourself sorcery thus resembles do-it-yourself psychiatry in that either nothing much happens at all or what does happen is more than the amateur practitioner is prepared to handle. But this, of course, was what the young did not understand.

I saw the return of magic as evidence of a desire for the more hearty, more holistic conception of the world that we in the West came to lose sight of when, three centuries ago, we accepted the myth of progress through the machine. But such a restoration of consciousness was possible only if magic was not perverted by the hucksters or by the thrill seekers—or by the military. What troubled me was the possibility that sorcery might well provoke a new era of censorship that would attempt to silence any talk at all of magic. Married to a witch, I would not welcome the return of witch hunts, yet many of my young friends by their experiments were perhaps setting the stage for a Salem in the style of 1984.

With these considerations my detective story assumed a new importance. I had the task, on the one hand, of convincing many already into the occult that they should avoid too casual a solicitation of the forces contained within the world of magic, and, on the other, of persuading quite ordinary people even to take this world seriously. To accomplish this I shall tell about Tanya and myself and about the people we have known, trace the different currents that have flowed together to make up the river of contemporary occultism, and try to assess the explanations offered by experts for the world of magic.

2.

So What Is a Witch?

ONE MORNING, after I had been discussing witchcraft in a class that I taught in ethics and religion, one of my coeds asked about the significance of having a prophetic dream. Many people, I told her, to her relief, have something like this occur at some time in their lives without it meaning that they too are witches. The witch is just a person who might have such things happen rather often.

A few days later, while waiting for class to start, she told me, still in shock, that she had mentioned my comments to her mother, only to be told that both her mother and grandmother were witches and she would quite likely be one also.

But what, for the older women in this particular family, did it mean to be a witch? For most people whose ancestors came from a rural European background it meant only that there was an inherited psychic capacity that might or might not be accompanied by the transmission of a particular set of practices for its utilization. Perhaps this capacity might skip a generation, or perhaps it might die out altogether in the New World, but it was a link with the past that was best not talked about too openly.

My stepmother, who shares this desire for secrecy, has contrasted this American outlook with the practices of her family in their native Italy. There, she told me, travelers would stop over and swap bits of lore with those people whom everyone in the village knew to be, well, "special." The following anecdote illustrates why traces of one or another regional practice might surface far away and so create the illusion of a common lore reaching back to pre-Christian times.

The father of one woman in my classes was a Hungarian rainmaker, and he had left her a "thunderstone" when he died. She had taken it to the anthropologists at the college, and they had identified it as a neolithic axhead. My stepmother, whose father was an Italian rainmaker, detailed the manner in which the rock would be thrown into a fire during a ritual for bringing rain, and my student recalled finally that this was the way her father had described his own activities to her when she was a very little girl. Both Hungarian and Italian practitioners used an object for magic which mythologist Mircea Eliade has shown possesses a universal significance—a Stone Age relic that more settled later generations would come to regard as holding occult powers when found buried in the ground as though implanted there at the end of a thunderbolt. Thrown back into the fire, a symbol of the powers of the sky, it would draw down the rain just as it had when it had first come to the earth.

Superstition? My stepmother assures me that her father was quite successful as a rainmaker in the old country, although in the mining town in Illinois to which he emigrated his powers were not quite so respected. He had once attempted in vain to warn his fellow miners not to enter the shafts on the fateful day that the mine collapsed. As the lone survivor of the crew he worked with, was he a witch? The other men in the town were now afraid of him, but they ridiculed him as well. One day while playing *bocce* on a wet field, the men lost their heavy wooden ball in a swampy area.

"Find the ball by your magic," they shouted to the one known as a witch. His eyes hard, he commanded the players to form a circle and dance around the hat that he threw on the ground. "Do not laugh," he grimly ordered the bystanders. The field was silent while the men danced. Finally my stepmother's father halted the dance and picked up his hat. The dumbstruck players saw that it had been covering the ball they had lost. His honor avenged, he then moved his family to California.

My Hungarian student's father also used a hat for an occasional piece of sorcery. After coming to the United States he had prospered as a rancher. A number of friends hunted in the woods adjacent to his property, and one day he invited a few of them to use his wide-brimmed hat for target practice. After murmuring a few words over the hat he set it on a fence post ten yards away from his guests, all of whom were crack shots. To their amazement they found themselves unable to hit the seemingly invulnerable hat. As much as his friends would attribute successful rainmaking to coincidence, this bit of magic defied their efforts to find a rational explanation.

Both my stepmother and my student vouched for these incidents as more than conjurors' tricks, although neither woman claimed to know how her father had done it.

Both stories are useful, I think, in demolishing half a dozen stereotypes about who and what witches are. From them we can see that (1) witches are not necessarily women, much less ugly old hags; (2) they are most definitely "mortals"; (3) their powers, while sometimes having a definite practical application, do not appear to grant the instant fame and fortune expected by most would-be sorcerers' apprentices; (4) witches do not necessarily regard their practice of magic as having religious significance of any kind; (5) the ability to manifest these powers may appear in quite whimsical settings with little or no ceremony; and (6) witchcraft appears as something quite ordinary even if unpredictable.

We Americans first learn of witches in our childhood fairy tales, and then we are taught a world view that excludes magic on a priori grounds. We may still have our private superstitions, but we are reluctant to see them as anything but playful departures from a basically common-sense outlook. If someone claims to be a witch, he or she has to be regarded as "odd," to say the least. In many communities such a claim can even be a basis for legal prosecution or other types of public harassment.

Although Tanya knows better than to mention in casual conversation that she is a witch, it is not always easy to avoid having it brought up. If it is known that I'm a writer as well as a teacher, Tanya will have to admit that I deal with witchcraft. How did I get into such a weird topic? I married a witch. After a double take, the questioner inevitably begins on a new round. Does she ride on a broomstick? Could she turn someone into a toad? Would she do something to prove her contention that she is indeed a witch?

I can easily understand the frustration that leads men such as our Italian and Hungarian rainmakers to prove themselves through unexpected displays of power. I can also understand the eagerness of many contemporary covenists to present themselves as engaged in a worship of the old gods displaced by Christianity. This assimilation of magic to non-Christian religions in the modern era does have the advantage that if there are paranormal events in connection with the worship of these old gods, why should they be regarded as any less respectable than the miracles claimed by the devotees of other faiths? And why should anyone call a witch crazy just because he professes the "Old Religion"?

Tanya, who for a long while regarded herself as at best an agnostic, has not been able to make use of this particular line of defense. Nor does it appear that the world of magic is all that well served by simply exchanging one stereotype for another.

In order to clear up the confusion caused by a public promotion of the covens as the sole practitioners of witchcraft it might be well to make a distinction between cult witches, those who do define themselves as professing the "Old Religion," and what I call genetic witches, individuals who display a capacity for paranormal phenomena of any kind. The existence of a coven tradition has offered many genetic witches the sense of identity otherwise denied them in a contemporary urban environment. At the same time it provides them an outlet for their religious feelings that is more compatible with their identity than is orthodox Christianity. But a witch is first of all a witch because of something he is as a person, not because of his association with any particular group.

An analogy with other human capabilities might be helpful here. While most of us can learn to play an instrument if we work at it, we also know that some individuals are born with a special genius for music. These born musicians may not always receive the training that will permit them to realize their talents, but the ones who do are able to go on to become our great performers, and they will most likely be associated with other musicians. These associations are the way the world acknowledges who is and who is not a musician.

How rare is the talent for paranormal phenomena? In each generation there are no more than a relative handful of individuals whose psychic capacities are so striking that they attract widespread attention. These are the virtuosos like Peter Hurkos and Jeane Dixon, people I would call genetic witches regardless of the fact that they are not themselves "into witchcraft" and may not have a strong interest in the occult as such. Yet there are a great many others who, if not of equal talent, fill out the ranks of the psychics, seers, healers, or what-have-you who make up the world known to devotees of one or another side of the occult. And finally there are the otherwise ordinary people who know that rather often things happen for which they are not able to give a rational account. If Colin Wilson (author of *The Occult*) is to be believed on this point, about 5 per cent of the population possess the extraordinary ability for paranormal experiences which he calls Faculty X. This would make one person in twenty a genetic witch. Most of these people might not be willing to acknowledge the extent to which magic touches their own lives and might, in fact, be quite troubled by their experiences.

If I seem to have had more than my fair share of witch friends and acquaintances, it is because, as I learned once Tanya entered my life, people with an involvement in the world of magic tend to find each other out, creating a kind of magnetic attraction.

This attraction, I must admit, has not always been beneficial. At times I could bring to some persons a certain peace of mind, but I could also become the occasion for others to attempt rather dangerous psychic adventures. Permit me to give examples of both.

Greg was the hip product of a Hollywood high school. He was sharp, argumentative, and perhaps overly cynical. One evening after we had talked about witchcraft in class he asked for a chance to discuss something that had been bothering him for a number of months.

"It began," he said, "several years ago. This other guy and I used to race our motorcycles over the back roads. We had been really close until my girl friend began liking him better than me. I was so angry that I felt I could have killed him, only I would never have really tried to. We went out on our bikes and he slammed into the side of a hill. He was dead but I never touched him.

"Things like that kept happening. Another guy was killed and several were badly hurt after I got mad at them. One time I was mad at my mother. She's always very careful with drugs, but that night she overdosed on her sleeping pills. I woke up in a cold sweat, just knew that something was wrong, and broke down the door of her bedroom to get to her. I got her to the hospital just in time, but that really scared me.

"Lately everything seems to be going wrong for me. I can't make sense of my life. School, work, and people all get to me. I'll flash on things before they happen, or I'll get angry and bad things will take place around me. What's wrong anyway?"

In a conventional counseling session Greg would have been told that there was no reason for him to let a tragic series of coincidences burden his conscience. Of course he should attempt to control his hostility, but he was not responsible for what had happened to others. But this was not a conventional counseling session, and the things Greg told me about himself, particularly about his experiences with ESP, suggested that he had to come to terms with something that most other counselors would have said was impossible.

"Okay," I told him, "from what you've said I'll have to call you a warlock, probably a very powerful one. Your anger is able to take on an objective form. Unconsciously you have acted out the feelings which consciously you have tried to repress, and because of something about yourself the things you act out inside become realities. You do have to take responsibility of some kind for what has happened, but it would be foolish to let yourself get hung up about it. The job is to face up to what goes on inside of you. Develop more positive feelings, and I think you'll find the world around you changing for the better."

Because of his makeup I argued that Greg had a special responsibility to understand the world of magic better. He had already developed a certain interest in occult literature, and I recommended that he should read Dion Fortune as perhaps the safest guide to follow in developing whatever capacities he possessed. I felt he might also profit from reading Aleister Crowley's *Magick in Theory and Practice*. There was a bookstore in Hollywood and also an occult shop whose proprietor seemed quite knowledgeable, but I had to recommend that he be cautious.

As it turned out, Greg's visit to the bookstore brought him into contact with a young woman able to guide him far better than I could. She too advised him to study Dion Fortune, but she felt that exposure either to Aleister Crowley or to the occult shop was quite dangerous to someone already so drawn to the practice of a black or harmful magic.

In the weeks following, Greg acknowledged that for the first time in a long while he was genuinely happy. His work at the college had picked up, his personal relationships were improving, and he was confident about his future. At the same time, he admitted, if he was in that part of Hollywood, there was an almost physical pull in the direction of the occult shop.

Since I had echoed the warnings of the girl in the bookstore, he was doing his best to resist it, having already been hurt enough, he felt.

Another young man, the boy friend of a witch whom Tanya and I regarded as one of the people closest to us, had not been so cautious. Kathy's sensitivities matched Tanya's, and she had gone through a series of relationships that had taken her to the center of the British rock music scene. One evening at our apartment Kathy had tried to ask for advice about a series of unpleasant dreams that indicated some type of psychic attack. Bob, her boy friend, feeling that he was being left out of something that touched on his relationship with her, angrily demanded to be let in on what was going on.

We found out that Bob too was experiencing the same type of phenomena. The source, we reasoned, was perhaps the musician to whom Kathy had once been engaged while in England. He was as much into the occult as into drugs, and he had previously made a number of efforts to coerce Kathy to leave Southern California and return to him in England. Should they attempt any ritual countermeasures? Tanya and I felt that it might not hurt.

The next day Bob visited the Hollywood occult shop already noted (it was, in fact, because of Bob's familiarity with this shop that I could later mention it to Greg). The proprietor was at first cautious when Bob asked about protective amulets, then suddenly expansive after he was told the situation. He had, he explained, been taught the Voodoo associated with Marie Laveau, the powerful *mambo* who dominated New Orleans occultism in the nineteenth century. Countermagic was his specialty; he was waiting for the warlock who could outdraw him in any exercise of occult gunslinging.

The psychic attacks did stop immediately. Bob was impressed and returned repeatedly to the shop. Now he found the practice of magic completely absorbing, and, as Kathy told us, he was as intemperate here as he was in his use of drugs. New phenomena occurred, but this time they seemed more likely to be the product of Bob's experiments than of some outside force.

One night we had a panicked call from Kathy. There was a sound at their second-story window that seemed like the scratching of a giant cat. Bob felt that he could control any of the forces that he had summoned, but Kathy, whose relationship with him had begun to deteriorate, was terrified. Later, after being involved in a serious auto accident, Bob surrendered his interest in occult rituals for things more down to earth, but by now he and Kathy had separated.

I admit that both of these stories read like fiction. On the surface they also seem to justify the type of community concern that led to the torture and slaughter of perhaps two hundred thousand people at the end of the Middle Ages. If there are individuals whose hostility can affect not just their own circumstances but those of the persons around them through the use of presumably occult powers, should they not be made accountable for these acts? This, of course, was the logic of the Salem witch trials, but if we have learned anything at all from this tragic episode it is that the courtroom is a most inappropriate forum in which to deal with the occult. Besides, as we shall see, the world of magic does seem to work out its own rough and ready justice.

But any consideration of how to deal with the results of witchcraft and sorcery presumes a reality that cannot be easily explained in terms of fraud or self-deception. I am obviously willing to assert that there is such a reality to account for what I have seen and have been told.

Assume that what we call extrasensory perception or ESP is perhaps not an extra (or sixth) sense so much as an extraordinary manner of utilizing our ordinary abilities. Since the "sight" is the most common of the paranormal phenomena associated with witchcraft, it seems reasonable to suppose that the possession of a marked capacity for ESP would be enough to make someone a genetic witch. I tend to agree that all of us have *some* capacity for ESP that can be excited under appropriate physiological and psychological conditions. Some people, either because of an accident such as a severe blow to the head (Edgar Cayce and Peter Hurkos, for example) or because of a special genetic disposition, meet these conditions as a matter of course; others meet them with sufficient frequency that the experience becomes almost taken for granted.

Tanya, for instance, has been told that she shows the brain wave patterns characterizing a person using hallucinogenics. According to authorities on ESP such as Andrija Puharich, some hallucinogenic materials, particularly that contained in the mushroom *Amanita muscaria* used the world over in shamanist rituals, excite the parasympathetic nervous system in order to produce a physical state highly conducive to telepathy. It is perhaps the cause, then, that Tanya as well as those others I have termed genetic witches are exhibiting spontaneously the effects that Dr. Puharich has obtained in the laboratory through the use of drugs.

But even granted that her physiology may be unusual, why label her a witch? Ought not we be getting away from this talk of magic in order to concentrate on an analysis of the chemistry of the paranormal?

One reason for using the word "witch" is that Tanya uses it herself as the daughter and granddaughter of witches. A more important reason is that, like the term "musician," it denotes the possession of a talent and it argues an identification with a specific tradition, a community with others who also inherit this tradition, and above all a certain role played out in society for the benefit of others.

There is at present a considerable amount of research into the strictly scientific aspects of paranormal phenomena. Much has appeared as a response to the work being done in the Soviet Union and Eastern Europe, and it has produced an excitement among hardheaded scientists paralleled only by the enthusiasm of the first generation of psychic researchers during the heyday of nineteenth-century spiritualism. The danger, however, is that in an effort to achieve a laboratory duplication of paranormal events we tend to lose sight of the cultural setting in which the meaning of these events is defined. Not only does this loss of an appropriate setting often prevent the phenomena from taking place, but the significance of the phenomena that do appear is distorted.

By our study of paranormal phenomena we are in a sense establishing that the events traditionally associated with the world of magic do occur even if we cannot yet reduce them to the neat sets of equations which are the ultimate goal of the hard sciences. But what do they *mean?* "Knowledge is power," wrote Francis Bacon, and in our modern age this has come to mean that knowledge is of value only in proportion to the power that it offers.

The traditions of magic have obviously been concerned with power of one sort or another. But they have also been concerned with knowledge as a manner of relating to the profoundest mysteries of human existence. The sorcerer, the shaman, the seer—we might use any of these equivalents for the word "witch"—is a person who because of his own makeup and his training in a particular type of lore is uniquely, to use the phrase which Carlos Castaneda's Yaqui sorcerer don Juan applies to himself, "a man of knowledge." The place of man in the universe, the importance of life and of death, the connection between a moral outlook and the harmony of nature —all of these are the backdrop against which the magician acts out the feats that we are today attempting to examine in the cold light of the laboratory.

This does not mean that the person who has secured entry into the world of magic is any more a philosopher or a theologian than he is a scientist. Magic is a way of seeing things that parallels a religious outlook, but above all it involves a mode of consciousness in which the individual acts at the interface of two worlds. The sorcerer may not himself understand what it is that he does, but, unless he is a fool who will find himself soon destroyed by his recklessness, he does know that the world of magic is not to be ventured into without the utmost respect.

The witch, then, is someone who finds the world of magic his by birthright and who then attempts to make his own the value system developed by those who have preceded him.

Those who have come forward as today's most verbal proponents of witchcraft—individuals such as Louise Huebner, Sybil Leek, Alex Sanders, and many others often unsympathetically regarded by other cultists as "celebrity witches"— typically have stories of a family background that corresponds to Tanya's. Mrs. Huebner, for instance, writes of the encouragement she received from her witchy Yugoslav grandmother, Mrs. Leek tells of an Irish-Russian ancestry that included a lady whose grave was defiled that a stake might be driven through her heart, and Alex Sanders began his own career in witchcraft as a child after a ritual initiation by his Welsh grandmother.

Tanya became aware of herself as a witch at the age of three, when she first experienced both prophetic dreams and astral projection. Earlier her mother had been hospitalized in the City of Hope with tuberculosis, and in the trauma of separation she had come to identify strongly with her Russian-born grandmother, who in turn tended to think of the little girl as the reincarnation of Tanya's aunt, who had died of cancer in childhood.

It was from her grandmother that Tanya first came to acknowledge that the phenomena she experienced linked her to a family tradition reaching back two centuries. Witchcraft for both her mother and grandmother had taken on much of the coloring of the Anglo-American covens with which they were associated.

Since Tanya's aunt, whom she so much resembled, had been an aspiring ballerina, her grandmother decided finally to send Tanya, also a promising dancer, to ballet school in England. This second separation from her mother had as strong an effect on the little girl as had the first. Tanya learned to define the meaning of her life within the narrow bounds of her art, finding escape from its discipline only through passage into a beautiful world of her own imagining.

Tanya usually returned home during the summer. One year, after her mother had remarried and was still establishing the rhythm of a new life, she remained in England and made friends with the Gypsies who camped in the area near the school. Here too she learned more of folk magic and, as it had been with her grandmother, she learned also the importance of secrecy, perhaps the most effective means of instilling into its neophytes a respect for the world of magic.

Two years later Tanya came home for good. With dancing no longer available as a means of channeling her energies, her pent-up furies erupted into a bizarre explosion that led finally to her stay at UCLA's Neuropsychiatric Institute. Here the doctors worked to distract her from the voices that alternately terrified and beguiled her as she created an internal universe which one psychiatrist was to describe as the most complex of any that he had encountered in his work with paranoid schizophrenics. Therapy was successful—or rather she was told in one final vision that she had the power to silence the voices if she so chose—and Tanya attempted to pick up the pieces of her fragmented education.

She was enrolled at Highland Hall in Los Angeles, one of the schools setting out to teach according to the principles of the Austrian occultist Rudolf Steiner. After her junior high school graduation she went on to a New England boarding school that belonged to the same system. In both schools she was again immersed in the atmosphere of magic, although the specifics of Steiner's occultism were reserved for those who would go on from the schools to membership in the Anthroposophical Society, a group Steiner had formed in the early years of the twentieth century. Tanya recalls fondly the techniques of "eurhythmy," the fluid movements by which dance was again made part of her life, and she cites the particular predilection of her instructors for pentagrams, the five-pointed stars which are an important part of ceremonial magic. As a teenager she danced through the pentagrams as part of her exercises, and through their power she came to the final definition of herself as a witch that she held when I met her.

Since early childhood Tanya's powers had matured considerably. Her schizophrenic breakdown, which in many respects became a terrifying initiation into the demonic, left her with an enhanced ability for telepathy, and her later interest in the tarot and astrology permitted her to express her magic through these classical practices of divination. She also continued with the spell-casting that she had first learned from her grandmother, and, if asked today whether such things as spells really work, she points to me, the professor she feels she won by magic, as proof that they do. (I tend to insist that sorcery had nothing to do with our relationship; she is an extraordinarily beautiful and talented woman quite able to get my attention all on her own.)

Tanya, like Pat, Kathy, Greg, and others I will mention, is a genetic witch; unlike the others, she has had the advantage of a family background in which her abilities were permitted a systematic development. Her one experience with a Hollywood coven has been enough, however, to deter her from looking for a full cult expression of her powers.

How important to herself is it for Tanya to be a witch? Curiously, in the years we have been together, the role of magic in her life has diminished considerably. She is, I think, potentially a great psychic, but despite my own increasing interest in witchcraft, I have agreed with Tanya that too intense a practice could be dangerous to her stability. Under stress, for example, she has shown a tendency to the phenomenon of multiple personality (described in *The Three Faces of Eve* and more recently in the book *Sybil* by Flora Rheta Schreiber) as well as to the type of schizophrenic retreat that occurred in her childhood. As far as we are both concerned, the rewards of being a cult witch do not necessarily justify the risks.

Still, despite the fact that Tanya has suspended many of the practices in which she engaged at the time we met, she most definitely remains caught up in the world of magic; her view of reality involves a dimension completely alien to the expectations of contemporary Western culture. It is at once childlike and ancient, filled with intimations of the spiritual and yet curiously earthly.

Life with Tanya is by no means a day-to-day round of spell-casting and spirit-chasing, but it does bring with it the continuing possibility of contact with a realm of other-worldly experience. And I have come to take for granted that I am to be ever more deeply caught up in the exotic subculture of the occultists, at least as an interpreter if not actually as a participant.

Tanya has told me that she had a clear mental image of me months before we met. She knew then that I was to influence the entire course of her life although she had no knowledge of how. Certainly it was to happen that my own life took on a completely different character. Contrary to the image of the flustered husband in the series *Bewitched*, most men married to women drawn to the world of magic never even realize that fact. I am something of an exception, even within Tanya's own family, but this I take to be part of whatever destiny provoked our meeting.

Marriage to a witch, again contrary to the Hollywood portrayal, has not brought about any striking changes in the circumstances of my daily living. Nevertheless, things do happen, even apart from the psychic encounters I will describe in later chapters, that make me quite aware of Tanya's witchiness. These include the coincidences that led to the appearance of this book, as well as the fact that Tanya herself causes a remarkable fascination in those who know her. It is not just that she is a quite attractive young woman; as we have often been told, even chance acquaintances will feel drawn toward her as though to someone who belongs to a different time, perhaps to the enchanted world of Camelot or to some other equally romantic era.

Living with magic, I have often wondered what would happen if I decided to pursue a further career in sorcery for myself. Can I, I've asked, remain just an observer and still have anything honest to say about the value of magic as either a basis for a deeper personal integration (the theme of many contemporary occultists) or the source of a truer vision of man's potential (the theme of my own earlier book)? So far, principally because of Tanya's concern for my welfare, I have avoided the type of commitment that would mark me as a practitioner of the arts I am writing about. Even though I am married to one born to magic, I have to admit that by our own choice witchcraft plays a quite minor role in our lives, and for now I must present myself primarily as the historian. Tanya has not remade me into a magacian (nor has she wanted to), but through her I have become aware of what the world of the occult is all about.

3.

Anatomy of a Legend

I KNOW THERE ARE WITCHES. They may not ride broomsticks—and I've known my mother-in-law to have used a cauldron only once—but they are quite real. In a more restricted sense of the word witches are the heirs of the various traditions of folk magic that preceded the age of the machine. They are the rainmakers, the fortunetellers, the healers. In many cultures they are also the courts of last resort, the hired guns, as it were, for those who demand extraordinary assistance in winning a mate or avenging a wrong.

The word "witch" derives from the Anglo-Saxon *wicca* (with the feminine form *wicce*), a word used today by many covenists as a synonym for the "Old Religion." It can be related to the words "wit" and "wise" and to a term meaning "bent" that continues in such terms as "witch hazel." "Wicked" suggests that in England the connotations of "witch" were largely negative. ("Warlock," often used by later writers to refer to a

solitary male witch, is entirely pejorative in its original meaning; it refers to an oath breaker or deceiver.) More neutral
terms were the "cunning man" and "cunning woman" used in
Renaissance England to refer to the village seers and healers
who engaged in what was thought of as "white magic."

Terms from other languages tend to show the same mixed
feelings for witchcraft. The harshest perhaps is the Italian
strega from the Latin word for a screech owl that had come to
refer to a vampire. The Greek *pharmakos* identifies the witch
with the expert in poisons. Generally, however, the words in
use relate simply to the fact that the witch is the one who
makes use of sorcery of one type or another. The French *sorcier*, the German *Hexe* and *Zauberin*, the Spanish *brujo*, and
the Russian *vedyna* all lack the sense of horror felt by the peoples of the Mediterranean for the kin of the dread Circe, who,
according to Homer, turned the sailors of Ulysses into swine.

As in the Anglo-Saxon *wicca*, the concept of the witch refers
to a man as well as to a woman, but a frequently cited English
distinction between witchcraft and sorcery is by no means
universal.

The word "witchcraft" has typically been used in a negative
sense for historical reasons that indicate the prejudices of the
medieval churchmen who condemned anything from the world
of magic as a sign that the Devil was being worshiped in the
place of Christ./Twentieth-century covenists have worked to
rehabilitate this image of Wicca or the "Craft of the Wise"
by granting the church its point that medieval witchcraft was
in fact a religious exercise. My own contention is that the entire effort to separate witchcraft from sorcery tends to obscure
the constant interaction between a folk magic (low magic)
and the practices of a more intellectual occultism (a so-called
high or ceremonial magic). Contemporary coven practices

cannot, for instance, be understood without reference to the ceremonial magic of the Renaissance that was revived in the nineteenth century through groups such as the Golden Dawn. On the other hand, the tradition of ceremonial magic, which we shall discuss later, is shot through with folk practices that mark the debris of a number of older outlooks.

What do we really know about the tradition of witchcraft in the West? What I learned was that there exist two separate legends and one factual history. The first legend developed through the centuries of persecution that culminated in the almost unbelievable savagery of the sixteenth and seventeenth centuries. The second is the legend of the "Old Religion" adhered to by the cult witches of the twentieth century. The factual history is a complex story in which the folk magic of ancient Europe was mingled with the residue of the collapsed Hellenistic civilization to create the basis both for the first legend and for the covert beliefs and practices of today's hereditary witches.

Since I found myself working backwards from the second legend in my own effort to penetrate Tanya's world of magic, this is perhaps the best place for us to begin. In this chapter we shall sketch the story of the "Old Religion" as recounted by folklorists in the nineteenth century and transmuted into a reality by modern covenists. In the following chapters we shall examine first the legend created by the medieval church and then the geography of the world of magic that lies behind the legends of both the past and the present.

Shakespeare's greatest plays, it might be noted, share the themes that made *Rosemary's Baby* a box-office success: sex, violence—and the occult. An Elizabethan audience, no less than a contemporary one, reveled in a presentation of ghosts

(*Hamlet*), witches (*Macbeth*), and supernatural beings (*Midsummer Night's Dream*). This, after all, was still an age in which men and women could be prosecuted for damage resulting from the practice of black magic. The king who ruled England in the years after Shakespeare's death, James I, could himself write a theological treatise on the evil of witchcraft. Some rationalists, like Reginald Scot and Thomas Hobbes, might dispute the prevailing doctrine on the reality of witches as individuals in league with the Devil, but popular sentiment continued the prejudices of the past.

In time the outlook of men like Scot and Hobbes would become the norm of an urban, educated population. In rural areas, however, old beliefs—and old fears—disappeared much more slowly. Tanya recalls, for example, that the people in the lovely Devonshire countryside where she went to school continued to accept the presence of elemental spirits, the fairies, in all the growing things around them.

Such rural beliefs and practices are characteristic not just of England but of the entire West. Early folklorists such as Jacob Grimm had suggested an association between such patterns and the paganism the church had attempted to exterminate in the Middle Ages. Witchcraft in particular was seen as a relic of the older European religions, especially of the worship of Diana, goddess of the moon.

In the late nineteenth century the American journalist Charles Godfrey Leland, who produced several volumes on the folklore of northern Italy, felt that he had found conclusive proof that *la vecchia religione* (the "Old Religion") had survived even beyond its last recorded appearance three centuries earlier. With the assistance of a young *strega* named Maddalena, he assembled a remarkable little collection of materials which he entitled *Aradia, or the Gospel of the Witches*.

It included a self-styled *Vangelo* or Gospel recounting the birth of Aradia, the goddess of witchcraft, directions for a ritual meal in honor of Diana and Aradia, a collection of spells, and assorted legends attesting to the existence of a counter-religion.

The references to oppression in *Aradia* suggest the same type of troubled period that had produced both the Franciscans and the heretical sect of the Waldenses (the Poor Men of Lyons), a twelfth-century group that had stressed asceticism and a highly personal piety in sharp contrast to the lavish and overly formal style of the institutional church. Waldensian influence remained strong in northern Italy throughout the medieval and modern periods, and it is quite possible that it contributed to the general mood of Leland's manuscript. Yet beyond this I tend to doubt that the legend of Aradia had roots as ancient as Leland supposed. The entire nineteenth century was an age of romantic reconstructions of the era of Greece and Rome, and the structural simplicity of the myth, so unlike the confused versions of most folk tales handed down through the centuries, suggests the hand of someone who knew his classics and had a flair for poetic expression as well as a fervent hatred of the church and of the landed aristocracy.

Leland mentions his belief that witches' sabbats (ritual meetings) still took place, even within the Holy City itself. Nevertheless, the spells and the stories he adds to his basic text suggest only the individualistic practices that generally characterize European folk magic. Were there covens in northern Italy? In an area where witchcraft was practiced with little fear of official reprisal, the absence of more explicit references to group activities seems a clear enough indication that they just did not take place. Leland, it would seem, thought otherwise, because as founder of the Gypsy Lore Society, a practitioner as well as a student of magic, he was the true romantic, more at home with a reconstructed antiquity than with the mechanized world around him.

This nostalgia, marking many of the occultists of the period, is the key to understanding how seeming men of the world could dress up in exotic costumes, pronounce incantations in an impossible language, and in general act as though the future of mankind lay elsewhere than in the expansion of industrial civilization. Yet the fact is that the end of the nineteenth century saw the existence of many groups dedicated to the study and practice of magic. Witchcraft, in the view of the devotees of England's Hermetic Order of the Golden Dawn or Germany's Order of the Temple of the Orient, was a debased Christianity, a worship of the Devil, beneath consideration by educated men.

Leland's *Aradia*, published in 1899, received little attention and was soon largely forgotten. Margaret Murray, the lady who made witchcraft intellectually respectable, never refers to it in her two major books, and it does not appear in the pages of Gerald B. Gardner's *Witchcraft Today*, which inaugurated the contemporary round of revelations regarding the "Old Religion." Thomas C. Lethbridge, whose book *Witches* reintroduced Leland's work to a modern audience, commented that it "appears to be rare and it seems probable that it was smothered in some way by vested interests." A more likely explanation is that even the discovery of a sect dedicated to Diana in the back country of Italy would not prove that the coven witchcraft of the Middle Ages, if it ever existed at all, had survived into the modern world.

There is an interval of two decades between *Aradia* and Margaret Murray's *The Witch-Cult in Western Europe*. Un-

like Leland, Miss Murray made no claim that organized witchcraft had outlasted its persecutors. What she did present was a
thoroughly remarkable study supporting the idea that witchcraft, while it existed, was a distinct religion that co-existed
with Christianity throughout the Middle Ages. This claim did
not require a belief in the possibility of miraculous occurrences.

Despite the title of her book, Miss Murray, largely confined her study to the British Isles. She begins with a critical
distinction between "operative witchcraft" or the various
practices of folk magic and "ritual witchcraft" or the forms of
a religion rooted in a stage of civilization preceding the development of agriculture. Her argument is that this religion,
which she describes as having a god in the form of either a
man or a beast, well-defined rites, and a highly developed
organization, survived the advent of the Christian church.
The great witchcraft trials, which began in Britain with the
prosecution of Dame Alice Kyteler in 1324, marked a conscious and ultimately successful effort on the part of the Christian clergy to suppress their ancient rivals. Still, as Miss Murray
reconstructs them, the prosecutions were not solely religious
but also involved the contest for political power between the
original peoples of Europe and their Rome-oriented successors.

What distinguished Margaret Murray's study from earlier
works on witchcraft was her total acceptance of the material
provided by the "confessions" of those tortured as witches.
Earlier writers had either taken them at face value as evidence
of a perverted Christianity or had rejected them in their en-
tirety as the product of clerical imagination. In *The Witch-
Cult in Western Europe* they are regarded as factual state-
ments about what Miss Murray termed the "Dianic cult." The
devil—or god—of the witches that was alleged to have been
worshiped at ritual convocations was a man either garbed in

black to conceal his true identity or dressed in animal skins to represent the nature divinity (the Horned God) that was the object of the cult. The thirteen-member covens (twelve worshipers and the one costumed as the god) were organizations designed to carry out cult business.

Ten years after her first book's publication, Margaret Murray presented *The God of the Witches*. By now she accepted completely the idea that the fairies of legend were the aboriginal pygmy inhabitants of Western Europe. They were also the heirs of the "Old Religion," and the conquerors who wanted their allegiance learned to adopt their ways. This was the reason that the Dianic cult was likely to find its adherents among the highest members of the royal courts of England and France.

Miss Murray already had presented her thesis that both Joan of Arc and the notorious Gilles de Rais, executed in 1440 as a mass murderer, had been the leaders of covens. In this second book she added the names of William Rufus, the English king slain in the New Forest in 1100, and Thomas à Becket as individuals professing the "Old Religion." All four were described as having been the human sacrifices demanded at the end of each seven-year cycle of a king's reign. William Rufus, according to this thesis, died in his own stead, but the other three, two of whom ironically were canonized by the church they opposed, were ritual substitutes. Joan and Gilles de Rais died for Charles VIII, and Becket died for Henry II.

This extraordinary assertion meant that not just the kings of France and England but even high-ranking members of the Catholic hierarchy, such as the sainted archbishop Thomas à Becket, were only nominally Christian. It meant also that the idea of the divine victim was basic to an understanding of medieval politics. As might be expected, this thesis lost Margaret Murray much of her reputation as a serious historian.

But undaunted, in 1954, the year of Gerald B. Gardner's *Witchcraft Today*, she produced *The Divine King in England*, a final statement of her belief that British royalty had accepted the "Old Religion" from Roman days down to the seventeenth century.

Margaret Murray's books have become as much a gospel for contemporary witches as Leland's *Aradia*. More than anything else they have created the legend of the "Old Religion" continued by Gerald Gardner, Sybil Leek, Alex Sanders, Raymond Buckland, and the many others who have announced themselves as latter-day worshipers of the Horned God and the goddess of the moon. What remains completely unknown is the extent to which Miss Murray not only legitimated the covens that were to surface after the Second World War but even made their creation possible. There is no hard evidence that there were English covens in existence before the 1921 appearance of *The Witch-Cult in Western Europe*.

Early in the eighteenth century English law, reacting as much to the tragic experiences of the colonial magistrates in Salem as to a new climate of rationalism, reversed the stand that it had taken throughout its history. No longer would individuals be prosecuted as witches because of the charges made by others. Now it would be their own claim to occult powers that was outlawed.

This last witchcraft statute remained on the books until 1951. It was repealed primarily because of the lobbying of the spiritualists and not because anyone thought that there really were witches who should be free to practice the Craft without fear of punishment.

In 1954, however, Gerald B. Gardner, a former plantation owner and customs official in Malaya who had retired to the

New Forest in England, published *Witchcraft Today* as a statement that covens did exist and that the time had come for details of the Craft to be made public. His book, for which Margaret Murray provided an introduction, rehearsed the story of the "Little People" presented in *The God of the Witches*.

As Gardner saw it, neolithic patterns of worship, specifically the cult of the Horned God, came to be influenced by the worship of the Great Mother as a Celtic population succeeded the aboriginal pygmies of Western Europe. This Druid cult in turn tended to take on the coloring of successive waves of invaders until in the Middle Ages, contrary to Margaret Murray's thesis, most witches would have thought themselves true Christians. The Craft, however, had lived on even through the age of persecution.

Gardner's own introduction to the Craft makes a fascinating story in itself. As Doreen Valiente recounts it in her *An ABC of Witchcraft Past and Present*, Gardner found that neighbors of his in the New Forest area were members of an occult group begun by the daughter of the Theosophist Annie Besant. This was the Fellowship of Crotona, named after the esoteric group begun by Pythagoras in ancient Italy. Some of the members of the Fellowship eventually confided to Gardner that they had made contact with the last members of an old coven. Gardner in turn met the elderly woman who headed the coven and was initiated into witchcraft by her. After her death he wrote a novel, *High Magic's Aid*, in which he revealed the continued existence of the coven tradition. This was in 1949, still two years before witchcraft would cease to be illegal. Then in 1954 he published *Witchcraft Today* and lifted the curtain of secrecy from the activities of his own coven.

Gardner, who earlier had been a student of Malayan magic,

by now had fashioned a whole new career for himself out of the study of witchcraft. Besides supervising a host of new covens, he opened a Museum of Magic and Witchcraft on the Isle of Man, a place whose inhabitants he felt showed the racial characteristics of the "Little People." Gardner claimed throughout to be transmitting the Craft rather than remaking it. But Sybil Leek does not accept that the nudity and ritual sex characterizing Gardnerian covens (as well as the breakaway groups associated with Alex Sanders) are at all authentic. Francis King, one of the most knowledgeable of contemporary writers on modern occultism, suggests that Gardner was simply indulging his own voyeuristic and sadomasochistic tendencies in the rites he proposed, citing that, in the early 1940s he commissioned the somewhat disreputable Aleister Crowley to prepare four of the rituals to be used in a revived witch cult.

The late 1950s and early 1960s were the heyday of new covens, although there was not yet the widespread publicity that would permit the "Old Religion" to fragment into a hundred heresies. Sybil Leek received her own induction as a high priestess from a coven near Nice that had been headed by an elderly Russian aunt; she then returned to the New Forest, where she operated an antique shop, to develop the Horsa Coven. Alex Sanders, who had begun his study of witchcraft with his Welsh grandmother and then dabbled in black magic before joining one of the new Gardnerian covens, started off on a highly public career which led him to be named "King of the Witches" by admirers.

Gerald Gardner died in 1964. The man who came forward to continue Gardner's work, particularly in the United States, was Raymond Buckland. Also a writer as well as a publisher of old materials such as Leland's *Aradia*, Buckland began his own version of a witchcraft museum on Long Island.

In 1969, a year after Sybil Leek's *Diary of a Witch*, June Johns wrote *King of the Witches: The World of Alex Sanders*. One of those converted by this description of Sanders's concept of Wicca was Stewart Farrar, a journalist who in 1971 presented *What Witches Do: The Modern Coven Revealed*, a book in which he both described his own rapid initiation into the Craft and published the full text of one of the "Alexandrian" rituals.

How much is there left to tell? Francis King, who shares my suspicion that modern covens did not appear until after Margaret Murray's first book, accepts that there were two English covens in existence when Gardner arrived in the New Forest. What they were like might possibly be determined from the contents of the Book of Shadows, any of the various manuscripts in which the high priestess of a coven is to record the rituals used by her group.

I have seen two printed versions of the Book of Shadows. One is a rather standard set of incantations offset from an occultist's own manuscript. The other is the copy prepared by "America's Witch Queen," Lady Sheba, and offered through Llewellyn Publications. Lady Sheba's manual is divided into three parts: laws, rituals, and sabbats. Included in the text of the laws are admonitions on the conduct of a witch under torture. If these are genuine, they would suggest an origin for the Wiccan laws going back at least to the early eighteenth century.

The rituals follow what has become a standard form for the vast majority of covens. The witches are to perform their rites in the nude within a circle nine feet across prepared by the high priestess with her consecrated knife (athame). Inside the circle is an altar with the implements (candles, water, salt, a censer, a bell, a cord scourge) to be used in the rites. There are eight Great Sabbats or major festivals (Halloween, for instance) and twenty-six Esbats coinciding with the new and full moons, and each is to be celebrated with appropriate symbolism. At the festivals on which new witches are to be initiated into any of the three degrees of the Craft, there are additional rites which require, among other activities, the "fivefold kiss" (upon the feet, knees, groin, breast, and lips), a mild flagellation, and suitable admonitions.

Apart from the nudity and the flagellation, which are not necessarily erotic in tone in the more serious covens, there is little in Lady Sheba's text that should offend the ordinary person. Certainly there is nothing of the stress on harm to another person that appears in the stereotype of the witch. Taken at face value, the rituals of the latter-day covens that she describes are gentle, poetic evocations of the rhythms of nature. The Devil is conspicuous by his absence.

Since any version of the Book of Shadows is necessarily the product of a living tradition, it is impossible, as I have already suggested, to say just how much of Lady Sheba's work is relatively recent and how much antedates the career of Gerald Gardner. Tanya tells me that her grandmother's "Black Book" was known as the "Book of Calls" and contained various demonic invocations, written in what seemed to her to be a backwards Latin. This suggests that the originals of what is now known as the Book of Shadows were nothing more than the grimoires or manuals of black magic in use since the Middle Ages to which had been added bits and pieces of an oral tradition regarding coven procedures.

This oral tradition could have been begun as one solitary witch passed on his lore to another; the rules for a coven could have developed gradually as a result of these witches coming to take for granted that ideally they were supposed to meet in groups. One form or another of the Book of Shadows might then have preceded all the historical covens. Still, there is perhaps no way of ever knowing for sure what is the true history of the modern covens, and I advance this simply as my own resolution of these questions.

No discussion of contemporary witchcraft would be complete without reference to the tongue-in-cheek Satanism of Anton LaVey, who regards all traditional religions as both fraudulent and psychologically destructive. A longtime occultist who had followed careers as varied as those of a lion tamer and a police photographer, LaVey in 1966 converted an occult discussion group into the First Church of Satan. His San Francisco home became the center for highly publicized Black Masses that had all the expected paraphernalia: a nude woman for an altar, dramatic invocations of the Devil, and counsel to practice the "seven deadly sins."

LaVey, whose showmanship exceeds even that of Alex Sanders, has proven himself a master of the occultist put-on in the best tradition of Aleister Crowley. *The Satanic Bible*, one of several books that he has written, expresses a coherent philosophy in which the Devil is seen as the symbol for all the human drives repressed by orthodox Christianity. Worship of the Devil in the Satanic Church is intended to satisfy a human need for ritual while permitting a therapeutic expression of the lusts and hostilities that are part of man's condition. LaVey's conception of witchcraft as a set of techniques for focusing latent paranormal capabilities may be nothing more than a hip updating of Aleister Crowley's "Magick," but predictably it has angered other cult witches.

The question of whether witchcraft has to be thought of as religion came up soon after the death from cancer of Tanya's beloved grandmother. Tanya had begun to experience a recurrent dream that stressed the sense of loss which is central to most theological conceptions of hell. The loss, in the dream, was brought about by her refusal to commit herself to a religious belief of any kind. To her psychiatrist, to whom she had gone for therapy on and off since adolescence, the significance of the dream was that Tanya had not yet come to grips with the specifically religious dimension of human mortality. Shocked and saddened by her grandmother's death, she was unable to give it meaning.

How, the doctor asked, was it possible for Tanya to call herself a witch and *not* identify with some type of religious experience? She insisted on her atheism and he just as resolutely pointed to the evidence of the religious concern emerging from her unconscious. She had to admit finally that she did believe in God and that the view of magic she held took on a new quality because of this belief.

It is, after all, difficult if not impossible to draw a line between the spheres of magic and religion. Both relate to the world in terms that reach beyond the narrow limits of what we today think of as a waking consciousness, the distinction being between a discovery of transcendence to which man responds with worship and the recognition of a harmony to which man attempts to attune himself through his symbols. From this perspective it is understandable that magic should continually make use of a religious framework in its practices and that religion should make itself more visible by assuming the garb of magic.

Tanya, finding herself religious after all, in this respect shares the mood of the cult witches who, from the days of Gerald Gardner onward, have argued for an intrinsically religious perspective in their rites. Sybil Leek may possibly have gone the furthest in this direction; in *The Complete Art of Witchcraft* she even develops a theology for the "Old Religion" by mixing in the Asian motifs of the duality of nature (as in the Chinese concepts of Yin and Yang), karma, and reincarnation with the theme of the lunar worship already familiar to us from *Aradia*. This religious earnestness indicates the extent to which today's covens are the natural heirs of the moralizing secret societies of an earlier era.

Is this a religious experience at all compatible with the more familiar Judeo-Christian tradition? Anton LaVey has chided those who accept the "Old Religion" for lacking the will to see themselves as true anti-Christians, but his own view relies on a quite one-sided presentation of Christianity. Gerald Gardner saw no problem in a person being both a Christian, however heterodox, and a witch, and I know of no coven in his tradition that calls for the explicit renunciation of Christianity that was part of the medieval legend. This may be an outlook many Christian fundamentalists find upsetting, but it is a quite common view of the witches themselves.

In the first chapter I mentioned that the young who have accepted the idea of witchcraft as part of the counterculture have not typically thought of their practices as holding any religious significance. Many are quite willing to follow Anton LaVey and Philip Bonewits (author of *Real Magic*) in a totally materialistic outlook on magic. But this, to my mind, has not kept the return of magic from being a religious phenomenon. Witchcraft may not always be a complete belief system in itself, but it is something functioning in the absence of other beliefs in order to satify a specifically religious need— the need to find a significance to the person that transcends the limits of ordinary experience and to achieve a kind of experience in which the reality of this transcendence is confirmed.

Religious needs are not equally strong for all persons or in all cultural settings. They appear in their most striking forms when other institutional forces are weakening. The first covens of the 1950s coincided with a dramatic increase in the appeal of the church after the chaos of World War II and the tensions of the Cold War. In both periods men were looking inward, and religion and magic alike gained a new hearing. The costumed occultism of the counterculture, born in the reaction to Vietnam, gained a remarkable hold on the public imagination at the same time that a powerful new fundamentalism began to take shape with the self-styled Jesus People.

As a historian I have had to point out that the legend of the "Old Religion," no matter how beautifully presented, remains a quite recent addition to the mainstream of Western occultism. Nevertheless, to the more serious covenists, Wicca fulfills a real need, and it is for them alone to judge the worth of the religious experience they derive from it.

4.

Brother Heinrich's Wicked Ladies

TANYA MAY CALL HERSELF a witch today, but three centuries ago such an assertion in the Christian world could have brought her an invitation to appear before the local magistrates. In the offing might be torture and the prospect of death for having committed the most heinous crime known to the medieval mind.

Of course, this was not true everywhere or at all times. In the Russia of her ancestors, for instance, there were never the widespread witchcraft prosecutions that characterized Western Europe, simply because Russia had not yet outgrown the pogroms that in Europe had preceded the massacres of those accused of witchcraft.

Tanya's grandmother once recounted the manner in which almost all the people of her village were slaughtered in a pogrom that occurred when she was a tiny child. It was not necessary to look for those who trafficked with the Devil while the

Jews were at hand to absorb the aggressions created by an unmanageable environment. And, to recall the horror of the age in which I was growing up, Europe found itself quite able to return to a use of the pogrom when again it was necessary to procure victims for the dark gods of material success.

It is only a coincidence that Tanya should be both Jewish and a witch. The irony is that, were we still living under medieval standards, Tanya would probably be acquitted of the basic charge of witchcraft because she is not a baptized Christian and so cannot be the apostate which by definition the witch is made out to be. Nevertheless, her acknowledgment of the world of magic in both belief and practice would damn her under the laws that prohibit sorcery, and under torture she might still be asked what she knows of the renegade Christians who attend the "sabbaths" and "synagogues" of the witches. In some areas, if she were to be let off gently for a first offense, she might be forced to wear a headdress known as a "Jew's hat" to mark her public disgrace.

Although contemporary presentations of witchcraft typically propose romantic origins for the term "sabbat" that would distinguish it from the Jewish Sabbath, the slightest acquaintance with medieval sources indicates that a crude anti-Semitism dictated both this and other usages. Groups of witches were, for instance, consistently referred to as "synagogues"; the term "coven" does not appear in the trial literature until it is used in Scotland in the late seventeenth century. The leader of the witches' ride, in the areas and periods when this concept was central to the picture of the witch, is often none other than Herodias, the scandalous Jewish queen who provoked her daughter into asking for the head of John the Baptist on a platter.

In the worst periods of the witchcraft panic of the sixteenth and seventeenth centuries, witches were frequently accused of the same anti-social activities (poisoning wells, murdering infants) that were earlier attributed to the Jews. And finally, like the Jew, the witch is damnable not for what he does but for what he is—the one who has turned against Christ.

The implicit association of Judaism and witchcraft is, I think, the key to an understanding of the medieval legend of the witch that eventually would give rise to fantasies such as *Aradia* and the Celtic reconstructions of Margaret Murray and Gerald Gardner. It also explains why in a country such as Spain there were few prosecutions and no hysteria at the time when Western Europe generally was convulsed by the fear of witches. The Spanish church was too busy with the *moriscos*, the Jews and Muslims who had only nominally converted to Catholicism after an edict by Ferdinand and Isabella that required the exile of non-Christians. In Italy, another country in which the witchcraft craze never really got started, it was enough to fear the Protestants. (This association is also, as we shall see later, the key to an understanding of the tradition of ceremonial magic that penetrated all talk of witchcraft both in the Middle Ages and again in modern times.)

Although the actual history is far more complex than the legend of the "Old Religion" developed by Margaret Murray, there is a measure of truth in her assertion that the lore of the witch reflected a pagan background. There were two social classes able to resist enforced Christianization in the early Middle Ages. One was the people of the countryside (the *pagani*, from the Latin word for a country district) who, like the Indian and *mestizo* populations of Latin America today, made Catholicism a veneer for more ancient practices. The other was the educated aristocracy.

Many non-Christian aristocrats, men of wealth and culture,

held out until the sixth century, two hundred years after Constantine, largely by taking on as house chaplains the displaced professors of Greek philosophy, which had already been integrated with the remnants of Greek religion in the first centuries of the Christian era, and by sending their sons to be educated at the still non-Christian schools of philosophy in Alexandria and Athens. When the Muslim invaders overran what was left of the Roman Empire in the south and east they found the magical traditions of alchemy, astrology, and sorcery quite alive despite persistent Christian efforts to suppress them. It was through Islam, we might note, that the highly intellectualized Hellenistic magic was again made available to Western Europe.

The population of remote rural areas presented two problems. There was always the resistance provided by the continuation of ancient practices, and the danger of a relapse into heathen beliefs was only partially eased by the church taking over feast days (such as Candlemas in place of a pagan fire festival), "baptizing" local divinities ("Saint" Christopher or "Saint" George), and adapting old customs (erecting a fir tree at Christmas or decorating eggs at Easter). Orgiastic fertility rites were not so easily assimilated, and in the old literature there are the cases of parish priests reprimanded for their part in sponsoring such festivals.

The other, eventually the more difficult, problem was the appeal of the heretic or the visionary for a people already resentful of the power and privileges of the Catholic clergy. Even more formidable than reformers such as the Waldenses who went from Lyons to Italy was the dualist orientation of Persian Zoroastrianism (the idea that good and evil, light and darkness, spirit and matter, God and the Devil are distinct realities in a contest for the souls of men), which had been prevalent in many of the groups that came to rival the new Christian church.

The Persian prophet Mani utilized this dualism when in the third century he structured a church of his own along the lines developed by the Catholic hierarchy, and his philosophy (Manicheanism) was kept alive through a succession of medieval movements, including the Bogomils in the Balkans and the Cathari or Albigenses in southern France. The Dominican order was organized originally to battle the influence of the Cathari through more effective preaching, and it has been argued that the combative stance of these priests carried over as a principal factor in the prosecution of witches after the Cathari had been destroyed.

Country people barely able to keep straight the fine points of an orthodox theology were not likely to avoid a certain distortion of heresy as well. A cry against the wealth of the church, for instance, could be translated into a murderous uprising against all those who held power in the name of Christ. There were quite literal devil worshipers in isolated areas of medieval Europe, and this gave credence to the legend of witchcraft as it was later developed.

The church itself was hardly in a position to appreciate the manner in which both the survival of pagan forms and the influence of heresies such as that of the Cathari ("the purified") had mingled to create the belief in witches. All acts of sorcery, no matter how trivial, had been regarded as diabolical by more orthodox theologians, and the presence of both folk magic and actual diabolism in the same era led to an understandable identification of the two. It led also to an ecclesiastical paranoia that was operative even when the more usual reasons to fear witchcraft, such as an epidemic or devastating weather, were absent.

This identification was not complete, however. The old attitude toward paganism and the new fear of heresy produced a curious contradiction in the church documents themselves. At a time when the church was concerned with downgrading the influence of older practices, there had appeared an ordinance from the court of Charlemagne which denounced the popular belief that there were women who rode the skies in the troop of the goddess Diana. According to this *Canon Episcopi*, priests were to explain that any such ride was an illusion created by the Devil to seduce the Christian from his faith in God as the sole source of miraculous powers. Through a misreading of the collection of decrees in which the *Canon Episcopi* appeared in the tenth century, it was understood as originating from the fourth-century Council of Ancyra and so holding the force of dogma. If read strictly, it appeared to condemn one of the essential beliefs of many later prosecutors: the marvelous transportation of witches to the remote areas where they would hold their "sabbaths." Undaunted defenders of the proposition that witches did make such nocturnal flights insisted on a distinction between the pagans noted by the *Canon Episcopi* and a newer, more dangerous *secta strigarum*, a cult of witches that had appeared at the beginning of the fifteenth century.

The fact that theologians could still debate the details of witchcraft (was the witches' sabbath a hallucination or an awful reality?) may have been one factor contributing to the decline of mass trials by the end of the seventeenth century, but seldom did it help those accused of witchcraft, the witch was damnable for what he was, not for what he did. For the church it was as sinful to take pleasure in an entirely imaginary orgy as it was to attend such revelries in person.

If we keep in mind that sorcery had been actionable even in

pagan Rome, we are in a better position to appreciate how trials that were taken for granted in the remnants of the battered Roman Empire could be expanded over a space of centuries into a legalized slaughter of gigantic proportions, an avalanche that swept away the last safeguards of personal liberty. Tragically, it was only when that happened that public opinion would begin to reverse itself and the hysteria would cease. How many died before that? Many writers accept the inflated body counts of overly zealous prosecutors and talk of nine million deaths; the horrendous figure of two hundred thousand is perhaps closer to the truth.

The legend of witchcraft as an evil distinct from mere sorcery began gathering momentum in the eighth century. In 1022 a trial for heresy in the French city of Orléans rehearsed the accusations of sex orgies and cannibalism that had already been used by Romans against Christians and by Christians against Jews. It also cited the claim that there was an instant transportation to obscene rituals where the Devil was adored in the form of a black man (a charge that was not then particularly racist, although a later racism would borrow from it).

In 1335 trials notable for two reasons were held by the Inquisition at Toulouse and at Carcassone, old centers of heresy. First, there is the use of the term "sabbat" indicating specific days for cult worship; second, torture was applied to extract the confessions needed for suspects to be delivered from the church to the state, "the secular arm," for execution. Within a century and a half the procedures and the charges for witch trials were fairly well defined, but the trials themselves were hardly as common as some could wish. In fact, it often seemed that local officials failed to appreciate the enormity of the diabolical conspiracy that had appeared since the advent of the fifteenth century and it would take an enthusiastic prosecutor to wake them up.

The Joseph McCarthy that the era required turned out to be an energetic middle-aged Dominican named Heinrich Kramer, otherwise known as Institutoris. He appears to have been a somewhat ruthless man who had made many powerful friends in Rome and through them gained himself a papal appointment in 1474 as Inquisitor for southern Germany. By 1476 Institutoris was well into his career as a witch hunter, but he often found his hands tied by the procedural niceties that restricted the scope of the Inquisition.

Ten years after his original commission, Institutoris obtained a document from Pope Innocent VIII that granted him and his fellow Inquisitor, Jacob Sprenger, full authority to hunt down witches, thus freeing their peculiar church tribunal from the limits set by more conservative bishops and magistrates. Two years later Institutoris persuaded Sprenger, who was also a professor of theology at Cologne, to lend his name as co-author of a new treatise, *Malleus Maleficarum* (*The Hammer of Witches*), through which Institutoris hoped to win back some of his reputation lost because of his excesses.

Not content with obtaining Sprenger's collaboration, Institutoris also made it appear (apparently through forgery) that the prestigious theological faculty at Cologne endorsed the work, when in fact only four professors were found willing to accept its extremism. It was not long before the somewhat more reasonable Sprenger and Institutoris had a falling out, and eventually, after the Dominicans had ordered him out of Germany, the Pope found Institutoris a new mission in eastern Europe.

What is tragic is that the widely reprinted *Malleus*, a long work written in the formal style of medieval discussions, became a classic reference for anyone who wanted to see witches in his own back yard. Skeptics found it easier to ignore than to refute—and, after all, it was printed together with a papal bull and a letter of approbation from the famous faculty of Cologne, documents enough to intimidate anyone.

Most of the spice of the book is provided by the early consideration of the beliefs that demons could function as sexual partners (the incubi and succubi) and that women, given the perversity of their nature and the insatiability of their lust, would readily accept the delights of demonic intercourse. Obviously a woman who would desire sex with a fallen angel is capable of the most horrible crimes, but Institutoris specializes in depicting their interest in abortion and infant sacrifice, a description which was to be cited against many a hapless midwife at the height of the hysteria. Moreover, witches not only caused impotence (a curiously recurrent theme in the early literature of witchcraft), but they could even simulate castration for some of the men unlucky enough to cross them. This was all in addition to the usual disasters of bad weather and poor crops.

Oddly enough the idea of the "synagogue" is absent, probably because it had not yet come to characterize the German lore with which Institutoris was most familiar, but perhaps also because it might have been counterproductive. The Inquisition, as the sex-obsessed Dominican saw it, was concerned with the discovery of the women who had consorted with demons and, in order to continue their infernal amours, had consented to act as instruments for the destruction of their Christian neighbors. Consequently, the fact of any personal misfortune, especially a sexual one, should be enough to encourage a "witness," whose anonymity could be protected throughout the trial, to denounce a witch. The witch hunts, as H. R. Trevor-Roper notes in his own analysis of the period, only continued the logic of the pogroms that earlier in the century had ravaged the same part of Germany in which the *Malleus* appeared.

The references to a "race of witches" are particularly disturbing in their suggestion that what may have been a voluntary transgression on the part of the parent could become a metaphysical stigma with the child, which could easily be used to rationalize genocide.

Brother Heinrich is a frightening manifestation of the kind of hysteria that we have come to expect whenever there is talk of an alien conspiracy. Were he a priest today, we might find him whipping up the local Knights of Columbus against the Communist peril and writing richly documented analyses of the subversive messages to be found in rock music. The Inquisition, which normally was an investigative body under the jurisdiction of the local bishop, was given a free hand by the Pope, and in his lethal efficiency Institutoris taught the West how really to hunt witches.

The documents from the France and Germany of the next two centuries attest to the manner in which over and over communities, following the example of trials in other areas, would decimate themselves and then recoil from what they had done. The lore of the *Malleus* presented witches as sex-starved women, and, as H. C. Erik Midelfort points out in his own study of the witch hunts, this was the period when earlier marriage patterns were breaking down and there were far greater numbers of unmarried women to provoke the suspicions of concerned officials.

Unattached or unfaithful women were by no means the only victims once the hunts began in earnest. Since each victim had to confess who else had surrendered himself to the Devil, lists would be compiled that included men, women, and children as well as the elderly. Innkeepers and midwives were among the individuals most likely to be named in a first round of accusations, but unpopular landlords and businessmen would come soon after. Dissident officials, particularly those who criticized the conduct of the trials, were also easy marks for their colleagues, but often enough one or another of the prosecutors was caught in his own net. The confession of a prosecutor, named perhaps by vengeful suspects, was typically the signal for a last burst of panic before the community recognized the absurdity of its position. Even afterward it would take years for the factionalism caused by the trials to subside, and the prevailing bitterness might permit still new witch hunts to take place. And all this in the name of religion and the public order!

It is important to note that despite the picture we have of Heinrich Institutoris the majority of trials in Europe were not conducted by the Inquisition, and they made little use of the ponderous *Malleus Maleficarum*. The divisions introduced into Christendom by the Protestant Reformation only strengthened the conviction of French and German communities that the Devil had in fact come to play a terrifying new role in human events. Protestants and Catholics, divided on other matters of doctrine, agreed that those who made a pact with Satan had committed the worst of human crimes, one so horrible and yet so hidden that it justified the use of extraordinary procedures for its detection. Neither malicious action (*maleficium*) nor physical attendance at a sabbat was as significant for continental prosecutors as the fact that someone out of lust or greed had renounced his baptismal vows to become the Devil's own.

One of the persistent ironies of the trials is that the confessions were accepted as reliable indicators of the extent of diabolical activity within a community. Repeatedly the witches would admit that they had been deceived by the Father of Lies when his promised gold would turn into dung or broken pottery or when demonic sex proved painful rather than pleasant. Even the sabbats had to be regarded as quite possibly illusory. But when a person, no matter what his age or position, was named a witch by several suspects, he too had to face the torturers.

Seldom did a suspect fail to say whatever he felt was expected of him, and the circumstantiality of his confession was used to rebut any later recantations. The only alternative—absolutely unthinkable to these pious men—would be to accept the possibility that the trials themselves were a lie.

Up to this point we have been talking about the development of the witchcraft legend in the areas of Europe where there had already been persecutions of the Cathari and the Jews. Of the various theories as to why the witchcraft craze began as it did in the late fifteenth century, Trevor-Roper favored the idea that it represented a perennial conflict between the townspeople of the plains and the often racially distinct population of the hills. Midelfort saw it as following from the dislocations produced in part by the socioeconomic changes at the end of the Middle Ages, in part by the conflicts between Catholics and Protestants brought about by the Reformation. And, of course, there are the old and now discredited theories that the trials resulted from the sexual frustrations of the clergy or from the eagerness of the prosecutors to confiscate the property of the condemned.

What we have to keep in mind is that the medieval idea of the witch had been developing for centuries. At first it was the stereotype of the ugly old woman riding a broom (as in a late thirteenth-century illustration) with a demon by her side in the form of a cat or a toad. In the sixteenth and seventeenth centuries that stereotype broke down completely. In this dangerous new age, it was thought, the Devil could buy the worship of anyone. The great astronomer Kepler, for instance, was helpless to prevent the arrest of his mother as a witch; perhaps fortunately, she died in prison before her trial. In the early seventeenth century a group of Ursuline nuns at a convent in Loudun exhibited signs of demonic possession, and an unpopular priest, Urban Grandier, was executed as a sorcerer who had committed their souls to the Devil. Yes, Satan could be anywhere, even in the church itself.

I agree with Midelfort's argument that the witch hunts in general reflected an uncertainty as the medieval era gave way to the modern, but also a witch hunt could occur simply because a community aware of their existence elsewhere found itself with evidence that the Devil had struck them as well.

What happened at Salem in the colony of Massachusetts is a good case in point. All told, less than fifty persons would die in America on a charge of witchcraft, but twenty of these victims were from Salem in the one horrendous panic of 1692.

In order to understand Salem we should note that in the sixteenth and seventeenth centuries England and her colonies appeared far less preoccupied with witchcraft than was continental Europe. There was never, for instance, the concern with heresy that had become the substance of the continental trials, and torture was not used to extract the type of confession that had perpetuated the witch hunts of France and Germany.

Chadwick Hansen's book *Witchcraft at Salem* is a belated effort to rescue the Puritan leadership of Massachusetts, especially Cotton Mather, from the charges laid against them by unsympathetic chroniclers. What happened, as he tells us, is that a dabbling in divination did lead to hysterical reactions in a clique of teenaged girls. The initial charge of witchcraft seemed vindicated when one of the women accused by the girls (Tituba, a Carib Indian slave) freely confessed to diabol-

ism. Subsequent investigations produced evidence suggesting
that several more of those who were later tried also engaged in
the practice of witchcraft, even to the point of black magic,
but this in itself would not have marked Salem—or its trials—
as any different from other communities in America or England.

What did distinguish Salem was that the court opted to accept "spectral evidence"—the descriptions given by the girls of
how they could "see" various members of the community
engaged in malicious actions against them—contrary to the
strongly worded advice of Cotton Mather, who had earlier
been quite successful in dealing with similar cases of hysteria.
Since hysteria thrives on attention, a number of men and
women were indicted, convicted, and executed before the
judges realized that the multiplying accusations, which soon
began reaching to some of the most influential citizens of the
commonwealth, had to be delusory. This about-face squelched
the phenomena that had precipitated the trials, and the Salem
experience was one factor in the rewriting of British law by
which all such prosecutions were ended. Witches could still be
arrested, but only as frauds.

Salem today has become a tourist attraction for those eager
to see mementos of this rather dark chapter in American history. Episodes in the television series *Bewitched* were filmed
there in order to mix together old and new legends—the medieval conception of the witch as the devotee of Satan and the
Hollywood rendition of the witch as a kind of fun superbeing.
But the truth is that something ugly happened there, and no
amount of laughter can undo the evil that was done in the
name of God and the Crown.

All of this talk of witches as the consorts of the Devil became unfashionable once a new scientific mentality had ap-

peared. The trials themselves began to fade away even before this happened, the result of a growing realization, as at Salem, that the law was not an appropriate vehicle for dealing with what people called the supernatural. Moreover, as Trevor-Roper points out, a general decline in the use of torture as a technique of interrogation meant that there were fewer confessions, and the fewer the confessions the less likelihood there would be of further trials.

But in the areas where old views die slowly, as in the countryside of Devonshire that Tanya recalls so well, a fear of witchcraft can still lead to violence. Doreen Valiente recounts the story of a Devonshire farmer who assaulted a woman he accused of bewitching his pig. His intent had been to draw blood to break her spell, and he had threatened to kill her. This was in 1924, but I would not doubt that the same outlook continues today.

Tanya is perhaps lucky that as a schoolgirl in that area she did not speak of her own witchcraft; she too might have experienced such an assault. Even now one reason for our continued use of pseudonyms is that we are not so sure that someone somewhere will not blame her for whatever private misfortunes are taking place.

The American philosopher George Santayana once remarked that men who are ignorant of history are condemned to repeat its lessons. I have the strong suspicion that the reverse is true also. We often need the experience of the present to appreciate the meaning of the past.

The witch hunts that took place in the twilight of the Middle Ages can be seen as a special case of the great spy hunts that occur whenever people fear subversion by a strong and cunning enemy. The psychology that provoked them would not change, however, even though an old metaphysics might give way to a new. As Arthur Miller was to suggest through his play *The Crucible*, the fear of sabotage remains pretty much the same whether the setting is seventeenth-century Salem or Washington during the McCarthy era. Only the gods and devils are different.

One of the least appealing things about any spy hunt is the manner in which the behavior of the patriots mimics the image held of the enemy. We find, for instance, the John Birch Society and the Minutemen replicating some of the more odious features of the Communist Party of the Soviet Union. The same can be said of the dictatorships of Greece or Brazil or South Vietnam when we read of the tactics, including indiscriminate arrests and often lethal torture, used to stop a real or imagined Communist menace.

In England, which was otherwise spared the worst features of the continental witch hunts, one of the unlovely characters brought forward by the prevailing fear of witchcraft was a somewhat unsuccessful attorney named Matthew Hopkins, who, beginning in 1644, systematically terrorized the county of Essex with a pretended commission from Parliament naming him Witch-Finder General. He offered his services for a fee and proved quite successful in extracting confessions when he circumvented the laws prohibiting the torture of suspects. Hopkins, who at one point claimed to have the Devil's roster of all the witches in England (one can imagine him standing in a village courtroom and proclaiming, "I have a list"), based his own image of the witch on the volume written by King James I shortly before his accession to the throne of a united England and Scotland.

James intended his book *Demonology* to counter skeptics such as Reginald Scot, author of *The Discovery of Witchcraft,* and in it he anglicized the European image of the witch as the Devil's paramour. The Statutes of 1604, passed a year after James came to England, expanded the definition of the actions constituting witchcraft and strengthened their penalties. The King was gradually to become far more of a skeptic himself, particularly after he saw one clear case of fraudulent bewitchment, but his book and his laws remained to haunt a later age. For the Essex lawyer they proved a shortcut to fame and fortune.

Following the descriptions given in the *Demonology*, Hopkins spent two years running down women whose pets might be taken to be incarnate demons ("familiars") sent to advise them in their evildoing. As well as using the psychological torture of round-the-clock interrogation, he revived the medieval ordeal of "swimming" a suspected witch—tossing the woman into a stream to see if she would float or sink on the assumption that the Devil would keep his servant from drowning. It was not long before his activities were halted by higher authorities, but, if we are to accept the old statistics, Hopkins was responsible for several hundred executions before he was brought to account both for his illegal procedures and for the profits he had made through his career of witch baiting.

One of the more curious aspects of the entire age of witch hunting is that, just as the fear of Communist terror can be used to justify an extraordinary degree of political repression, the fear of magic was one of the things leading otherwise God-fearing citizens to undertake the forbidden practice of magic in their own defense. Doreen Valiente tells, for instance, of a glass-covered box alleged to have been sold by Hopkins as a protection against witches, among its contents some of the materials used in witchcraft.

Hypocrisy? The story is, I think, far more complicated.

What the ordinary person accepted, quite apart from the preaching about the intrinsic evil of sorcery that he might hear in his parish church, was that the practice of witchcraft did exist—and that it seemed to work. As in the thinking of the good Christians who borrowed money from Shylock in Shakespeare's *The Merchant of Venice*, it might be damnable to engage in a certain type of activity, but it was not damnable to take advantage of that activity. The pogroms ended, for example, when the European Christian found the Jew "useful" as the only one willing to engage in the forbidden but needed practice of moneylending. In England a mitigating factor in the witch hunts was that no one, apart from the most fanatic prosecutors, wanted to be free of *all* witches, lest he have no recourse against some new assault of the Evil One.

Jeffrey Burton Russell, a historian who has stressed the origins of the full witch craze in the beliefs and practices of earlier centuries, has suggested that only about 20 per cent of the witchcraft charges represented "theological embroidery." The rest followed from a lore that the theologians, including men like Institutoris, had learned rather than invented.

It is to this lore that we shall have to turn our attention next if we are to penetrate the legends of the old and the new witchcraft in order to find out just what was the truth about witches in the past and how it might help us understand the possibilities that magic holds for the present.

5.

The Truth About Witches

WE HAVE NOW LOOKED at two legends, one the reconstruction of the "Old Religion" by Margaret Murray and the latter-day covenists, the other the medieval image of the devil worshipers run to ground by zealous prosecutors stretching the limits of church and civil law. Although Tanya does not accept the contemporary coven as an appropriate vehicle for her own magic, nor does she fit the picture of one of the Devil's consorts, she still calls herself a witch. I have encouraged her and others in this usage, primarily because I have no adequate term to substitute but also because it connotes the sense of tradition which, I feel, is indispensable for effective magic. What, then, is the true history of those we today call witches?

The legends we have already discussed have dealt with a European background, and I am going to confine the considerations that follow to Western and especially to Celtic sources. Later we shall have to look at the meaning of magic in non-Western contexts, but for the present it may be enough to note that there is little in the lore of Africa, Asia, or the Americas that differs substantially from the lore of an older Europe.

Europe itself may be thought of as a beach hit by successive high tides, each depositing new materials. We know almost nothing about the first tides, since the bulk of our archeological evidence and all our written history is a product of the waves that broke afterward. By the second millennium, however, we can trace these metaphorical tides with greater precision. Several, such as the Achaeans and the Etruscans, developed civilizations that rivaled the more ancient cultures of Egypt and Syria with which they traded, but they in turn were submerged as new peoples pushed out of the area to the north of the Black Sea. Greeks and Romans poured into the peninsulas to the north of the Mediterranean, Iranians and Aryans into the Mideast and the subcontinent of India, and the Celts into the unspoiled territory of western Europe.

Once again contact with the Egyptians and the Phoenicians of Syria taught some of these new peoples patterns of culture that quickly brought them to the same cultural level. The Greeks used the Phoenician invention of the alphabet in order to preserve the memory of their Achaean cousins and predecessors in unparalleled literature as well as to transmute a fading Egyptian theology into the remarkable new vision of man that we find in the philosophies of Pythagoras and Plato. The Romans, who were master organizers rather than littérateurs like the Greeks, crushed their Etruscan rivals, destroyed the power of Phoenicia (the former ally of the Etruscans) in its North African colony of Carthage, and then moved on to annex first Greece and then the rest of the Mediterranean.

Organization, however, has its drawbacks. The Romans,

who were forced to contend with threats of a Celtic invasion as the people of the area known as Gaul were pushed south and west by their Teutonic relatives, began to look admiringly at the valor of their enemy. In sharp contrast to the self-indulgence that seemed a natural consequence of their successes, they saw the Celts living close to nature with a far greater honesty in their personal relationships. Caesar, for instance, wrote of the Druids, the Celtic priests, as philosophers who inspired Gallic warriors to new heights of bravery with a vision of reincarnation; and Tacitus a century later repeatedly cited Celtic exploits in what has to be the earliest version of the myth of the Noble Savage.

Eighteenth- and nineteenth-century writers were to accept these seemingly incompatible presentations of the Celts as unspoiled primitives and as mystics. The result was a fair measure of nonsense that anticipated the romanticism of Margaret Murray and Gerald Gardner and led to the appearance of reconstructed Druidic orders even before there were reconstructed covens.

The truth about the Celtic religion, which I also accept as the truth about Europe's first witches, is that it reflected a culture less barbaric than it appears in the presentation of Tacitus but also far less sophisticated than it was seen by Caesar. The Celts had already made contact with older cultures through their dealings with the Etruscans and, shortly before the beginning of the Christian era, were in a position analogous to that of the Indian tribes challenged by English colonists on the Atlantic seaboard. There were enough settlements and communication to permit the possibility of a new national unity, but the process was as yet incomplete. Just as European encroachments disrupted the timetable for the Iroquois to become a single united power in North America, Roman encroachments destroyed the budding nationalism of the disparate peoples of the Celts.

One of the critical engagements in this conflict took place in A.D. 61 at Anglesey when the Roman Paulinus subdued a British Druid center despite the efforts of black-garbed women to screech his troops into retreat. Just how powerful the Druids were in England before this time is uncertain. There is absolutely no evidence, for instance, to connect the Druids with the ruins at Stonehenge, and, despite Caesar's conjecture that their center was in Britain, it may be that they were only lately arrived from the continent. We do know that they formed a priestly caste in Gaul that shared the privileges of a heroic aristocracy with the warriors. It is quite possible that the standardization of ritual training for the Druids through a period that might take up to two decades had already developed a sensitivity to interests transcending the limited concerns of any one tribe. The consolidation of Druid power in England would have been an important step in achieving a Celtic unity in the face of the Romans. Their enemy sensed this, and the destruction of their stronghold was seen as a major achievement.

One of the factors that might have permitted the Druids to achieve some sort of Celtic unity was the worship of the god Cernunnos (the Horned One) who had more than just a regional appeal. This pastoral divinity was conventionally represented as possessing either antlers or horns and attended by a stag and a ram-headed serpent. The legends about Cernunnos depict him as lord of the animals, a status shown in Celtic art by having the god sit squat-legged among a retinue of beasts. He also appeared as lord of the underworld and therefore the source of wealth for his worshipers.

Suppression of the Druidic cult of Cernunnos was important

to the Romans for purely political reasons. With the advent of Christianity the Horned God found stubborn new enemies. Images of the squatting Cernunnos were taken over to depict the Devil, and the stories in which Cernunnos appeared as a huge black lord of the beasts were passed on as part of the folklore regarding the manner in which the Devil was seen by his followers. The color black, it should be noted, was a Celtic means of representing the supernatural; the color of death for a Celt was red.

Other gods and goddesses fared better under the Christians than Cernunnos. The best example of this is the threefold Brigantia (the High One) or Brigid, a Celtic mother goddess often associated by the Romans with Minerva, who became Saint Brigid of Kildare. Attributes of other divinities were attached to prestigious saints such as the monk Columba, who was supposed to know the language of the birds and to have a white horse that foretold its master's death. Lesser local divinities, such as the figures originally venerated as the protectors of wells and rivers, became the fays or fairies which theologians would think of as being either minor demons or souls of the unbaptized. Even a great pastoral festival such as Samuin (November 1) was Christianized into All Saints Day.

According to Roman accounts, the Druids engaged in animal and human sacrifice, and we know that the cult of the severed head was the most usual expression of Celtic religion. There is, however, nothing whatsoever to support Margaret Murray's contention that the Celtic priests engaged in the worship of Cernunnos by dressing in costumes to simulate his appearance, just as there is nothing to suggest the existence of covens as a kind of religious bureaucracy. Cernunnos is occasionally represented nude in his role as a god of war (the Celts fought stripped as a display of bravery against their heavily armored enemies), but again there is no reason to suppose that Celtic festivals required their participants to be "sky-clad."

The bloody festivals of roving bands of warriors hardly fit the image of the sabbat that developed finally in medieval lore, and it seems safe to say that the image of the "synagogue" or coven is part of the 20 per cent of witch lore that is strictly a clerical fabrication. Even the number thirteen associated with the sense of this word "coven" can be explained quite easily if we keep in mind that the term is only a variant of the word "convent." As the Scottish witch who contributed the term in her confession would most certainly have known, religious groups such as the Franciscans preferred to maintain their communities or convents as close as possible to the number made up by Jesus and his twelve apostles. The medieval trials at no time argued any specific size for the "synagogues."

Although shifting shape from human to animal form through some type of enchantment is an occasional motif in Greco-Roman mythology, for the Celts it is a major feature of a lore in which the worlds of birds, animals, and men continually interpenetrate.

It is also the source of the belief in vampirism, which the Celts shared with the Greeks and Romans. Warrior goddesses, particularly those who assumed the form of crows or ravens, might assault their enemies and literally tear them apart. In Greece these were monsters known as *lamiai*, in Rome either *lamiae* or *strigae* (from the word for an owl). Later tradition would somewhat demote these supernatural beings by presenting them as blood-sucking ghosts seeking to restore their lost vitality. In the Christian era what had been a fearsome characteristic of pagan goddesses would finally become one of the charges leveled against the baleful old women who fit the first stereotype of the witch.

The witch's cauldron, familiar to any reader of *Macbeth*, is another instance of Celtic lore cut down to size. Throughout the myths there are references to a cauldron of immortality. Moreover, since the Celts revered water more than any other element, it was only natural that buckets and cauldrons would also play a role in their conception of how to do a proper spell. "Boil and bubble, toil and trouble."

The Druids, although their worldly power was broken in battle with the Romans, did survive for several centuries into the Christian era, offering a lore which even on purely secular terms local warlords found superior to the learning of the first Christian priests they would have known. The development of a highly intellectual order of monks in Scotland with the sixth-century Columba meant that the Druids, already close to extinction, would no longer have even the advantage of their poetry against Christian priests who knew Latin and Greek literature as well as systematic theology. Myth deteriorated into a folklore which the Christians themselves felt free to take over for their own purposes, and the magic of the gods and goddesses underwent a process of infantilization to emerge as a set of rural superstitions for healing and divination.

Witchcraft itself was not yet a source of terror for the Christian. Quite the contrary. Charlemagne, who was crowned ruler of the new Holy Roman Empire on Christmas Day of 800, enforced prohibitions against belief in the old magic in his capitularies, as in the *Canon Episcopi* discussed earlier. True witches—beings able to effect marvelous actions by their own powers—did not, could not exist.

Despite these official disclaimers there was a body of Germanic folklore in which we can hear echoes of the roving war bands of a less settled age. According to these tales, a spirit, most commonly a goddess named Perchta or Holda and identified with the Roman Diana, led a band of spirits in a wild hunt that brought destruction to whoever would be in its path. In time these supernatural hunters were regarded as actual persons made capable of flight by the goddess—the belief which the *Canon Episcopi* attempted to suppress. In short order, however, belief in Diana gave way to belief in the Devil, and one of the components of the myth of the sabbat was established as medieval clerics decided that it was within the power of Satan to transport his followers to their obscene revelries. Diana, after all, did not exist, and the heresy rejected by the *Canon Episcopi* consisted in granting a pagan deity marvelous powers. The Devil was quite a different matter, and here the heresy would consist in denying his capabilities rather than in affirming them.

It was always understood that the Devil was not an entity independent of God. For the Christian, the depredations caused by Satan were to be understood as trials of the just permitted by the Lord. The Book of Job was here a basic text. Witches—those who accepted the mastery of Satan for whatever reason— were guilty of the crime of treason against the true lord of the world, and this was so even if the orgies attended by the witches were entirely hallucinatory, a delusion created by the Devil to entrap the wicked.

At this point the legend and the history intersect in a rather curious manner. Over and over in the trial literature there are accounts of voluntary confessions in which suspects claimed to have attended the sabbats even though they were known to have been asleep. For those who believed in malevolent witches this permitted the idea of "spectral evidence," as in the trials at Salem in which it was the astral bodies of the accused that supposedly engaged in mischief.

For the skeptics, however, it marked a chance to comment on the unusual properties of the ointments used by the witches. Since aconite, belladonna, and hemlock are among the drugs mentioned in traditional recipes for flying and for shape-shifting, the skeptics would appear to be quite correct in their assumption that the only "trips" taken by the witches were those caused by the salves. The question in my own mind is the extent to which recipes of this sort were in actual use.

Except for Margaret Murray and her followers, it has been conventional for students of the history of witchcraft to attribute the uncoerced confessions appearing in the literature to mental disorder. Excited descriptions of the sabbat, for instance, have been regarded as a hysterical response to. the bleakness and repression that characterized much of medieval life. Could it be, however, that they are expressions of a drug subculture rooted either in antiquity or in the more recent experiments of the people looked to as rural pharmacologists?

I venture this hypothesis rather cautiously. John M. Allegro in *The Sacred Mushroom and the Cross* has already argued the extreme view that much of the mythology of the ancient world, including the stories of the Old and New Testaments, reflects a drug and fertility cult that utilized the hallucinogenic mushroom *Amanita muscaria* (known in Europe as fly agaric). According to Allegro, this cult was still alive in the first century A.D. Officials of the nascent Christian community, ignorant of the true beginnings of the sect to which they had been converted, accepted documents such as the Gospels and Epistles at face value rather than as a coded initiation into the secrets of the cult. Heretics such as the Gnostics did keep the truth alive, but in time they were ruthlessly suppressed.

I would strongly dispute Allegro's basic thesis, but I must admit at the same time that a covert drug cult *could* have existed in the ancient world. It is possible that the knowledge of poisons, which was bound up with the meaning of witchcraft in the old imperial order, included a knowledge of how to use the same materials in limited dosage or through external application in order to create hallucinogenic effects. Such a knowledge might have been passed on with only the most limited of formal organization and survived more or less intact into the Middle Ages.

Regardless of whether the skill is concocting hallucinogenics was ancient or relatively recent, it apparently did exist in the Middle Ages. Memories of old Celtic cult practices, many of which survived in various folk practices, as well as a distorted understanding of Catharism would then have provided the basis for private reveries which, in an altered state of consciousness, assumed the form of a thoroughly satisfying "separate reality." This would be an experience far less spiritual than the ecstasy approved by the medieval church, but it would have proven highly functional for the men and women who lived on the margins of the society of the Middle Ages.

What of the more repugnant aspects of the recipes—the use, for instance, of the fat from the bodies of infants or the marrow from the bones of children? Most likely this is embroidery by the demonologists. But possibly there were individuals who did accept the necessity of such substances, and there *could* have been actual cases either of infanticide or of the desecration of graves to obtain them.

I would repeat that all of this is pure conjecture. The one reason that I am interested in this idea of the medieval witches as adherents of a drug cult is that I am aware of the role drugs have played in the occultism of more recent times. Aleister Crowley scandalized his former associates from the Golden Dawn by his own acceptance of opium and cocaine as legitimate adjuncts to the practice of magic, and the revival of a more free-lance witchcraft in the late 1960s is intimately connected with the use of drugs by the young. This could also have been the case in the Middle Ages. Celtic religion flourished in an atmosphere of unbelievably hard drinking, and the Dionysiac cult of Greece—itself an underground religion that co-existed with the more respectable worship of the temples—required alcohol as a vehicle for ecstasy. Could not the systematic use of hallucinogenics have functioned similarly for even less orthodox subgroups within the worlds of Greek and Celtic magic?

Even if this hypothesis could be substantiated, it should be kept in mind that Celtic beliefs and practices were so disparate that there was nothing that even approached a universal cult. The poet Robert Graves, for instance, has argued to the contrary that there was a cult of the "White Goddess" throughout ancient Europe and, following Margaret Murray, that the medieval covens kept this "Dianic cult" alive in a later age.

It is true, of course, that a lunar motif appears in Greek lore in the triplicity of Artemis-Selene-Hecate (waxing moon, full moon, waning moon) and that Celtic representations of a mother goddess (the Magna Mater) often paralleled this Greek image. But the Celts generally favored the idea of triads. Moreover, unlike their Greek counterpart, the Celtic mother goddesses are seldom depicted with the attributes that would mark them as goddesses of the hunt—a vital feature in the cult of Diana as it has been understood by modern covenists. If not even the Druids, the servants of Cernunnos, appeared everywhere in the Celtic world, the existence of a widespread matriarchal cult dedicated to the Celtic equivalent of Diana seems rather unlikely.

I tend to follow Jeffrey Burton Russell's presentation of the medieval understanding of the witch as marking a gradual humanization of the characteristics of the older Celtic deities. There was doubtlessly a great amount of sorcery in the Celtic world even apart from the arts practiced by the tribal shamans we know as Druids. This witchcraft did, I believe, outlast the fall of the Druids and the preaching of Christian priests. Its practitioners were more likely than not to be women, who were otherwise excluded from both Druidic and Christian ministries.

By the time of the Middle Ages these witches, often holding their practices secret because of the prohibition of sorcery, would themselves be Christians, although theirs was a Christianity with strong Celtic overtones. As in the Voodoo of Haiti, even the language of sorcery might change in order to reflect the official beliefs superseding the more primitive religion of a subjugated people, but the sorcery itself presumed a mythic structure drawn from an all but forgotten era. Ironically, again as in Haiti, the ways of a vanished priesthood would be preserved by individuals who in an earlier era would have been excluded from such a ministry. To this extent, then, it is correct to speak of the "Old Religion," but it is hardly the sense intended by Margaret Murray.

There were obviously many other influences at work in shaping the witchcraft of the Middle Ages. The legend developed by the prosecutors, injecting as it did a reading of the world in Catharist terms, would have led the witches themselves to substitute the Devil for Cernunnos in their recollection of a Celtic past, but it was the Devil seen as a friend of mankind rather than as its implacable adversary.

Another influence was the tradition of ceremonial magic reintroduced into the West by those familiar with its continuity in the hybrid culture of the Islamic world. The grimoires, for example, strongly paralleled Celtic witchcraft even though the magicians, typically men from an urban intellectual background, consistently interpreted their sorcery as a manipulation of the occult powers of nature rather than as the erotic devil worship attributed to ignorant peasant women. In time, however, bits and pieces of the lore of the grimoires would have become intermingled with Celtic practices in such a way as to reinforce the image of the witch as the one who cultivated demonic powers.

Along the way, one potentially damning element had been introduced into the lore of what witches could and could not do. This was the idea that the soul of the witch could in some manner separate from the body in order to attend the sabbats or to work *maleficia*. The concept of the *lamia* or *striga* from Greco-Roman folklore came to be applied to witches in general. It was no longer a question of shape-shifting, as in lycanthropy, but of the insidious action of the astral or spectral body of the witch.

In keeping with this idea it was felt that demoniacs were persons infested by the alien powers worshiped by the witch. Through the ceremonies connected with exorcism the bewitched party could be compelled to reveal the source of the evil that troubled him. He might even be able to witness what happened with the witch's spectral body regardless of what was known about the location or activities of the physical body.

In Loudun in the 1630s a hysterical French prioress, Soeur Jeanne des Anges, convinced enough responsible individuals that she was possessed to bring about the arrest of a priest, Urban Grandier, who had earned the enmity of Loudun's principal citizens. During his trial the prosecutors heard testimony to the effect that the priest, despite his internment, had still been able to assault the nuns in their convent. Convicted as a *sorcier*, Grandier was tortured, then burned alive.

Soeur Jeanne, whose frantic recantation had been regarded by the prosecutors as further evidence of the intensity of her possession, was finally freed of her demons and became som... thing of a celebrity in the court of Louis XIII. The King's son, the future Louis XIV, was born with the nun's supposedly miraculous chemise upon his mother's stomach, and even the worldly, ailing Richelieu granted her an audience at a time when his door was barred to everyone else.

For Aldous Huxley, whose *The Devils of Loudun* is a classic retelling of this incident, Soeur Jeanne had only been playacting at possession in order to gain attention but became so caught up in her role that she was perhaps unable herself to tell where reality left off and a morbid world of her own imagining began. This would not have made her unique within her age. I mentioned earlier that James I, the king who was determined to rid England of the plague of witches, was persuaded to change his views after witnessing one clear case of fraudulent possession, and always there is the tragedy of Salem at the very end of the century.

What is horrifying to us in retrospect is not so much that frauds and hysterics were granted the attention they desired, but that innocent men and women had to undergo torture and death because of their testimony. If it was a curse upon an age that hysterics who thought themselves witches could die violently, it was an even greater curse that hysterics could present themselves as possessed and have others die as a result.

When we look back on so much unrelieved horror, would it not have been better for the tradition of Celtic magic to have died out with the Druids? Had no one been left to tell the old stories or perform the old spells and so give credence to the church's legend of the witch, would not the Middle Ages have known a greater peace than it did? This I doubt. Even before the days of the *Malleus Maleficarum* there had been pogroms, and in Eastern Europe after the witch craze had ended there would be a comparable panic because of alleged incidents of vampirism. The men of the Middle Ages, raised in an atmosphere of crusading, would have persisted in finding adversaries, especially ones determined on a supernatural basis. As far as the history of that period is concerned, it could not have mattered that much whether there really were witches (in the sense of individuals keeping alive old practices) or not.

Principally because of what we know of the cunning men and cunning women of England, I do accept that there were witches who to some extent sustained an outlook that antedated Christianity. Included in this outlook were a certain amount of practical knowledge, including techniques for utilizing paranormal capabilities (as in divination), and a fair measure of poetry. The large-scale witch trials, as Midelfort concludes, were in the long run dysfunctional for the societies in which they occurred, but witchcraft itself served quite real needs. At the very least, as the anthropologists point out, it often provided a substitute for physical aggression.

Would the same be the case today? True, many of the functions of an older magic have been taken over by the scientist. Physicians prescribe compounds that are often derived from the materials used in witchcraft, and psychiatrists and psychologists attempt to cope with the same terrors and anxieties that brought the witch his clients.

We shall attempt later to assess what it is that we have lost with the departure of magic from the modern consciousness and what we are offered by its return. But first we must look more closely at the complex tradition that was developing in the Mediterranean world even while the Druids were experiencing their decline and fall.

In the chapters that follow we shall enter more deeply into the world of Hellenistic magic, the source of most of the lore that contemporary witches accept as their heritage without knowing its true origin. This is the world of astrology and alchemy, the world too of ceremonial magic. It is the world that is Tanya's even more than the "fairy arts" derived from the Celts. And with its study we may also begin, I think, to understand something more of the true significance of occultism in the development of Western thought, here including even the scientific viewpoint that by definition would seem completely opposed to all that is meant by magic.

6.

A Brief History of Ancient Magic

THE PICTURE WE HAVE of Celtic society as it survived well into the Middle Ages is that of a heroic aristocracy not too different from the society of the Achaeans described by Homer or the world of the Hindus before the coming of Islam. The magic of the Celts, apart from the powers attributed to various supernatural entities, rested with individuals at either end of the social scale. At the top of the society there were the tribal shamans or priests carrying on practices that required lengthy training; at the bottom were the otherwise burdensome "old wives" who possessed a cruder lore of their own. This, I think, is a pattern replicated throughout the world.

There is another pattern as well. An elite priesthood tends to become inaccessible, and the outcast who mimics the rituals of the priest takes on a new importance, particularly when the outcast in some manner represents the priesthood of an earlier time. The Voodoo of Haiti is a classic example of how this pattern functions. The same pattern can be found in the Mediterranean world in the period immediately before the era of international power politics begun by Alexander the Great. What happened afterward was that there was an explosion of occult interests as the lore of the much older world of the Mideast began to circulate throughout the Mediterranean and into the back country of Europe. A later age looking backward would, if anything, tend to exaggerate the extent to which Mediterranean sorcery was part of the early Hellenistic period. Even Alexander himself was presented in medieval romances as the natural son of the sorcerer Nectanebo.

In the same spirit, historians who were several centuries removed from the days of Pythagoras and Plato developed increasingly elaborate accounts of the manner in which Greek philosophy had preserved the occult teachings of the Egyptian priesthood.

The Neoplatonists also systematized an outlook toward magic in which "theurgy," a white magic relying on the demonic forces intermediate between the gods and men, was opposed to "goetia," the typically malicious sorcery of individuals such as Nectanebo. This was a distinction that would continue through the Middle Ages as a way of separating an acceptable occultism from the varied practices associated with the witch and the black magician.

The actual story of the transmission of the magic of Egypt and the lands to the east is far less romantic than the versions known to a medieval audience. In order to understand it, we should keep in mind that Alexander's achievement created an atmosphere in which the parochial outlook of someone like Aristotle, Plato's most famous student and Alexander's tutor, was superseded by a new cosmopolitanism. Heirs of the Magi, the priests who specialized in dream analysis for the rulers of

Persia, and of the Chaldeans, the priests who had preserved Babylonian astrology through the succession of empires that ruled on the Tigris and Euphrates, mingled in new cities such as Alexandria with Hindu ascetics and Buddhist missionaries.

There were also the inevitable charlatans. The legends of a former Egyptian greatness always improved in the telling, and instead of a forgotten technology occult powers were given the credit for monuments such as the Sphinx and the Pyramids.

The oldest and most respected of the various bits of magic then in use was astrology, the art of divination through the stars. In its origins it appears to have been concerned only with the positions of the sun, moon, and five visible planets; and the significance of the number seven throughout the ancient world is usually explained by this fact. Within the first millennium, however, the concept of the zodiac, the belt of constellations through which these heavenly bodies seemed to move, was made the key to a more complex science of divination. Now, in addition to the characteristics associated with each planet (counting the sun and moon), there were the characteristics of the constellations already standardized in terms of an elegant procession of animals. Depending on what stars were in the sky when a person was born and on the constellations in which they were located, a horoscope could be prepared that would detail a person's fortune down to the time of his death.

The first horoscope that we know of was prepared in the fifth century B.C. Two centuries later the priest Berosus, an émigré from the turbulence of Persia, opened a school for astrologers on the Greek island of Cos, and it was not long before the average citizen of the Hellenistic world paid as much attention to his chart as does the average citizen today. Such interest was not always acceptable to those who ruled the Mediterranean. Claudius, for example, banished the astrologers because of their readiness to predict the time of his death. A dislike for all astrologers but one's own came to mark a number of the Roman emperors.

Many of the philosophers, anticipating the outlook of the Christian theologians, felt a similar distaste for astrology. Like Shakespeare, who wrote, "The fault, dear Brutus, is not in our stars but in ourselves," they found a certain incompatibility between the logic of astrology and their own conceptions both of human freedom and of divine providence. A horoscope, it seemed to them, risked becoming an excuse for avoiding the rigors of a virtuous life. And it still remained to be seen how it was possible for the stars to influence human events with the degree of detail posited by the astrologers, especially when so many individuals with the same chart would lead such different lives.

Astrology obviously survived all the efforts of both princes and philosophers to outlaw it as physically impossible, morally suspect, and politically dangerous. Still, by comparison with other practices, astrology possessed a quiet dignity. For anyone who wanted to engage in the business of sorcery, even if on no larger a scale than the preparation of amulets, there were lists upon lists of minutely detailed prescriptions drawn from a dozen cultures. Pliny, a contemporary of Claudius, in his *Natural History* recorded a number of volumes of the lore regarding the supposedly occult properties of almost anything that one could think of that was animal, vegetable, or mineral. Writers such as Pliny, in other words, regarded the magic of the time as the product of an ancient science rather than recognizing that their own science, such as it was, had been an outgrowth of magic.

Some of these prescriptions reflect the type of concerns that might lead someone to consult a magician in the first place. The fact that some of these recipes call for slightly impossible ingredients, such as dragon parts, created still new possibilities for ambitious frauds.

Much simpler than the prescriptions calling for more or less exotic materials were the amulets that had become a universal feature of everyday magic in the later Hellenistic world. Most were of Egyptian origin, and the most popular was the scarab, a stone, paste, or glass representation of the dung beetle that was the emblem of the god Khepera, the divinity who rolled the sun across the heavens. Since the sun was the source of all life, the scarab was taken as a source of immortality and thus as a powerful protection against bad luck of all kinds. The basic idea of any amulet—and of magic in general—can be seen in this example. A concrete object (the beetle that rolled its eggs into balls of dung that would provide a low heat for their hatching) is seen as corresponding to a spiritual force, and the power of the spirit is encapsulated in a representation of the object.

Later ages saw an increasing sophistication in the types of amulets in use. Already the Gnostics, the great rivals of orthodox Christianity, had made extensive use of semiprecious stones inscribed with the names or figures of various divinities, most notably the god Abraxas—one possible source of the all-purpose magical word "abracadabra." These seals might also be inscribed on parchment or on anything else that would take an image, and in time their usage developed into an exotic shorthand that is still important for those engaged in ceremonial magic.

All of this, however, was just a minor part of the occupation of those who were professional magicians. Anyone might read a collection such as Pliny's *Natural History*, and amulets were available everywhere; the real work of the sorcerer lay in his

conjuration of demonic forces after the manner of good King
Solomon.

The basis for this more serious ceremonial magic lay in a
belief common to most primitive peoples that a name in some
manner incorporates a person's being. Knowledge of someone's secret name, like possession of bits of his hair or parings
from his nails, could be a source of power over him. Babylonian magic, which attributed illnesses of all types to the activity of demons, had utilized a knowledge of the names of
these demons in order to develop exorcism into a fine art.
Only the most depraved or the most foolhardy would undertake to reverse this process and command the demons to appear for whatever benefit they felt this might bring them.

This Babylonian concept had been refined by the introduction of the alphabet and the subsequent use, as in Hebrew and
Greek, of the letters of the alphabet to function as numerals.
The traditional Jewish refusal to pronounce the name of God
(Jahweh or Jehovah) had given the four letters composing it
(the Tetragrammaton JHVH) a particular mystical significance. Later exegesis would, by substituting words whose letters added up to the same numerical value as the letters of the
Tetragrammaton, develop a whole list of the supposedly secret
names of God. The validity of this procedure was reinforced
by Pythagorean and Platonic speculation on the "numbers"
constituting the five regular solids and through them the five
elements (earth, air, fire, water, and the ether) that made up
the visible universe. Science and religion alike seemed mysteri-
ously linked through numerology, and the magician was only
following the lead of the philosophers and the scholarly rabbis
when he attempted to develop elaborate lists of the angels,
fallen and otherwise, and their specific powers through this
same type of analysis.

To the intellectuals of the ancient world, neither language

nor the properties of numbers seemed quite as arbitrary or as irrelevant as they might to us. In the early centuries of the Christian era, for instance, a Palestinian named Nicomachus of Gerasa could write *Theologoumena Arithmetica* (*The Theology of Numbers*). In the same period there appeared the Hebrew *Sefir Yetsirah* (*The Book of Creation*), a numerologically inspired discussion that gave a precise accounting of the spirits associated with the stars and seasons, times of the day and points of the compass, locations and operations. Even though neither volume was concerned with magic as such, both contributed to sorcery. The work of Nicomachus became one of the sources for the theurgists, who were the last heirs of Plato's Academy; and the *Sefir Yetsirah* was the primary source for the Cabala, which reached its peak in the twelfth century and was quickly adopted by non-Jewish occultists.

The true sorcerer, the practitioner of the "goetic art" condemned by Roman law and later by Christian theology, was the man who argued that the names of the demons could be known and that they could be conjured through interminable recitations performed according to unbelievably exacting requirements. In order to accomplish this task, through which he would have access to perpetual health and to the treasures of the earth that were also in the charge of demons, he would have to live a life as exacting as that of any monk. Only a man of great moral purity could hope to subdue the demons, and it is easy to see that for the more moralistically inclined the preparation for sorcery could become an end in itself.

Clad in white linen, chaste and fasting for days at a time, the true sorcerer would present a formidable image of a man in full control of himself and thus in control of the occult powers of the world. There are no indications that this picture was anything more than fantasy. The usual feeling of the writers of the period was that the so-called sorcerers of their acquaintance were only clever frauds, conjurors capable, for instance, of changing water into wine through the use of jugs equipped with special valves.

Numerology is one clue to the desire of Hellenistic intellectuals to create a universal synthesis. The development of astrology during the second century of the Christian era is another. The great name here is Claudius Ptolemy, the man who by his summary of astronomy in the *Almagest* ensured that Europeans down to the time of Copernicus and Galileo would continue to think of the earth as stationary.

The dominant authority of Aristotle in the area of natural science had by this time submerged the concept, originally proposed by the philosopher Democritus and taken over by the school of the Epicureans, that the world could be understood as composed of atoms moving in a vacuum. The prevailing view was that the earth had four basic elements (earth, air, fire, and water) differentiated in terms of the mix of the opposed qualities of hot and cold, dry and moist. The fluid "stuff" in which these qualities resided was called prime matter, and the qualitative changes of prime matter accounted for the changes in substance as one element was transformed into another. Living organisms were made possible by the transmission of a life principle (or soul) which could act as the organizing form for a physical body.

For the Aristotelian, the ceaseless round of substantial changes taking place on the earth depended on the more perfect motion of the heavenly bodies. Since it was axiomatic that motion had to be explained by finding a source on either the same or a higher plane, the movement of the stars was seen as resulting from the action of pure intelligences which played the same role for the heavenly bodies that physical souls did for earthly ones. The earthly processes of generation and corruption were caused by an innate desire to approximate the purity of the stars, and the stars were in motion because of the innate desire of their intelligences (or "gods") to attain the ultimate purity of what Aristotle termed the Prime Mover, an intelligence that was completely at rest because of its total perfection.

An acceptance of the Aristotelian outlook explained the metaphysical connection between the stars and terrestrial events that was needed if astrology was to become more intellectually respectable than it had been earlier. Ptolemy, in a work called the *Tetrabiblos*, made good use of it in order to discuss the "triplicities"—the designation of each constellation in the zodiac as representing successively the operations of fire, earth, air, and water. In addition, improving on an Egyptian practice by which the constellations of Aries, Cancer, and Libra had been regarded as "cardinal" or particularly influential, Ptolemy proposed the "quadruplicities" by which the signs of the zodiac were also seen as either cardinal (outgoing), fixed (resistant to change), or mutable (adaptable).

Thanks to Ptolemy, the characteristics of the signs of the zodiac were handed on to later tradition as follows:

ARIES (the ram)—cardinal and fire
TAURUS (the bull)—fixed and earth
GEMINI (the twins)—mutable and air
CANCER (the crab)—cardinal and water
LEO (the lion)—fixed and fire
VIRGO (the virgin)—mutable and earth
LIBRA (the scales)—cardinal and air
SCORPIO (the scorpion)—fixed and water

SAGITTARIUS (the archer)—mutable and fire
CAPRICORN (the goat)—cardinal and earth
AQUARIUS (the water bearer)—fixed and air
PISCES (the fish)—mutable and water.

What have lasted in the lore of later generations are the ideas of associating each planet with one or two of the constellations and of dividing the sky into "houses," segments that relate to distinct considerations within a person's life (his family, his business, etc.).

One astronomical fact that Ptolemy himself was aware of (it had been discovered by Hipparchus several centuries earlier) but which was not incorporated into his astrology was the precession of the equinoxes. The vernal equinox marks the point in the sky where the sun seemingly crosses the equator on its return to the north—the end of winter and the beginning of spring. Because of the slight wobble in the earth's axis, this point shifts infinitesimally each year. In the two millennia since the time of Hipparchus this has amounted to twenty-eight degrees, enough to move the actual zodiac almost a full constellation back from where it appeared in the sky when the tenets of astrology were being formulated. Spring now begins under the sign of Pisces rather than under the sign of Aries, and by the end of the century—depending on how the zodiac is divided by different astrologers—it will be under the sign of Aquarius. Later Western astrologers canonized the zodiac as it appeared to Hipparchus and Ptolemy, and this so-called tropical system has remained the norm down to the present despite a recent and often abrasive challenge from those who profess what is termed a sidereal astrology.

The Hellenistic age also developed an intricate lore in which the different signs of the zodiac were related to parts of the body, to precious and semiprecious stones, and to plants. Much of this lore appeared in Pliny's *Natural History* and was accordingly transmitted to both the ceremonial and the folk magic of the Middle Ages.

Aristotle's conception of the divine intelligences causing the movement of the stars was also taken over by the early medievals in order to link astrology with the lore of demonic forces already given impetus by the Pythagorean numerologists. Jewish and Christian thinkers alike quickly converted the pagan divinities with whom the Babylonians, Egyptians, and Greeks had identified the planets into the angels known from the Bible. The Gnostics went even further, and by the time of Albert the Great in the thirteenth century it seemed almost self-evident to assert that angels, stars, and material objects were all linked together by occult connections. Those who knew these connections—latter-day versions of the Persian Magi who were typically horrified (and worried) if anyone compared them with commonplace sorcerers and witches—would be able to achieve effects that to the uninitiated would seem miraculous but were really no more than a matter of applied science.

As always, the stories of what any of these intellectuals could accomplish through occult means improved in the telling. For example, Albert the Great, actually a Dominican professor who was one of the first to use Aristotle as a basis for a Christian metaphysics at the University of Paris, inadvertently became an example of the medieval magician because of the fact that he wrote extensively on occult properties. One of the feats attributed to him was the creation of an artificial man (a homunculus or golem) which provoked Albert's student Thomas Aquinas to the point of dismantling it in order to gain some peace and quiet for his studies. Also attributed to

Albert, who together with his brilliant protégé has been accepted as a saint by the Catholic Church which he served, was a grimoire for black magic—an indication that the lines between natural philosophy, occult philosophy, and an illicit sorcery were never too clear in the medieval imagination.

The particular contribution of the Gnostics was the theme of emanation, the idea that creation was accomplished by a kind of diminution of the divine nature, a type of downward filtering of the spiritual into the alien spheres of matter. The physical world was seen as a prison for the souls of men. It was created by demonic forces (such as the Jehovah of the Bible) which had betrayed their own divinity. As such the earth represented a place of trial that could be surmounted only by a mysticism that lifted the initiate above the levels of the stars to be filled with gnosis, the redemptive knowledge of the true God who was entirely beyond the physical world.

The early Christians had to struggle against Gnosticism in order to assert the religious validity of a normal human life, but Christian thought itself was subtly infiltrated by the mood of its antagonists. Saint Augustine, who had been a Manichean before his conversion to the Christianity of his mother, was only one of many thinkers who were never quite able to free themselves from Gnostic tendencies.

The first Neoplatonists also resisted some elements of the Gnostic orientation, but they did take over the theme of emanation and the implicit downgrading of normal human experience. Plotinus, an Egyptian mystic who initiated this last stage of Greek thought through his teaching in Rome, argued that all we mean by reality is a downward radiation of the sublime unity of what he termed the "One." On its way down to the world of man, the bridge between the spiritual and the physical, this "energy" was responsible for the existence of independent realities termed "Mind" and "Soul." The goal of philosophy was the "complete return" of the human soul to its own essence and through this to a mystical union first with Soul, then with Mind, and finally with the One. The visible world, according to this outlook, was no more than a symbol of the invisible, an opportunity for contemplation.

This concept of emanation was later to find an axiomatic expression in the phrase "as above, so below" so dear to Western occultists, and it is not difficult to see how writers such as Jamblichus, the philosopher whose version of "Hellenism" influenced the policies of the Emperor Julian (the Apostate), interpreted it as a rationalization of the magic that had been damned by pagan and Christian intellectuals alike. The magician worked with the symbolic links among physical objects to achieve the presence of the spiritual forces they represented. Through his ritual ingredients and his incantations he united his will to that of the gods. The result would be that the magician held the power of the gods with whom he was linked.

In the early part of the Middle Ages Jewish and Muslim thinkers were more strongly exposed to this outlook than were Christians. The Islamic onslaught may have destroyed what was left of the great library at Alexandria, but it also encouraged the translations that guaranteed that Greek philosophy would stay the norm for an intellectual life in the world of the caliphs. Since the Greek philosophy found by Islam was uniformly Neoplatonic, both Muslim and Jewish intellectuals came to take an emanationist approach for granted, even if it did not quite agree with the separation between Creator and created stressed by the Bible and the Koran.

The most significant contribution of the thought developing in the later history of Western occultism was the doctrine of the *sefiroth*, the emanations of God discussed in the teaching of the Cabala ("tradition") that reached southern France in the late twelfth century. As adopted by Christian occultists, the Cabala was to play the same role for a new style of theurgy that the thought of Jamblichus had for the theurgy practiced by the last of the Greek philosophers. For the present let me just point out that the magic in the Middle Ages and the Renaissance was largely that of the counterpoint to orthodox philosophy and theology provided by the doctrine of emanation originally taken from the Gnostics.

We have been considering the development in the Hellenistic world of two of the three aspects of magic most important to later Western occultism—sorcery and astrology. The third is alchemy, the "science" that qualifies, at least etymologically, as the original "black art."

The word "alchemy" is an Arabic contribution and derives either from Chem (the black land), the old name of Egypt, or from *chymia* (pouring), one of the techniques used in the laboratories of men who were completely unsure of where science ended and mysticism began. The first is the more romantic explanation; it may also be the more probable when we consider that *chem* also referred to a black substance appearing in the refining of metals that, according to some authors, was thought of as the stuff of the mystical body of Osiris.

Today everyone knows that the dream of the ancient alchemist was to transform lead into gold by means of a mysterious catalyst that was generally termed "the philosophers' stone." In an age when the actual transmutation of metals is taken for granted (we do, after all, understand the process by which radium spontaneously decays into lead, and we have reversed it to create a handful of substances lying beyond the original periodic table), we tend to smile at the manner in which these would-be scientists failed to grasp that the real differences among metals lay in the nuclei of their atoms rather than in the fancied distinctions of hot and cold, dry and moist. What we do not appreciate, however, is the degree to which alchemy, like the astrology we have already discussed, sums up not just the ambition of an age but a way of relating to nature, including the mineral world, as something alive.

For its remote origins we must look back some fifteen hundred years before Christ when the Hittites, a people who lived in what today is Turkey, began the smelting of iron ore to produce a material superior to the bronze which for about two millennia had been used in place of stone for both agriculture and warfare. The techniques of metallurgy, which probably appeared as a natural development of the potter's art, had become increasingly sophisticated from the time that copper (used in the ratio of eight or nine to one with tin to make bronze) was first extracted from the copper compounds already in use as coloring agents, but their application to ironworking now created a new profession—and a new mythology.

Mircea Eliade, one of the foremost students of the entire area of myth and religion, has detailed the manner in which this occurred. Until the advent of smithing, iron was regarded as sacred because of the fact that it was to be found in a pure state only in meteorites. It was a material that came from the sky and thus from the gods, a source, then, of powerful magic. The natural magnetism of certain iron oxides would have bolstered this view, and it has been suggested that Thales, the father of Greek philosophy, was thinking of magnetism when he argued that all things were full of gods.

The development of ironworking altered this view only slightly, and it made the smith, who drew the divine iron from the ground rather than from the sky, a natural rival to the priest. The operations of smithing were readily compared to childbirth; the smith was the man who hastened the labor by which the earth brought forth her minerals. The old, generally quite public mysteries that celebrated the sexuality of nature in an agricultural era were challenged by newer mysteries that were limited to the craftsmen who were the hereditary masters of a far more difficult technology.

In the Greek world, the fact that craftsmen more and more tended to be slaves had the double effect of intensifying the secrecy of those who did understand metals and leading the philosophers to expound theories that became increasingly remote from the actual workings of nature. This segregation of the theoretical and the practical brought about the loss of much of the advanced technology of the ancient world when the Roman Empire broke under the onslaught first of the Germanic tribes from the north and then of the Arabs and their allies from the south. It also ensured the perpetuation of even the most outlandish Greek theories as a type of secular revelation paralleling the Bible and the Koran. Alchemy was the result.

To their credit, the men of the Middle Ages did not share the ancient world's contempt for experimentation. What was unfortunate was that few of these medievals felt confident enough to challenge the basic theory of nature formulated by Aristotle, although they did make ever more sophisticated modifications in it. First in Islam, then in Christian Europe, thousands of private forges were set up in an effort to duplicate the processes of Mother Earth by which metals were gestated.

Further complicating this situation was the peculiar understanding held of Aristotle by the Neoplatonists. According to these last successors of Plato, qualitative physics could readily be fitted into a theology that stressed the existence of man as a microcosm of the entire universe and a theory of causality according to which all of nature was an unfolding of the logical order contained within the divine Mind. What the alchemists would especially remember was that the physical world was itself a living organism, and both animate and inanimate substances followed an essentially biological model for their production. (The revolution of modern thought was only in part in the conception of a quantitative physics to replace Aristotle's idea of qualities. The most significant difference between the old and the new science was the transition from a biological to a mechanical viewpoint.)

The urge to syncretize characterized not only the Neoplatonists, but all of the intellectuals in this the twilight of the Hellenistic world. Just as magic in general came to be attributed to the Persian Zoroaster, the legendary reformer who crystalized the old Iranian fire worship into a logically appealing dualism, alchemy came to be attributed to a legendary Hermes (or Mercury) who had been the teacher of Pythagoras. This Hermes quickly became indistinguishable from Hermes Trismegistus ("the thrice-great"), the Hellenistic version of the Egyptian god Thoth who had brought mankind the art of writing.

For Jews, Christians, and Gnostics whatever the pagans said of Hermes Trismegistus was applied to Enoch, Adam's grandson and the founder of civilization. In the name of Hermes-Enoch all the occultist tendencies of the period could be coalesced into a presumably consistent tradition. The result was an incredible outpouring of writings attributed to Hermes Trismegistus (or to Enoch), most of which stress the importance of transcending the physical world and all culturally derived understandings of "truth" by means of a theosophy or gnosis available to the true believer.

Attempts at alchemy had begun in Egypt in the centuries before Christ. Bolos Democritos presented a treatise that argued for transmutation on the grounds that already by various processes metals could be altered to look like silver and gold. (The prevalence of these practices for outright counterfeiting was the occasion for Archimedes chancing upon the law of specific gravity in his search for a means of detecting the difference between real and spurious gold.)

In the early Christian period the Egyptian Zosimos wrote an encyclopedia that included a measure of good chemistry with an abundance of allegory. Byzantine writers, particularly the seventh-century Stephanos (from Alexandria) and the eighth-century Archelaos, kept the ideas of Zosimos alive in Eastern Europe, but they anticipated later Renaissance writers by seeing alchemy as far more a mental than a physical science.

The Muslim heirs of Hellenistic thought were somewhat more practical in their approach. They did maintain the conception of alchemy as an occult science—the brief *Emerald Tablet* allegorically expressing Hermes's own view of alchemy is an early Arabic writing—but at the same time they were meticulous in their efforts to catalogue any novel phenomena that they observed in their laboratories. Less bound to the past than the Neoplatonists or the Byzantine commentators, they ventured notable additions to the basic Aristotelian theory.

The first Islamic alchemist was the prince Khalid, who early in the eighth century studied under a man who had himself been a student of Stephanos. Khalid was also the first to order translations from Greek sources, and later in the century this same interest in the world of Greek thought led the great Jabir (Latinized as Geber) to continue the practice.

Jabir, a Sufi writer at the court of the fabled Harun al-Rashid in Baghdad, is the man who formulated the specific theory that made alchemy seem far more than a pipe dream.

Aristotle had proposed that inanimate materials were the products of the action of the sun creating "exhalations" by heating water or earth. The vaporous exhalations from water, when trapped inside the ground, were dried and compressed into metals. All other minerals resulted from the imprisonment of smoky exhalations.

Jabir adapted this by arguing that Aristotle's elementary qualities became the "compounds" hot, cold, dry, and moist by their union with pure substance. Two materials, sulphur and mercury, represented the combinations of hot-dry and cold-moist and, consequently, were the elements that, under the appropriate planetary influences, came together to form all the metals.

The differences among metals were due to the fact that two of the qualities were "external" and two "internal," the result of varying purity and proportion in the sulphur and mercury that all had in common. The perfect metal, gold, was hot and moist outside, but cold and dry inside, while lead was cold and dry on the outside and hot and moist inside. How would someone proceed to convert lead into gold? Simply readjust the qualities, a process to be accomplished through various elixirs whose constituents could be determined numerologically.

Fundamental to all alchemy is the idea that metals grow in the earth and that gold represents the final product of the earth's natural pregnancy. "Inferior" metals are in a sense premature births that can be returned to the artificial womb of the crucible. Such metals might also be considered diseased, and transmutation would be a type of medicine aimed at removing impurities (the purpose, after all, of any elixir). It was also possible, given the frequently presumed connection between disease and sin, to argue that this purification of the metals was a moral process requiring an appropriate purgation on the part of the alchemist.

Jabir's particular significance is that he gave all these metaphors a new relevance by fixing attention on two substances that were already known to be involved in the chemical changes witnessed in metallurgy—mercury because of its liquid state and its utility in extracting gold from other minerals, and sulphur because, unlike the gases, it was a visible by-product resulting from the refining of various ores. Jabir also provided the basis for an even more powerful metaphor: the idea of the chemical wedding, with gold the offspring of a perfect union of mercury (considered a female principle) and sulphur (considered male).

Not all Islamic thinkers supported the idea of alchemy. Aristotle had not discussed it, and a "pure" Aristotelian would accordingly have little to do with it. The philosopher Avicenna, for one, rejected the possibility of humanly manipulating the specific differences of metals, even though he accepted the idea that mercury and sulphur were their basic constituents. He did, however, add to the stock of theory by his assertion that gold and silver resulted from the union of a pure mercury with varying degrees of a pure white sulphur, while an impure mercury and good sulphur resulted in tin, a pure mercury and a corrupt (because combustible) sulphur produced copper, a pure mercury and a very impure sulphur gave lead, and iron was the unfortunate product of both an impure mercury and an impure sulphur.

Still, despite the skeptics and the obvious frauds, alchemy was sufficiently well established in Islam to be one of the main arts of interest to those hardy medieval intellectuals, such as

Gerard of Cremona, who ventured south of the Pyrenees for direct contact with the more sophisticated world of Arab thought. Through their efforts as translators the Latin world was once again made aware of its own Greek inheritance. In the twelfth century that inheritance came to include the "truths" of alchemy.

The Christian West had long thrived on allegory; and the absence of an adequate technical vocabulary, together with the conspiratorial aura surrounding attempts to create fantastic wealth through a powder or potion, made metaphor a quite natural mode of expression for Christian alchemists. It also made alchemy much more "occult" than it had been with the Arabs, and it permitted a shift in emphasis away from alchemy as a more or less empirical enterprise to alchemy as a technique for personal enlightenment.

Most of the allegory was obvious enough. From Hellenistic times there had been an association of the sun and moon with gold and silver, of Venus and Mars (gods and planets alike) with copper and iron, of Jupiter and Saturn with tin and lead, and, naturally, of Mercury (the great god Hermes, patron of the alchemists) with the quicksilver or mercury that was the key to transmutation. There was also the idea that in the creation of the elixir there would be a sequence of colors from black to white to yellow to red, and this permitted a further association with a progression through the influence of the planets from Saturn (a symbol of blackness or death) to Jupiter and the moon, then to Venus and Mars, and finally to the sun.

Some of it becomes more esoteric. *Aqua regia,* a mixture of nitric and hydrochloric acids, was the green dragon; a pelican (which in legend sucked blood from its own chest for nourishment) referred to a circulating still; and the philosophic egg was the vessel that would contain the finished product of the elixir. Various steps in "the great work" of the alchemists were compared to the ordeals of the ascetic seeking moral purity, to a retreat to the womb (a symbol of prime matter), and above all to the marriage of the white moon and the red sun.

Moreover, nothing is quite what it seems. The sulphur present in gold, unlike ordinary sulphur, cannot be burned. Antimony, "the gray wolf" that is usually a poison, can be a medicine. The true alchemist, despite his ceaseless drive to transmute metals, will not care about material wealth. Perhaps most striking of all is the image of mercury itself as a hermaphrodite containing within its dual nature the seed of all other metals.

One of the first Western writers to set off on a particularly thorny path of allegory was the highly influential Arnold of Villanova, a Catalonian physician who was a younger contemporary of Thomas Aquinas. Even while discussing the mystery of the elixir, Arnold could not resist comparing its preparation to the conception, birth, crucifixion, and resurrection of Christ. From Arnold on, a parallelism appears between Christ, the resurrected Savior, and the philosophers' stone, the source of a metallic salvation.

This Christian imagery, which had long since been interlocked with ancient pagan themes, was too powerful a lure for most later writers. It was, of course, only a matter of time before the allegory would be reversed. If Christ was first a metaphor for the philosophers' stone (which was also seen as the elixir of life offering physical immortality to the one who would drink it), why could not the philosophers' stone be a metaphor for Christ? The psychiatrist Carl Jung observes, in his own study of the history of alchemy, that once this happened the alchemists were forced to choose between paths. Those who saw the identity of the elixir with Christ abandoned the laboratory, and those who didn't abandoned mystical language altogether. (We might note in passing that the alchemy of China underwent a similar transition from a laboratory effort to a set of exercises for meditation.)

All the bits and pieces of the occult lore of the present have specific starting points in history, and those starting points can generally be found in the chaotic world that followed on the conquests of Alexander the Great.

What we see from the occultist legends are several occasionally interlocked approaches to the reality of man in his universe. All four are "magical" in the sense that they presuppose a harmony between how men think and the way things are which lies completely outside what a modern scientific outlook says is possible.

By a strictly rationalist criterion they are all unequivocally superstitious, or at best they can be regarded as misguided substitutes for science. In the next chapter we should, I think, balance out this view as well. The world of magic may not be a "secret wisdom" handed down from Egypt, Atlantis, or anywhere else, but it is as much a clue to human potential as the world of science which is too readily said to supplant it.

7.

Why Magic?

WE HAVE DEALT with history to show that the beliefs and practices that mark today's occultism have quite well-defined origins in the thought patterns of an older Europe.

What we have not looked at, however, is why thoughtful men in the Mediterranean world after the days of Alexander should have accepted astrology and sorcery, or why their descendants in medieval Europe should have developed an almost unreasoning fear of witchcraft. What was the power of occultism in the past—and is this a clue to its attractiveness for thinking men of the present? Might there be some kind of cycle here, a spin from outlooks that are less rational to those that are more so and then back? Is the contemporary feeling for magic an effort to escape modernity by retreating into the intellectual darkness of an older age?

These questions have more than just academic importance for Tanya and myself, who continue to live in a world where any talk of magic retains the stigma of unacceptable gullibility if not of fraud. In 1972 all hell broke loose in a Northern California district (ironically in a place called Diablo Valley) when a community college English teacher offered a course in the literature of the occult. An elementary school district in Orange County in the same year banned *Jonathan Livingston Seagull* from its libraries because of the author's use of the theme of reincarnation. No, my interest in the occult just might not be thought of as a healthy replacement for my earlier support of student radicalism, and perhaps I should explain more fully why I found magic an intellectually respectable topic for myself.

At the risk of a certain immodesty, I would suggest that in some manner my own succession of outlooks recapitulates the history of our modern West. I began with a strongly religious orientation that led me to spend ten years studying for the priesthood as a member of the Society of Jesus. After leaving the more or less sheltered life of a Jesuit scholastic I went through a period of disillusionment with the verities of church and country that left me something of an atheist and an anarchist. Then, attempting to reconstruct a more positive outlook, I began considering the significance of what some have called "parallel institutions," social forms that provide alternatives to the large-scale organizations that otherwise seem to monopolize our human consciousness.

My experience as a Jesuit had already given me a certain insight into how consciousness works in order to create whatever it is we take to be "reality." I entered the Society of Jesus because of the glamorous legend of the order and left when I recognized that emotionally I was not cut out to be a priest, even if I might make a very good cosmopolitan intellectual. Too many needs that I had as a child had gone unfulfilled for me to be able to regard the celibate priesthood as anything but a kind of martyrdom, hardly an outlook for a good priest. But during the decade with the Jesuits I lived in a remarkable atmosphere of faith in which my feeling for the world I had left behind was replaced with the supernatural outlook demanded by St. Ignatius Loyola, the sixteenth-century founder of the Society.

In the Jesuit novitiate this change was accomplished through a systematic process of resocialization. We had minimal contact with "the outside"; there were no newspapers, radio, or television, and on rare visits to town we always went in pairs to keep each other in line. Except for recreation periods our communication was to be in a fractured Latin. The specifically Jesuit perspective of our reading was reinforced by still another half hour a day in which the master of novices lectured us on what we were to become.

In the first few months of the novitiate we went through what was called the "Long Retreat," the month-long version of the Spiritual Exercises developed by Loyola as a powerful device for remaking a man's consciousness. These teachings of St. Ignatius were to be reinforced through the daily periods of meditation that we were expected to observe the rest of our lives along with our other religious obligations, including twice-daily examinations of conscience. In case some trace of worldliness still remained, there were various devices by which we publicly advised one another of our faults.

All of this spiritual training was, except for its length, similar to that expected of any Catholic religious before he or she pronounced the vows of poverty, chastity, and obedience. But even after the novitiate, we Jesuits had five more years of education, two in the study of Latin and Greek and three devoted to the philosophy of Thomas Aquinas (much of it taught in

Latin), which only reinforced our separateness from others our own age. We did study French and Shakespeare and chemistry also, but more in the way of accommodations to contemporary expectations for an educated man than as subjects to be taken up with any particular seriousness. The fact that we were twentieth-century Americans very easily took second place to the fact that we were Jesuits.

By the time I began the three-year period of teaching that intervened between the study of philosophy and that of theology I found it almost unthinkable to contemplate just how it would feel *not* to be a Jesuit. We had our dropouts, of course, men who even after taking their vows had chosen to go back into the world, but always there was a sense of mystery about how this could happen. Some might go on to become quite prominent (Robert Blair Kaiser as a writer, Edmund G. Brown, Jr., as a politician), but still we found them just a bit incomprehensible. "Leaving" was just not talked about before it happened. To do so would have been too great an admission of the ordinary humanity that we attempted to live down.

I never did see my own name on the list of the *defecti*, but I know it was there and that my departure created its share of comment. My idiosyncrasies were probably recalled as indications of why I couldn't make it, and perhaps one or another pious friend prayed for me while I stumbled uncertainly through quite different steps than those I had learned as a cassocked seminarian.

Things are very different after the Second Vatican Council. Jesuit scholastics in California now go directly from a less closed-in novitiate to classical studies at Loyola University in Los Angeles. They dress casually, attempt to come to grips very soon with the inconsistencies of natural feelings and religious expectations, and in general live much more human lives than I did in my time. There are also not too many of them, and lists of dropouts were for a while taking on the look of a *Who's Who* of Jesuit superstars.

The point, of course, is that in the days before Vatican II our own world only partially intersected with the world of the outsider. Today, in an effort to superimpose the two, the young seminarian is forced to handle the phenomenon that psychologists refer to as "cognitive dissonance," the state of being confronted simultaneously with inconsistent perceptions. If he rationalizes (the normal manner of coping with cognitive dissonance), odds are that it will be in favor of the community that impinges most strongly on his everyday awareness. And that is probably no longer the Society of Jesus.

This is not meant as a criticism. The human cost of turning out sixteenth-century Europeans in the United States of the present was perhaps even higher. There may have been more of us, but too frequently we were emotionally and intellectually stagnant. This had been one of the most depressing realizations within my own training as a Jesuit, and it was a principal factor in my decision to withdraw from the Society rather than risk such hollowness for myself. The challenge for the Jesuits—and for the contemporary Catholic Church—is to see how the type of consciousness that marks one as not just a believer but as a committed religious can be maintained with a minimum of the often deadening routine that makes one into the true believer at the price of the vitality required to make his witness significant both to himself and to the person who is still just "of the world."

Religious belief is, I think, rather like a love affair. While it's alive one's whole being takes on a new dimension. But if one becomes disillusioned, what may follow is a cynicism that shrinks the horizons of life. This, I admit, happened to me, just as I feel it has happened to the Western world. Science is not enough of a substitute, and existentialism (in the style of Sartre and Camus) is no more than a passageway either to a new belief system or to utter nihilism.

Something of the answer for myself (and possibly for my age) began to emerge when I began a reconsideration of what it was that had been lost in the process of secularization. I found myself unwilling to accept the argument of many writers, from Richard Bach in *Jonathan Livingston Seagull* to Colin Wilson in *The Occult* and George B. Leonard in *The Transformation*, that what humanity requires is a quantum leap forward in evolution. Instead it seemed that the job was to recover something that men are born with but somehow forget when they learn to view their world mechanically rather than organically, as an assemblage of bits and pieces rather than as a living whole.

One clue that I was on the right track came from Claude Lévi-Strauss, the anthropologist in whose work I first read of the ability of so-called primitive peoples to relate to their environments through logical systems that are multisensory rather than just visual. Instead of describing the world solely in terms of what can be seen, we find tribal men using the more subtle cues of sound and taste and smell and touch in order to detect types of logical relationships which escape even the most trained eye. They are not pre-logical, as even Carl Jung saw them to be; rather they are *more* logical.

Another clue came from other anthropologists who noted that the frequency of extrasensory perception appears to be in inverse proportion to the sophistication of more normal communication by sight and sound. Australian aborigines, presumably one of the least culturally developed groups within the family of man, seemed particularly good at telepathy. Could it be, I wondered, that Colin Wilson's "dominant minority" were not the forerunners of some new species of man but instead were individuals who had somehow not yet lost man's psychic birthright? A certain reinforcement for this view came from the work of psychologists who were examining extrasensory perception in small children. Again there was the same indicator that development of other abilities, at least in the manner dictated by our kind of culture, is at the expense of psychic sensitivity.

The most significant clues came from the work done by Carlos Castaneda as a participant-observer in the world of Yaqui magic. I had first read *The Teachings of Don Juan* at the urging of my students, most of whom saw it as a confirmation of their own usage of drugs to arrive at what were coming to be called "different spaces." The book was stimulating, particularly in the relationship Castaneda drew between sorcery and the use of hallucinogenic materials, and I found it a valuable crosscultural reference when I discussed yogic practices in my class in Asian philosophy.

I had already met Tanya and begun my own cycle of odd experiences when Castaneda's next two books appeared. *A Separate Reality* and *Journey to Ixtlan* dealt more explicitly with sorcery as an outlook entirely transcending any question of hallucinogenics. Especially significant was the stress put on unlearning more familiar patterns of perception in order to permit the type of experience don Juan referred to as "seeing." Drugs functioned as a device to break down these old patterns, but "seeing" was no longer, as in Castaneda's original understanding, made to follow from the drugs themselves. The world of the sorcerer was quite literally *another* reality, one that by our Western criteria should not exist except as a type of fantasy.

Such a proposition is quite disturbing to anyone used to the idea of a universe, of reality as something that is single and internally consistent. What if we do live in a plurality of worlds simultaneously, and yet in order to be fully present in any one of them we must somehow dampen our awareness of the others? Most of us experience that to sense fully we must shut down our thinking, and to think we must turn off our senses. Would it then be the case that to "see" we have to take leave in some manner of both sensation and thought? And could it be that what we call a "schizophrenic break-down," such as Tanya went through as a child, is in some manner a forced entry into the world of "seeing"?

If these tantalizing and yet unsettling hypotheses could be proved out, it meant that literally anything was possible, even the shape-shifting that appears in Castaneda's repertoire of experiences as well as in the lore of European magic.

And where was I in all of this? Although Tanya disagreed, I felt that psychically I was close to being tone deaf. All I could do was listen and read and compare—and hope that somehow through all of this I might get closer to the truth about magic. And, of course, my own life as a Jesuit as well as further training in the social sciences had sensitized me some-what as to what to listen for, and how to read, and where to draw comparisons.

The beginning, it seemed, was to go back into the settings that provide the particular "atmosphere of faith" in which magic thrives. I knew already what it had taken to make me see the world as a Jesuit. Carlos Castaneda had provided an invaluable analysis of how he had come to see the world as a sorcerer. And above all I had Tanya to guide me with her own insights on what it means to be a witch. Perhaps I was in a fairly good position after all.

Where and when does magic appear in a society? What we are concerned with is not just the kinds of beliefs and practices we outsiders might consider "magical" (the way, for instance, that the strict Protestant used to look at the rites of the Catholic) but with the way insiders see themselves. Secondarily, however, we are looking for evidence of paranormal phenomena associated with these activities. Does telepathy appear to take place, for instance, or are there other "manifestations" (to use an all-purpose term favored by the spiritualists) that cannot be discounted as entirely hallucinatory? In other words, we are asking not only if a group believes in magic but also if there seems to be a solid experiential basis for this belief.

I need rain. Do I celebrate a votive Mass, do I engage in a rain dance, or do I seed the clouds with crystals of silver iodide? By a simple application of traditional rules, the first is religion, the second is magic, and the third is science. The trouble, of course, is that a simple application is not always possible. The rural European Catholic may think of the Mass in much the same way as the Hopi Indian thinks of his rain dance. Is the Mass magic or is the rain dance religion? If it happens that more often than not a properly conducted dance leads to rain, does this mean that the dance is any less scientific a procedure than the use of silver iodide, especially if the pilot who seeds the clouds hasn't the slightest idea of why this substance will work and another won't? The conventional distinctions between religion and magic and between magic and science must be used cautiously. The questions we are dealing with in this book cannot be resolved by semantics alone.

It is also necessary to be quite cautious about grand syntheses that explain magic in the context of some particular understanding of mythology. Long a forte of occultists themselves, this style of explanation gained new respectability with Max Müller and Sir James Frazer, the nineteenth-century pioneers of comparative religion. For a while everything seemed reducible to a discussion of how our ancestors thought of the sun as divine or how they felt the need of a divine victim. Though such hypotheses can be fascinating, the difficulty is that, in contrast to the physical sciences, simple explanations tend to be quite misleading in the social sciences. Human behavior, as Aristotle noted in his discussion of ethics, cannot be treated with the precision of mathematics. The way men think is not completely unpredictable, but it defies overly facile generalizations.

The work of Mircea Eliade represents a less sweeping yet more productive approach. As a young Jesuit I had read the French edition of Eliade's *Cosmos and History: The Myth of the Eternal Return* and first discovered the suggestion of the manner in which the linear thought patterns of the modern West differed from the more holistic orientation to be found at other times and in other places.

° From Eliade I learned that we moderns see time as moving in a straight line; the reality of an event is determined by our ability to situate it along this line. For primitive man, for the archaic societies of the West, and for Asia there is not the same feeling for history. Instead time moves in a circle, and reality is determined not so much by what happens physically as by the manner in which a sacred "then" can be recognized as a paradigm or example for the profane "now."

Eliade's other works, most notably his *Patterns in Comparative Religion*, have illustrated similar themes in which the sacred is discovered in the profane in order to provide not just an explanation but a sense of purpose. Objects or events that are unusual, places that are awesome, times that seem to echo with meaning—all of these can become manifestations of the sacred.

There is no one motif present everywhere, but there are families of motifs in which elements appear to separate and then recombine in order to create the kaleidoscope of human beliefs. The importance of any given theme appears to depend on the needs of men in differing environments as well as on strictly cultural factors, such as the contact one group has with another. But always there is the effort to transcend the limitations of the present, above all the limitations of mortality itself.

This style of analysis contrasts sharply with the nineteenth-century interpretation of primitive man attempting to rationalize his fear of natural phenomena and so moving through stages from mythology to philosophy to what we today think of as science. Rather than making science the sole criterion for "real" knowledge, we find it a type of specialized understanding that includes only a part of whatever men have known to be significant for the great bulk of their history on this planet. It is only in the lore of both religion and magic that we can look for the rest.

From a contemporary scientific perspective any explanation of the world which invokes feeling is invalid. Scientific answers by definition are objective—free, that is, of the intrusion of human subjectivity. Religion and magic alike deal with those features of human experience that *are* subjective. They are not amenable to the techniques of public verification by which the scientific method is defined. Science is necessarily impersonal; religion and magic are inconceivable without the factor of personal response.

All three are valid within their own spheres. The sphere of

science, because it is objective, can be understood the most easily. The spheres of religion and magic, precisely because they are concerned with modes of consciousness rather than with external behavior, are almost incomprehensible except in the one case to the believer and in the other to the type of person I call the witch.

The scientist, in other words, can show the nonscientist what it is that he knows. The believer and the witch must rely on a more indirect presentation in order to communicate what they feel. Their approach must be more phenomenological in its tone; it must attempt to bring the outsider to share vicariously their modes of consciousness, as in the testimony given by St. Augustine in detailing his conversion or in the kind of reportage that characterizes the works of Carlos Castaneda.

For the strict rationalist, of course, the only path to knowledge is through the scientific method, and in his eyes religion and magic are indistinguishable as illusions.

Again I would caution the reader to avoid thinking of any generalizations about human behavior as some type of necessary analysis. Like all such concepts, they should be regarded solely as points of view that are useful in coming to grips with a reality that ultimately defies verbalization even as it invites it. This is particularly true when we are dealing with the intellectual and affective structures that make up religion and magic.

One of the best recent efforts to respect the complexity of religious and of magical experience while still attempting to fit them into a framework of scientific understanding is in the work of the English anthropologist Mary Douglas. In her book *Natural Symbols: Explorations in Cosmology* Douglas considers the manner in which men see their own bodies as organic symbols of their society. The relationships within the society come to be expressed through "natural symbols" drawn from the body itself.

One quite useful scheme that she presents is in the form of a Cartesian graph. Two intersecting lines indicate positive and negative values of the strength of social boundaries (group) and the intensity of hierarchical relationships (grid). Zero represents a minimal structure in social relationships (hermits, for example). Societies with both strong (positive) group and strong grid are marked by a highly structured view of the world that is reflected in their collective rituals. Societies with a strong group but a weak (negative) grid tend to a dualistic outlook with an emphasis both on a malevolent witchcraft and on a protective countermagic. Where there is a strong grid but a weak group there is a view of the world as ultimately amoral that can lead either to the use of magic for personal advancement or to a religious millennialism.

The Hellenistic magician scrambled for success in his shifting environment by using a manipulative magic. The continental witch hunter attempted to secure the bounds of his world (his body) against diabolical subversion. Magic in the first case is seen as beneficent, one source of power among many. In the second it is clearly negative, a type of disease which must be cured. And in both it represents something highly individualistic that appears (or is thought to appear) when there is a weakness in either group or grid, the normal forms of social control.

Mary Douglas also makes a point that may sound familiar to those who have read Carlos Castaneda. The successful sorcerer, the one who has made his manipulation of the amoral forces of the world pay off, moves into a rarefied atmosphere that approximates the setting of those at the intersection of the axes on her graph. Within his perspective there is no longer any division among men except in terms of those who have knowledge and those who do not. In other words, there are sorcerers and there are fools.

What is the situation in a "normal" society, one in which both group and grid are strong (people know who they are collectively and each person knows his place individually)? Here there is a reliance on ritual as a device for reinforcing the perceptions of social integrity. From an outsider's point of view these rituals might seem to be magical, but to one who is a member of the society there is probably no clear distinction between magic and religion (and I would include here the civic worship we understand as patriotism). Gestures are regarded as efficacious, as bringing about a right order to things *ex opere operato*, because of the actions performed regardless of the presence or absence of strong feeling in the persons performing them. This is the unrecognized magic of parades and holiday dinners, of christenings and flag raisings. We act as though things are ordered and we expect order to follow from our action.

The failure to perform the expected gestures is already an indication that something of the order of society is breaking down. To continue with Douglas's language, either group or grid is weakening. At this point magic, now recognized for what it is because it is seen as something individualistic, can take on a new significance. In a society that still accepts its boundaries this can assume the form of a fear of witchcraft and the employment of countermagic against those who are presumed to be the source of disorder. In a society that prizes success but has lost its sense of unity there will be sorcery of one type or another. The astrology buff knows when to make a smart move and when not; the love-struck lady buys a pair of candles that will get her the boy friend she wants; the fledgling members of a pick-up coven solemnly hex an enemy. In each case an ultimately amoral power is solicited by the person cunning enough to know it exists and to find out how to use it.

From a rationalistic point of view these are only individualistic superstitions. People seem to have a need to believe in something, no matter how absurd. If it makes them happy . . .

Such an argument obviously assumes that there are no occult powers to be solicited. My earlier comments on the limits of science will have prepared the reader for the fact that I do not completely accept this interpretation. I have no argument against the possibility that in time all paranormal phenomena will be explained through an expanded understanding of the laws of nature, but my point is that they cannot be explained within the mechanistic models we now have available. And if there *are* paranormal events connected with the belief in magic, something which remains to be seen, it is simply not enough to invoke either the psychological principle that people tend to see what they expect to see or to call on the concept of the self-fulfilling prophecy.

Later in this book we shall have to consider just what is known about paranormal phenomena from a scientific point of view and come to grips with the moral issues raised by an analysis such as that of Mary Douglas. In other words, we shall have to deal with how "real" magic is and, regardless of whether it is objectively real or not, how "good" it is.

From an older theological perspective, which I learned in my catechism, God alone could act outside of the laws of nature. There were preternatural occurrences, "marvels" but not miracles, that could be attributed to the Devil, the fallen angel who might with divine permission still exercise a certain power over the physical world. Paranormal events, then, had to be understood as either divine or diabolical in origin.

I did outgrow this theology. Looking back, I realize that as a Catholic student and even more as a Jesuit I lived in a setting that was actually quite magical even if we could never recognize it as such. There was an axiom of Loyola's to the effect that we should pray as if everything depended on God and yet act as though everything depended on ourselves, but at the same time our reading was filled with the stories of how God seemed to make things work out for his servants who made use of the appropriate symbolic links to divinity (the cross, relics, etc.). We may have called it providence, but the point is that we were not content with saying that coincidences just happened. We were not to expect miracles, but we always had before us the examples of the saints for whom they were routine. In this particular atmosphere of faith there was meaning to be found in the most seemingly inconsequential events.

The principal reason for many of the changes in the church was a desire to increase its relevance for the mechanized world of the twentieth century. The old rules requiring abstinence on Friday and the celebration of the Mass in Latin were abolished, and the hope was that in place of ritual for its own sake there would be a new stress on finding spiritual meaning in the rites that remained. If it did not quite work out that way, it was perhaps because the theologians' distrust of magic caused them to overlook its place in the psychology of the more ordinary Catholic. A protective bubble had been pierced, and American Catholics quickly found themselves lamenting the loss of their distinctiveness.

The occult, in fact, has one advantage over religion for the sophisticated skeptic: it offers all the charm of exotic doctrines and rites without the need of commitment. With very little effort it can even become the religion of choice for the type of person who is a constitutional heretic.

Much of the untold history of the development of Western thought is based on this appeal of occultism for disaffected intellectuals. In a few spectacular cases these have been individuals who have become the spokesmen for a later non-occultist orthodoxy: Plato, the student of the Pythagoreans; Newton, the alchemist once described by John Maynard Keynes as "the last of the magicians"; Carl Jung, the observer of paranormal phenomena. All three were men who looked into the occult for patterns that exceeded the more rationalist expectations of their times. The feeling for magic expressed in these interests is often forgotten in order to concentrate on their contributions to a more conventional philosophy and science, but it is useful to keep this feeling in mind.

Occultism has always served, and is doing so at present, as a counterpoint to Western rationalism. It may be the case, as Mary Douglas points out, that magic appears when something is amiss in what we think of as the normal controls of society, but this need not mean that magic itself is without an extraordinary redemptive value.

"Magic is alive." A long time ago a Jesuit classmate friend who had left the priesthood for a career in social work gave me a handmade poster inscribed with this haunting phrase. I was to hear it later in a song recorded by Buffy Sainte-Marie, and in its mood it seemed to sum up the best of what the occult has to offer a world that seems too in love with its machinery.

What, in summary, is a magical outlook as distinguished

from the outlooks of religion and science? Science, as we have seen, is the most easily defined. Magic and religion alike are holistic, concerned with the relationships by which men situate themselves within the largest possible contexts.

To cite theologian Paul Tillich's classic phrase, the sphere of the religious is determined by that which is of "ultimate concern," the final questions of the source and purpose of whatever we consider to be real. In a sense, it looks upward and inward simultaneously.

Magic is far more limited in scope, dealing with the interdependence of elements on differing levels of reality. Sorcery, which we shall be considering in far greater detail in the chapters to come, operates through a manipulation of supposed symbolic connections between spiritual forces and physical objects. Astrology, for instance, presumes a connection of some sort between patterns in the sky and events on the earth. Alchemy, which depended on astrological themes for its development, came more and more to identify the physical processes involved in its *opus magnum* with changes in the state of the alchemist's soul.

This book is predicated on the idea that magic is more than metaphor, but even if I am wrong, the return of magic would still be significant. In an age that has prized facts over fantasy to the point of losing all sense of spiritual worth, even a poetry gone wild would be of value.

8.

The Occultist Counterpoint

THROUGHOUT THIS BOOK I stick to the broad description of the word "witch" for the reason that it has become part of the vocabulary of the counterculture and so is more familiar to the generation with which I am in contact than are other terms.

This problem of language was just as bothersome in centuries gone by. In the last part of the Middle Ages "witch" was most definitely a term of contempt, but "magician" was going through a process of transition as an increasing number of intellectuals began to flirt with doctrines that had until then been part of the underworld of medieval thought.

We might identify three more or less distinct streams flowing together to create this new outlook. The first was the feeling for Neoplatonic philosophy stimulated by the revived study of the Greek language. The second was the appearance of new manuals of black magic modeled on the sorcerers' recipe books dating from Hellenistic times. The third was the complex mystical approach of the Cabala synthesized in the late twelfth century.

The importance of Neoplatonism lay in the fact that, like Gnosticism, it presumed the existence of numerous levels between God and man. For the Gnostics, the magician—like the Simon Magus who confronted Simon Peter in the first years of Christianity—was the one who mastered the powers of these levels in his own upward return to divinity. For the Neoplatonists, who had taken over the body of literature attributed to Hermes Trismegistus, identification with the gods was similarly a source of power.

Christian thinkers, particularly the more adventuresome, had long been attracted to Neoplatonism because of the manner in which it appeared to reconcile mystical delights and intellectual curiosity. A more orthodox theology had demanded that the mysteries of Christianity, such as the dogma of the Trinity, remain outside the type of emanationist speculation characterizing the Gnostics and the Neoplatonists. Mystical experience—the ecstatic union with God—would similarly have to be regarded as beyond man's natural capabilities; it was a free gift of God in no way to be attained through a man's own efforts. But with the rethinking of Christianity taking place in the centuries that preceded the Protestant Reformation, this orthodox position was coming under attack. It was even being suggested that magic, including the summoning of demonic forces, was not just compatible with Christian belief but in itself a superior path to salvation.

The manuals of black magic represent a curious literary genre. Anyone reading the *Key of Solomon*, the *Lemegeton* (the so-called *Lesser Key of Solomon*), or any of the later grimoires of this tradition (including the hair-raising version attributed to Pope Honorius) has to note that the life of the magician is not an easy one. His implements—all of which he must make himself, just as he must copy out his own manuscripts—require fairly exotic materials assembled under equally exotic conditions.

Imagine, for instance, the hardships of making a knife when its blade must be forged during an astrologically correct interval, cooled in the blood of a mole mixed with pimpernel juice, and fitted to a handle made of white boxwood that has been cut, also under the right stars, with the single stroke of a new sword. Even presuming that the magician can succeed in outfitting himself correctly, all of the rituals require equally elaborate performances, including lengthy recitations of the names of the demons invoked. Sorcery, as it is here presented, literally requires the patience of a saint. Curiously enough, considering the quite selfish goals proposed for these intricate liturgies, there is also a constant exhortation to the magician to purify his heart in a quite saintly manner.

These old horrific manuals promise incredible rewards for exact performance—even invisibility or a ride on a flying carpet for those not satisfied with the humbler pleasures of seduction, the discovery of buried treasure, or the inflicting of one or another disaster upon the magician's less favored acquaintances. And if the directions do not work, it must be presumed that some detail in the liturgy was either omitted or done incorrectly.

All of this might make good enough sense if there were the slightest shred of evidence that any of the grimoires were the results of actual attempts at sorcery. My own suspicion is that they were a peculiar type of romantic fiction that took on the quality of a self-fulfilling prophecy—rather as though the satirical novel *Don Quixote* had come first and then real knights appeared to do what the old gentleman of La Mancha had only imagined. They may even have appeared as efforts to further defame the Jew as the ally of the Devil—the medieval rationale for genocide. But this is pure conjecture, and whatever may have been the true purpose of their authors, they did hold a tremendous appeal for the later cosmopolitan occultists who felt themselves above all sectarian differences.

The grimoires perhaps contributed to the Christian occultist's interest in the Cabala, although Jew and Gentile were otherwise quite far apart in what they took to be the significance of a tradition that had its roots in the ancient *Sefir Yetsirah* and reached a literary height in the *Zohar* (*Book of Splendor*) of the thirteenth-century Moses de León. For theosophically inclined Jews, the Cabala provided a technique for using the Bible to reach toward mystical experience. For the Christian, however, it was made into a clue to the command of demonic forces through the use of the sacred Hebrew that was piously supposed to have been the first tongue of angels and men alike.

In practice, occultist familiarity with the Cabala generally was limited to the basics of the Hebrew alphabet together with the numerological associations of each letter. References to Cabalistic wisdom were typically an effort to inflate the shopworn lore inherited from the last centuries of the Hellenistic world. Again there may have been a certain measure of anti-Semitism in this, although this time it operated by ascribing extraordinary knowledge to the Jew and then claiming to have appropriated this knowledge for more pure ends. (Later, as we shall see, the Rosicrucian legend would deal with Islam in the same way, and in the nineteenth century occultists branched out to take the entire colonial world, particularly India, into their enlightened syntheses.)

It may be that the first non-Jews to refer extensively to the Cabala, humanists such as Pico della Mirandola, held no such bias, but no Jew would feel flattered by the manner in which they argued that the Cabala could be used to prove the divinity of Christ. For many of the more orthodox, in fact, it only confirmed the suspicion that the *Zohar* was better thought of as "the book of lies."

By the turn of the sixteenth century these three streams—Neoplatonism, the grimoires, and the Cabala—were converging. One of the products was the *Occult Philosophy* of Cornelius Henry Agrippa, a three-volume introduction done while he was still quite a young man and recanted in his later years.

Agrippa, who admitted that he felt "occult philosophy" would be a less offensive term than "magic," stated that he did not intend to repeat the unsubstantiated tales of wonders to be found in the writings of Albert the Great or the various authorities on alchemy such as Arnold of Villanova. The passion for classical citations common to Renaissance writers made a mockery of this resolution, however, and the most outlandish assertions from ancient naturalists such as Pliny were woven in with bits of folklore that supposedly demonstrated an experimental knowledge of the secret properties of nature.

The theory that binds all this together is an adaptation of Neoplatonism in which the harmony of nature calls for complete correspondences between angels, stars, plants and animals, materials, and the sigils that were a kind of exotic shorthand. It was entirely reasonable, thought Agrippa, to suggest that the specific virtues of the planets could be drawn down through seals, magic rings, or the burning of an appropriate incense. To take just one example (incidentally, one of the least offensive), anyone soliciting the power of Venus should use an incense made of musk, ambergris, aloes wood, red roses and red coral, all of which are mixed with the brains of sparrows and the blood of pigeons.

A basic theme of Agrippa was that Aristotle's four elements were present in all creation, including the angels, only in different manners. This view kept him apart from the alchemists, who were moving toward the theory that the key to nature lay in the operations of salt, sulphur, and mercury. But at the same time it reflected a somewhat more concrete view of magic than that afforded by the liturgical predilections of the grimoires.

Agrippa remained the major authority on sorcery until the nineteenth century. Then, in 1801, Francis Barrett published *The Magus*, a rehearsal of the same lore of sigils, rings, and the rest. Later in the nineteenth century Eliphas Levi produced his own interpretation of magic, significant primarily for the manner in which the Cabala became the core of occultism rather than a peripheral issue.

To me, one of the remarkable things about the course of magic from the Middle Ages to the time of Levi is that a basic theme of the Neoplatonists, the use of meditation to obtain a communion with higher intelligences, was almost completely ignored. Magic, as with Agrippa's discussion of "occult philosophy," was presented as an entirely rational enterprise. There was little room for mysticism.

The appearance of a more mystical interpretation of alchemy had already begun the process by which magic was redefined in more psychological terms. It also marked the emergence of a new mythic basis for sorcery. No longer was it the more or less free-lance adventuring of individual magicians into the spirit world. It was now the esoteric vision of enlightened adepts, who might or might not be purely mortal, handed on through a dedicated but elusive fraternity.

At the same time that Agrippa was formulating his reinterpretation of sorcery, Paracelsus was developing the basis for a similar reinterpretation of alchemy. This man, who dared to say that he had gone beyond Aulus Celsus, the great Roman authority on medicine, and who made his own middle name of Bombastus a synonym for pretentious language, appears to us today as something of a tragic genius.

Physically unprepossessing to begin with, Paracelsus gained a quick reputation as a tempestuous nonconformist who lectured in medicine at Basel in German instead of Latin and who wore the leather apron of an artisan instead of the clerical gown of his colleagues. He lasted in his one university position for only two years, but in that time he challenged the entire basis of medieval medicine by insisting on the use of various minerals in place of the racks of organic remedies handed down from antiquity. Understandably, he was hated by his fellow physicians and by the druggists alike, and he was forced into a vagabond career that ended only with his death (in 1541) before he was fifty.

Alchemy was for Paracelsus only secondarily a question of transmutation. Its first task was the understanding of the constituents of all natural things for the sake of medicine. With Paracelsus there is the last great expression of the ancient view that all the universe is alive. As he saw it, there was a direct connection between the stars and the human body, and medicine ought to be a matter of concocting remedies that were astrologically correct in order to re-establish a balance between man the microcosm and the universe enveloping him.

His special contribution was the idea that the hierarchy of forces in the universe included soulless spirits—sylphs with bodies of air, nymphs or undines with bodies of water, salamanders with bodies of fire, and gnomes with bodies of earth

—all of which were responsive to human manipulation. This, as far as I know, is the earliest expression of the modern idea of "elementals," although there are forerunners to it both in Neoplatonism and in the medieval conception that demons were able to make themselves illusory bodies out of air.

Paracelsus took over the idea that mercury and sulphur, together with the salt originally suggested by the Muslim writer Razi, were the primary ingredients of all metals, but he extended this conception to apply to other substances as well, and this too provided a new basis for the practice of medicine. These three "hypostatical principles" required a balance within the human body for good health, and it was this idea that lay behind his advocacy of non-organic remedies.

As I've mentioned, the tendency to identify the philosophers' stone with Christ was gradually forcing the alchemist tradition to choose between mysticism and science. The influence of Paracelsus succeeded in tipping the scales in favor of mysticism. In particular, the emphasis he placed on the spirituality of nature provided the basis for the Rosicrucian myth first presented in *Fama Fraternitatis* (1614) and *The Chemical Wedding of Christian Rosenkreutz* (1616) and then elaborated through the works of writers such as Robert Fludd and Michael Maier. It was perhaps well that this happened. Robert Boyle's 1661 publication of *The Skeptical Chemist* was the death knell for empirical alchemy as a completely respectable undertaking.

Although many of the classic writings of Western alchemy appeared within the same period as the ceremonial magic that reached a height with Cornelius Agrippa, the idea of conjuration seems only rarely to have been brought into alchemy. The particular approach of the alchemist, in turn, did not seem to affect the magician. There were, of course, remarkable similarities otherwise. Both had their roots in the world of Hellenistic magic, and consequently both continued the strong moralistic tone of the last Platonists. This itself may explain why neither the alchemist nor the sorcerer saw himself as having anything in common with the witch as he was popularly imagined at the height of the persecution.

It is also the case that both perpetuated an animistic view of the universe at a time when a more mechanistic and thus amoral conception was being formulated by writers such as René Descartes and Thomas Hobbes. And, finally, both succumbed to the attraction of seeing their lore as necessarily occult, always just out of reach of a clear understanding. For the alchemists in particular, paradoxical expression became almost an end in itself, and the unraveling of more and more elaborate paradoxes came to hold the same importance that the fashioning of intricate correspondences held for the magician. One obvious result of this fascination with complexity was that alchemy and sorcery, rather than appealing to the intellectuals as they had in the Middle Ages and the early Renaissance, came to be the private preserve of charlatans and the semi-educated *gentilshommes* who were their natural prey.

It is this fascination with paradox that has drawn the attention of contemporary writers, Carl Jung in particular. Jung, who very early in his career became interested in the work of Paracelsus, wrote extensively on the symbolism employed by the later alchemists. As a psychiatrist, Jung saw the entire effort of the alchemists, whatever their own intentions, as devoted to "the separation and synthesis of psychic opposites." The chemical wedding of sulphur and mercury, the male and female principles, expressed the desire for psychological integrity, the "individuation" that would come when a person rec-

onciled the *animus* and the *anima,* the masculine and feminine components of his own nature. Alchemical symbolism,
therefore, could be interpreted as a particularly profound expression of the archetypes that mark the psychic inheritance
of all mankind.

Agrippa and Paracelsus stand at the transition between
medieval and modern conceptions of reality. Both were flawed
personalities, the one, as Colin Wilson has remarked, characterized by self-pity and the other by self-assertion and anger.
Neither fit contemporary patterns of educated respectability.
Yet in their own eyes they were the heralds of a new era free
of the superstitions of the past.

The atmosphere of faith for Agrippa and Paracelsus can, I
think, be specified in the following manner. (1) Reality is to
be understood as a living organism, a hierarchy of interdependent material and spiritual forces. (2) Man stands at the
bridge between the material and the spiritual and so, through
his own operations, is able to recognize and even control their
interaction. (3) Reality is evolutionary in the sense that each
part is in a process of development appropriate to its own
nature; just as all metals are meant by nature to develop into
gold, man is meant to develop into the Christ figure. (4) God
is either the totality of reality or the One from which it all
proceeds through a process of emanation; these two aspects
are complementary rather than mutually exclusive. (5) History is a cycle whose spiritual rhythms, as in the appearance
of divinely inspired teachers, are far more significant than any
type of political transition; strictly secular concerns, therefore,
are not properly within the purview of the man who is looking to his own transcendence.

To the extent that the specific connections among the

forces of the hierarchy are not open to an entirely mechanistic analysis, their knowledge becomes the basis of an "occult philosophy" or "occult science" that is partly empirical, partly revealed, partly the result of a logical synthesis that transcends the techniques of theology and natural science alike. Set in a dualist context (the acceptance, that is, of reality as representing the conflict of two opposed forces), this framework was the Gnosticism of the Mediterranean and the Mideast. Superimposed on the metaphysics of Plato and Aristotle, it led to the Neoplatonism of the late Hellenistic age. In India it permeated all of the formal philosophies.

The development of more conventional Western thought patterns, specifically Western theology and Western science, has been in sharp contrast to this occultist framework. The Judaic emphasis on a transcendent God and on the moments of history forming a linear pattern led Christian intellectuals to adopt a view toward reality that tended to broaden the chasm between the spiritual and the material. There was a hierarchy of forces, but they were by no means interdependent. Language, for instance, could not be used to command spiritual powers; symbols were appropriate for meditation, but they were worthless for magic.

Organizational complexity in itself tends to break down a holistic view (any consideration of parts in terms of a greater whole) in favor of something more mechanistic (one in which the whole is only the sum of its parts, and the coordination of the parts becomes of greater concern than the meaning of what results). The Romans, unlike the Greeks, were organizational geniuses, and it was Roman law rather than Greek poetry that determined the mode of thinking of the Christians who inherited their empire. Like true bureaucrats, the theologians prepared organizational charts for the faithful that ensured that they would always know their place in the scheme of salvation.

During all this time, while the combination of a linear view of history and Roman legalism pushed the West relentlessly forward to a more mechanistic view of the world, occultism supplied a countervailing force that kept pulling it back.

In the Renaissance, Copernicus challenged Ptolemy in the field of astronomy, and artist-technologist Leonardo da Vinci opened new vistas of what might be accomplished through machinery. But at the same time astrology, which appealed to many scientific minds because of its stress on the order of nature, was experiencing a decided revival. Alchemy and ceremonial magic were also flourishing, although most educated men found them too close to witchcraft for their comfort.

With the beginning of the seventeenth century, in the era of Galileo, Descartes, and Francis Bacon, it was not at all clear whether occultists or mechanists would carry the day. In the next chapter we shall look more closely at the myth that came along to concretize occultist interests, but for the time being it may be enough to indicate that the excitement of magic was never stronger than in the age which learned that the earth was not the center of the universe.

The mechanists won, as we know, but this did not end the appeal of occultism. What became necessary was a new manner of accommodating the occultist framework, its particular atmosphere of faith, to a changing scientific outlook. The concept of intelligences guiding the stars while demons intervened in physical processes became totally unacceptable, as did the ideal of effecting a literal transmutation of metals. What came to take their place for most occultists were the ideas of spiritualism and an approach to sorcery as the conjuration not of theological demons but of Paracelsian elementals.

The occultist counterpoint, dominant in the Hellenistic world and in the Renaissance and revived again in the nineteenth century with Theosophy and groups such as the Golden Dawn, obviously continues into the present. Today, despite the fact that it is more likely to be couched in the language of Indian philosophy or in the terms of Soviet biophysics and American transpersonal psychology, it can be as credulous and as pretentious as it was in the days of Agrippa and Paracelsus. What counts, however, is that it exists. Wrongheaded or not, it is a reminder that the horizons of human experience need not be limited.

Any discussion of the occultist counterpoint would be incomplete without some mention of the manner in which magicians or pseudo magicians have been courted by the rich and the powerful. This was never more true than in eighteenth-century Europe at the height of the Enlightenment when the Comte de Saint-Germain became a favorite of Louis XV and Cagliostro inducted aristocratic ladies into his own orgiastic version of an occult fraternity. But it was a pattern that appeared also in the Roman Empire, was celebrated in the legends of Merlin at the court of King Arthur, and with Rasputin at the court of Nicholas V of Russia perhaps changed the course of history. It is part of the story of the Third Reich, and I would not be surprised if someday soon newspapers announce the discovery of an occultist Watergate somewhere here or abroad. But why?

I discovered something of the answer the day that our friend Kathy called and asked if I could get at the copy of the *Necronomicon* which, she was sure, was among the volumes in the forbidden section of the Los Angeles Public Library. The *Necronomicon*, as any reader of H. P. Lovecraft knows, is the book of sorcery prepared by the mad Arab

Abdul Alhazred. For her and for many others, as I soon learned, the circumstantial inclusion of this entirely fictitious work together with quite genuine materials on the occult in a number of Lovecraft's tales—as well as in stories by other authors who have drawn from this same "Cthulu Mythos"— has had an effect even greater than that intended by its author. The "Old Ones," the malevolent alien forces described in the *Necronomicon*, have become appropriate Space Age successors to the legions of Lucifer feared by earlier generations. How do I know, I have been asked, that dread Cthulu is *just* a figment of a pulp writer's imagination, or that the Old Ones are not the *real* explanation for all the disparate practices of diabolical sorcery existing throughout human history?

The true addict of Lovecraftiana, like the true believer in Frodo and the Fellowship of the Ring created by J. R. R. Tolkien, prefers to see his favorite author as a hierophant, a priest of the mysteries with access to a special knowledge which he would want all but the faithful to accept as pure fiction. But for the insider ("Let him who has ears to listen . . .") there will be a deeper message, even an invitation to seek out a mysterious fraternity striving for the salvation of the world against cosmic odds.

The pioneer sociologist Georg Simmel has quite accurately depicted the ideas of the secret and the secret society as basic drives within more complex forms of human interaction. Secret societies, moreover, are often the key to an emerging awareness that must be sheltered for the sake of the future; or, perhaps as often, they are the clue to an awareness that is a punishable relic of the past. Christians, for example, had to function as a secret society in pagan Rome even beyond the style of other mystery cults, and the pagans who wished to survive the eventual triumph of Christianity in their turn were to follow the methods of those whom they had once persecuted.

The social logic of secrecy is particularly applicable to any discussion of the world of magic. The most obvious reason for secrecy in the older traditions lies in the credit given the possession of particular sets of symbols. For many cultures, the world itself was made by magic, and the recitation of a particular phrase or the performance of a particular action would be enough not only to alter anything within the world but even to accomplish its complete destruction.

This outlook was certainly present within the Egyptian magic that was the source of many of the Hellenistic ideas that have been handed down to the present as the basis of ceremonial magic, and it was only strengthened by the development of Cabala and the appearance of the grimoires. The eventual surrender of the qualitative physics of Aristotle to a revived atomism may have weakened the occultist's interest in external nature, especially when the marvels of a seemingly limitless technology meant that the scientist was outperforming the wizard, but it did not destroy occultism in itself.

Instead attention was transferred from the mysterious operations of nature to the development of the human psyche through systematic indoctrination into a hidden wisdom. Alchemy and sorcery alike were now marked less by the efforts of isolated entrepreneurs than they were by the emergence of various clandestine organizations. The secrecy associated with magic in the past continued, but the reasons for the secrecy were considerably different. The focus was no longer on the power of a symbol but on the internal needs of groups that functioned as secular counterparts to both the ancient mystery cults and the religious orders of the Catholic Church.

The lure of magic has always been power. The coven tradition, particularly as it has been developed by Alex Sanders and Anton LaVey, has offered the prospect of cosmic power as well as erotic fun and games to individuals whose daily lives are characterized by impotence. The promise of power has also been the pitch of the ads for the Rosicrucians located in the California city of San Jose ("There are some things that can not be generally told—*things you ought to know*. Great truths are dangerous to some—but factors for *personal power and accomplishment* in the hands of those who understand them"), as well as for the numerous groups advertising in the pages of occultist magazines.

This lure is no less strong for those who are already powerful, even though the psychological dynamics explaining it may be somewhat different. But in the case of the people who make up "society" an offer to share in some secret wisdom can hardly be as democratic as it is with the covens or the various mystic fellowships. It must be made to seem quite exclusive—and expensive. Cagliostro was a master of this art, although his ambition led finally to a miserable death in prison. Aleister Crowley was also, even if at times he could not resist a measure of crude burlesque, as on the occasion when he defecated on the rug of a wealthy lady who had solicited some sign of his power.

It was the possibility of costly deception that gave the word "magic" its double meaning in the ancient world. When the historian Herodotus wrote of the Magi, the priest-diviners of Persia, he presented them simply as men who claimed a certain special power. The philosopher Heraclitus, however, spoke of them as charlatans. Roman intellectuals kept alive the tendency to think of magic, the art of the Magi, as an either-or thing, and Christian writers followed them in this. Magic was deception or it was genuine power, although in either case the Christian had to see it as evil.

The trap here is that any either-or outlook toward the occult creates its own alternatives of either a hopeless skepticism or a pathetic gullibility. Illusionist Harry Houdini, for instance, could never be convinced that there were genuine psychic phenomena, and Arthur Conan Doyle, the creator of Sherlock Holmes and one of the great supporters of spiritualism, was hard put to recognize even the most patent deceptions. What is for real in the world of magic and what is not quickly become indistinguishable.

I grant that a pragmatic option to protect the overly credulous by legislation makes good enough sense. Quack magic like quack medicine ought to be restrained, but at the same time it has to be recognized that the definition of quackery is a touchy thing. Blanket prohibitions of astrology, such as those that are still on the books in many American communities, like the English witchcraft statute finally repealed in 1951, probably serve only to create a black market in the black arts. I have the same feeling about laws like the one enacted in 1973 by the Tennessee legislature that requires the presentation of *Genesis* as an alternative to the Darwinian theory of evolution but prohibits "the teaching of all occult or satanical beliefs of human origin."

There is a good reason for secrecy in the occultist tradition. The Taoist maxim says it best of all: Those who know do not speak, those who speak do not know. This does not mean that verbalization is impossible, only that it is entirely inadequate.

Agrippa and Paracelsus were ridiculed in their own lifetimes, Saint-Germain and Cagliostro were lionized. One difference was the fact that by the eighteenth century a potent new element had been introduced into Western occultism. This was the legend of the Brotherhood of the Rosy Cross, a mysterious confraternity acting as a source of occult wisdom.

By the time of the two roguish "Counts" Europe had been sensitized to the possibility that such a group existed and that individuals such as Saint-Germain and Cagliostro were in some manner connected with it.

What we shall have to look at next is how this legend began and how it grew.

9.

The Traveler to Damcar

IN MY FIRST YEARS of Jesuit study I lived in a self-contained community. Tanya went through similar experiences in order to arrive at her particular outlook toward magic. But when it seemed that she would be unable to adjust to the quite different atmosphere of an American junior high school, she attended two of the schools that followed the teaching patterns developed by Austrian occultist Rudolf Steiner.

The specifics of Steiner's teachings, formulated in what he called Anthroposophy, were not part of the instruction given the students at the Waldorf schools, but the teachers constantly alluded to their existence. No less than the boys I once taught at St. Ignatius High School in San Francisco, Tanya and her classmates were encouraged to take shallow drafts of a different atmosphere in the expectation that at least some of them would go on to enter completely into the special world of their instructors.

Without quite understanding their significance, students engaged in elementary techniques for breathing and movement that represented the first steps in any occultist training. They were also exhorted to read Tolkien's *Lord of the Rings* not just as fantasy but as a hint of some further teaching about the lore of elementals. All of this contrasted sharply with the earlier efforts of Tanya's psychiatrists at UCLA to assert a more ordinary sense of reality, but the results were, I think, entirely positive.

What was explained was the importance of using imagination as a means to a deeper spiritual life. As an example, Tanya recalls a play based on Goethe's *Fairy Tale of the Green Snake and the Beautiful Lily*. She had taken the role of the lily and her best friend had been the snake. What she had not known then was that Steiner had seen the fable as a recasting of one of the themes to be found in *The Chemical Wedding of Christian Rosenkreutz* and that he had described its experience as setting one "in the outer court of the esoteric." Before we look at how Steiner developed his thought, we should look at the Rosicrucian legend, which Steiner apparently first met with in Goethe and then took over on his own.

There is, as Steiner points out in his history of the legend, a measure of uncertainty about the actual origin of the materials contained in the two documents, the *Fama Fraternitatis* (anglicized by Thomas Vaughan as *The Fame of the Fraternity of the Rosie Cross*) and *The Chemical* (or *Chymical*) *Wedding of Christian Rosenkreutz*. The printed texts appeared in 1614 and 1616 and are ascribed to the Protestant theologian Johann Valentin Andreä. In his later years Andreä repudiated these works as a youthful jest, a forerunner of a more serious effort to organize a Fraternitas Christiana in 1620. There is evidence, however, that a manuscript version of *The Chemical Wedding* was in circulation in 1603 and a manuscript of the *Fama* in 1610. Steiner's explanation of these facts and of Andreä's later repudiation of Rosicrucianism is that as an adolescent he had been able to write out of a spiritual intuition that he lost when he became more of a self-conscious intellectual.

Fama Fraternitatis begins with the story of how a young man, identified only as C.R.C., made his way to the Arabian city of Damcar and there was taught the occult arts. Afterward he traveled to Morocco for further studies. Then he returned to Europe and founded a fraternity dedicated to helping the sick. Each of the four original members of the fraternity was to recruit a new adept to fill his place, but otherwise the very existence of the group was not to be revealed for a century.

C.R.C. died in 1484 and was buried in a secret vault in the brotherhood's original home. In 1614 the successors of the original group discovered the vault with the uncorrupted body of their founder. This was taken as the indication that the time had come for the group to open itself to men of good will everywhere.

A year after the original *Fama Fraternitatis*, an additional document appeared to renew the appeal. Then the next year saw the printing of *The Chemical Wedding*, a first-person account by Christian Rosenkreutz (the Frater C.R.C. of the *Fama*) of the visionary experience that had occurred to him on Easter Eve of 1459.

The *Fama Fraternitatis* caused considerable excitement among those who read it. Gradually this excitement died down when no one was able to locate its authors, and in a few more years Andreä himself had embarked on new ventures.

Was all of this an elaborate satire on the mystical alchemy

of the time? Steiner rejects this possibility. From its virulent anti-Catholicism and the repeated citation of Paracelsus as an authority, it would seem likely that this tale of the mysterious fraternity was concocted to provide a Protestant answer to groups such as the Jesuits. Steiner, the Catholic seemingly turned Gnostic (a description he emphatically rejected but which I think fits) was not willing to accept this interpretation either. *The Chemical Wedding*, he reasoned, described an authentic spiritual experience which Andreä presented in the name of the legendary Frater C.R.C. As for the rest, Steiner had to admit bafflement.

In a recent edition of the original Rosicrucian materials, Paul M. Allen has noted various points which, if they are historically valid, make the legend of Christian Rosenkreutz somewhat more credible. Contrary to the occultist historian A. E. Waite, who stated that Damcar was an entirely imaginary place, it is identified as Dhamar, a city in Yemen that in the fifteenth century was a Muslim intellectual center. Moreover, Christian Rosenkreutz is identified as the youngest member of a family eradicated in the campaign against the Albigensians. Placed in a monastery for his own protection, he had assisted the Bishop of Utrecht in his study of alchemy and then, after the prelate's death, had traveled into the Islamic world. Could a young man of a Catharist background, exposed to alchemy and then trained in Muslim thought, have founded a secret fraternity whose future sympathies would be entirely with the Protestant cause? It seems rather improbable but fascinating all the same.

Throughout the seventeenth century the Rosicrucian legend continued to intrigue odd intellectuals. The allegorical presentation of alchemy found in *The Chemical Wedding* was particularly acceptable to the Cambridge Platonists, and through them it continued to influence English literature.

In the eighteenth century Freemasonry appeared as a real-life version of the type of secret society presented in the *Fama Fraternitatis*. The line between fact and fiction blurred as various Masonic groups came to consider themselves heirs of the Rosicrucian mysteries. By the nineteenth century the time was ripe for still new groups seeking to revivify the legend of a Hermetic wisdom—an alchemy of the soul.

Early in the nineteenth century, at the famous Parisian seminary of St. Sulpice, a young man named Alphonse Louis Constant ran into some trouble with his ecclesiastical superiors. Although he had already been ordained a deacon, the last step prior to ordination as a priest, Constant was dismissed. His clerical training stayed with him, however, and he contributed a volume to the Migne collection of patristic sources under the name of Abbé Constant, purportedly a former teacher at a Parisian minor seminary.

His scholarship was then turned to a more lucrative field and, using the pseudonym of Eliphas Levi, he produced several volumes, most notably *The History of Magic* and *Transcendental Magic*, which quickly became classics of occult literature. Levi mined a number of sources for his own theory of magic, and the result was an odd mix of Gnosticism, the Cabala, Rosicrucian alchemy, and the lore of the old grimoires.

To set Levi's work in perspective, it must be remembered that the discovery of the Rosetta stone during Napoleon's occupation of Egypt had spurred a new interest in the supposed mysteries of the world's first high civilization. All good classicists already knew of the legends according to which both Pythagoras and Plato had studied in Egypt, and the alchemist tradition had perpetuated the Hellenistic myth of Hermes Trismegistus as the Egyptian source of all occult wisdom. The sudden accessibility of the once mysterious hiero-glyphics accordingly seemed to promise a new era in which the lore that had inspired the best of Greek thought would also inspire a West that had already begun to outgrow the classics of Greece and Rome.

Levi, who interpreted the Cabala as the Jewish transmission of ancient Egyptian wisdom, had little more than his semi-nary Hebrew to guide him in his reconstructions, but his work did excite other amateur Orientalists, particularly in England. Following his example, the promoters of the Hermetic Order of the Golden Dawn and later Aleister Crowley were to pre-sent occultism dressed up in a curious patchwork of Hebrew glyphs and Egyptian images.

At this time the advent of spiritualism was provoking widespread enthusiasm for paranormal phenomena, and, in the same year that Levi died (1875), an even more exotic personality, the Russian adventuress Helena Blavatsky, was organizing the Theosophical Society in the United States as a way of capitalizing on American spiritualist interests. The an-tiquarianism that was Levi's specialty ultimately was no match for the two-pronged attack of an emerging parapsychol-ogy and an ambitious metaphysics that reached back to At-lantis rather than to Egypt for its mythic origins. Nevertheless, Aleister Crowley kept alive the image of the magus as the master of ineffable knowledge which he might use either for good or for evil. The lasting potency of this image might be seen from the fact that John Fowles's *The Magus* was a best seller just a few years back.

To understand how Levi's influence was transmitted we must realize that the nineteenth century was the great age for occultist fiction. And, as before in the history of magic, fiction had a curious way of making itself come true. One link between the quite philosophical *Frankenstein* at the beginning of the century and a ghoulish production such as *Dracula* at its end is the presence of a new type of protagonist—the scientist who, in contrast to his materialist colleagues, recognizes the reality of the hidden forces of nature.

The novelist Edward Bulwer-Lytton, best known for *The Last Days of Pompeii*, was among the first in the procession of litterateurs into the ranks of the occultists. In the middle of the century Bulwer-Lytton came in contact with Eliphas Levi and was inspired not only to borrow some of Levi's ideas but also to undertake the formation of a short-lived English society for the study of ceremonial magic. Then, when the Hermetic Order of the Golden Dawn was begun in 1887, a number of authors, W. B. Yeats and Algernon Blackwood the most prominent among them, quite eagerly joined in its rituals.

The actual history of the Golden Dawn will always remain somewhat uncertain, but the best reconstruction is that its charter as an "Outer Order" teaching the lore needed by recruits for a Second Order, that of the Red Rose and the Cross of Gold, was provided by a certain Anna Sprengel. The precise authority of this lady, whose Nuremberg address was included in a ciphered edition of Rosicrucian rituals that had come into the possession of an English minister named A. F. A. Woodford, remains a mystery. She does seem to have been a real person and a member of the tangle of groups that marked the European extension of the Theosophical Society. Woodford represented her as an adept of the Second Order and, as such, someone with access to the members of still a Third Order, the innermost circle of the Secret Chiefs, who were presumably the direct heirs of Christian Rosenkreutz.

Woodford and three others, all with a background in Rosicrucianism, were the members of the original Golden Dawn and its Isis-Urania Temple in London. The dominant personality proved to be that of a museum curator named S. L. Macgregor Mathers. When correspondence with Frau Sprengel broke off a few years later, Mathers claimed to have established direct spiritual contact with the Secret Chiefs and even instituted his own rituals for the suppositious Second Order. Two of the founders of the group, Woodford and Dr. W. R. Woodman, had already died, and one other, W. Wynn Westcott, resigned from the Golden Dawn a decade after its founding, perhaps because of official pressure in connection with his position as a Queen's Coroner in London.

Mathers soon proved a bit too abrasive for the remaining membership of the order, particularly when, over their objections, he advanced a brilliant young protégé named Aleister Crowley to the rank of Adeptus Minor, the level at which he too was a member of the Second Order. The resulting schism, heightened by magical attacks and counterattacks, weakened the effectiveness of the Golden Dawn, and scandal eventually demolished it. Crowley, meanwhile, also split with Mathers and founded a group of his own—again, as he stated, according to the will of the Secret Chiefs.

What I find particularly significant in this account is the manner in which four men—an antiquarian, a clergyman, and two physicians—jumped at the chance to link themselves with anyone who claimed to represent the mysterious brotherhood of the *Fama Fraternitatis*.

As Aleister Crowley was to comment, the group's reliance on astral contact permitted a great deal of fraud and self-deception, but Mathers was completely caught up in it. Whether Mathers ever intentionally deceived any of his followers is open to question, but certainly he was easily enough deceived himself. The classic instance of this was the successful imposture of Anna Sprengel by a lady known as Madame Horos. Madame Horos, who had already served time for fraud in the United States and was to do so again in England, absconded with various manuscript materials related to the order and used them to set up a spurious Golden Dawn as a front for seduction and swindling.

This, unfortunately, was only one of many incidents that came to blacken the order's reputation, although it took the genius of Crowley himself to solicit even more unfavorable publicity, most of which centered on the sex magic that Crowley incorporated into the rituals of foundations such as his Sacred Abbey of Thelema, a short-lived experiment in Sicily. Crowley reveled in his notoriety, but the result was that the serious side of his sorcery was almost forgotten in the shenanigans that brought about the self-styled Great Beast's expulsion first from Sicily and then from various other parts of Europe.

But there was still a more significant aspect of this dependence on astral communications than the misfortunes that befell the Golden Dawn. When utilized by individuals who feared the occult, as in the instance of the "spectral evidence" introduced against those accused of witchcraft at Salem, it could lead to fantastic assertions regarding the prevalence of evil. When utilized by the occultists themselves, it could lead to equally fantastic assertions regarding the possibility of good.

To my knowledge, no historian has yet examined adequately the role played both by secret societies and by occultist study groups in the formation of the consciousness of the modern West. Like the mystery religions of the Hellenistic world, these expressions of the occultist counterpoint appear to have filled a need for ritual and myth at a time when the social structure generally was opting for a less sacral legitimation. Formal religion, in other words, could be challenged in the name of Reason, yet many of the church's strongest antagonists submitted to being "hoodwinked" as part of their initiation into secular substitutes for the religious confraternities of an earlier era.

In the nineteenth century, spiritualism, which offered much of the emotional excitement of religion without a need for the encumbrances of theological commitment, spurred a revival of the Rosicrucian myth. If, on the one hand, this joined with the interests of Gothic romancers to bring about the creation of groups such as the Golden Dawn, on the other it led to a remarkable new effort to intellectualize occultism on a new basis. In place of the Cabala and the relatively simple pantheism inherited from the Neoplatonists "occult philosophy" looked eastward to the ancient—and complex—teachings of India and Tibet.

Madame Helena Blavatsky almost single-handedly accomplished this Orientalization of the occult through her work in the formation of the Theosophical Society. Her early career included an impulsive marriage, riding bareback in a circus, and acting as an assistant to the medium D. D. Home. In 1873, at the age of forty-two, she arrived in the United States in time to exploit the American fascination with spiritualism. Falling in with Henry Steel Olcott, a lawyer who doubled as a journalist, Madame Blavatsky insisted that her travels had taken her to Tibet and that she remained in spiritualistic contact with some very evolved adepts who had taught her "esoteric Buddhism." Two years later she and Olcott founded the Theosophical Society, originally in order to explore the

Hermetic secrets concealed in the proportions of Egyptian architecture. In two years more she had produced *Isis Unveiled* as a curious synthesis of almost all that was available in both Asian and Western occult lore.

In *Isis Unveiled* and the still later *Secret Doctrine*, written after the Theosophical Society had allied itself first with the Hindu movement of Arya Samaj and then with Theravadan Buddhism, Madame Blavatsky, always writing with the astral guidance of her Tibetan master, Koot Hoomi Lal Singh, proposed a completely new account of the genesis of humanity. This was the doctrine of "root races" that expressed the evolution of monads to higher degrees of intellectual capability.

A century ago, we must remember, the task of any philosophy was held to be the creation of elaborate intellectual models after the manner of George Hegel. *Isis Unveiled* and *The Secret Doctrine*, the latter a title that a few years back seemed particularly ominous when it was requested by Sirhan Sirhan while he awaited trial for the murder of Robert Kennedy, were nothing if not elaborate. Unlike Eliphas Levi, who had opposed the Cabala to the "idolatry" of India, Helena Blavatsky correctly surmised that the temper of the times called for a synthesis of Western and Asian motifs. For her, the Cabala and Hindu mythology alike reflected a deeper teaching that was transmitted through a spiritual brotherhood even more mysterious than the group supposedly formed by Christian Rosenkreutz.

Madame Blavatsky does appear to have been a capable medium, but the English society for Psychical Research, acting on the charges brought by a couple who had been in her employ while she and Olcott were in India, declared her manifestations to be suspect. Despite this rebuff, she made a believer of an indefatigable lady named Annie Besant. Mrs.

Besant, who had already made one career for herself as a prominent Socialist, later took over the direction of the Theosophical Society, repaying part of its debt to India by her work in the formation of the Congress Party. (Mrs. Besant also created the first cult that would surround J. P. Krishnamurti, a young man whom she adopted, educated, and proclaimed as a new messiah. Krishnamurti later rejected such a designation and began a career of teaching that is singularly free of the esoteric allusions of his English patron.)

By the beginning of the twentieth century, then, the lost continent of Atlantis, first mentioned by Plato in an allegory contrasting Greek freedom and Asian despotism and reinstituted in the 1860s by Ignatius Donnelly as the hypothetical link between the cultures of Egypt and South America, had been reintegrated into Western occultism as a source of the "truths" common to all later traditions. And if Atlantis were not enough, there was now also the myth of Lemuria—the Mu of James Churchward and science-fiction editor Raymond A. Palmer. Yet more important than the introduction of either of these lost continents is the evolutionary monadology through which Madame Blavatsky attempted a significant reconciliation of ancient themes—particularly the ideas of an astral body and a world soul—with the concepts of nineteenth-century science.

This reconciliation was to go even further with the occultists who followed Helena Blavatsky. The most remarkable of these was still another mysterious Russian named George Ivanovitch Gurdjieff, who like Madame Blavatsky, had traveled to exotic places, was familiar with Asian mysticism, and liked to postulate the existence of varied life forms throughout the universe. After the Russian Revolution, when he was helped financially through the writings of his disciple, P. D.

Ouspensky, Gurdjieff emigrated to France and established his Institute for the Harmonious Development of Man as a communal center for the attainment of what he termed a fourth stage of consciousness—the concentrated awareness of one's own essence.

The elaborate cosmology developed by Gurdjieff, including extensive descriptions of the residents of other planets, is ultimately of less significance than the techniques for altering states of consciousness that have become the basis of several contemporary movements. Central to these techniques was a stress on intensifying the personal output of energy as the means to gaining a creative freedom. Life, for Gurdjieff, was meant to be hard—and his own manner of exposition was calculated to be as demanding as any of the techniques he taught.

It was left for Ouspensky, whose *In Search of the Miraculous* and *Tertium Organum* are modern classics of occultist writing, to systematize Gurdjieff's ideas as well as to corroborate them through further analyses of his own. If the theory of evolution, no matter how adapted, was the vehicle through which Madame Blavatsky could renew the emanationist theories of the past, it was the mathematical discussion of the fourth dimension that would serve the same function for Ouspensky. Past, present, and future are functions of consciousness within a three-dimensional world; it is within the fourth dimension that all distinctions of space and time can be overcome. Occultism, then, is the science through which consciousness can be brought to the level of the fourth dimension.

It is always difficult to establish the precise influences at work in any piece of occultist literature. Historical recapitulations, for example, interject suggestions of relativity that occultists generally find disturbing unless, as does Madame Blavatsky, they can utilize them as *ad hominem* justifications for a deeper truth supposedly handed down from a wiser era through a coterie of chosen souls. Gurdjieff, as Colin Wilson points out, originally was as fascinated as was his countrywoman by the lure of an esoteric fraternity—in his case, the Babylonian Sarmoung Brotherhood dating back to 2500 B.C. Still, unlike the foundress of the Theosophical Society, Gurdjieff never claimed to have made contact with any mysterious adepts.

One of Gurdjieff's admirers, Rafael Lefort (in *The Teachers of Gurdjieff*, published in London in 1971), has, I think, suggested the most likely resolution of this question. His own investigation of the individuals and movements with which Gurdjieff came in contact took him finally to a Sufi master with whom Gurdjieff had studied before his appearance in Moscow as a potent but secretive magus. The Sufi's teaching— Cease to look for any master but oneself—was the same antiauthoritarian conclusion reached by Krishnamurti after his break with the Order of the Star in the East, the group that the Theosophists Annie Besant and C. W. Leadbetter had founded as the vehicle for his epiphany as the new savior of mankind.

On this basis, no description of "reality" would be significant except as a poetic hint for the individual to effect his own transcendence. Esoteric groups in the classical mold would be not only unnecessary but even counterproductive. If this reading is correct, Gurdjieff, the most mysterious of all modern occultists, ironically marks the end of mystery; a magician, as Colin Wilson makes him out to be, he also marks the point where magic is transmuted into mysticism.

At the beginning of the modern era the Rosicrucian myth and then Freemasonry offered a counterpoint to the rhythms of an advancing technology. In the nineteenth century, Rosicrucianism—broadened from a mystical alchemy to take in the ceremonial magic of the West and the meditative techniques of India and Tibet—became an even more potent effort to escape the limits of secular existence. The human sources of an esoteric wisdom—Jews in the Middle Ages, Arabs in the *Fama Fraternitatis*, Tibetans in the teaching of Madame Blavatsky—became increasingly remote even as they were seen as increasingly knowledgeable.

The myth of a Hermetic wisdom formulated in Egypt and preserved in the Cabala was absorbed into the myth of Atlantis and finally, as at present, into the myth of interstellar contacts. Imaginative extensions of various traditional practices (my interpretation of the grimoires that began with the *Key of Solomon*) became rules for elaborate rituals, and the rituals demanded the creation of closed groups, such as the Golden Dawn, that might see themselves as the outer shells of incredibly ancient fraternities.

Meanwhile, the paranormal phenomena evidenced in spiritualism facilitated a transition from Cornelius Agrippa's theme of "occult philosophy" to the theme of "occult science" found in Ouspensky. The Paracelsian idea of elementals, one of the things taken over by the Rosicrucian tradition, was given a new standing through Theosophy at the same time that it was conjoined with the idea of the astral body as an energy system. The jargon of Indian metaphysics and the novel presentations of twentieth-century science were brought together to formulate still newer syntheses of almost incredible complexity.

By the First World War, to be an occultist no longer required initiation into mysterious symbols that were supposedly efficacious within themselves; mastering the viewpoints of the Theosophists or of Gurdjieff and Ouspensky more than satisfied the need to maintain an esoteric perspective. And, accordingly, the old secret societies were no longer necessary in order to achieve the psychic satisfaction of having left an old world in order to acquire a new identity.

At present there is something of a movement back to a more ritual magic. This is the case even though parapsychology and groups dedicated to Transcendental Meditation or to various techniques of biofeedback attempt to provide altered states of consciousness without the use of the symbolism that involves an entry into the world of magic. For many, this is through the reconstructed witchcraft that is the heir of the now outmoded lodges of the Victorian magicians. For others, it is through a quite explicit sorcery that acknowledges the validity of conjuration without calling it either religion (as in the covens) or mysticism (as in the Rosicrucian secret orders).

Could there also be a movement back to accepting the existence of some "secret wisdom"? The urge to believe in Lovecraft's *Necronomicon* among many college-age devotees of the occult is, I think, indicative of the continuing allure of the mysterious at a time when secular culture has proclaimed the end of mystery. Magic, at its worst, is a private demand for the costumed heroes—or villains—and secret words of power that many of us remember from old-time comic strips.

The experience of altered states of consciousness effected through hallucinogenics has already prepared the young for the transformations expected from rituals derived from a more mystical alchemy. Why not then search out the work of the mad Abdul Alhazred, refusing to believe that it is fiction and fiction alone? This, after all, was what the straight world used to say about witches and their covens.

Perhaphs I'm overestimating the potential for a mystique based on "dread Cthulu," but I've already seen how seriously the old techniques of sorcery are taken by individuals who might have been thought too sophisticated for the business of double circles and inverted pentagrams. What's interesting is that the potency of belief has a curious way of making fiction become reality—as it did first with the secret orders and then with cult witchcraft.

There is, of course, a great difference between a faddish involvement and the total change of a life style in keeping with a new belief system. It is said that we have a need to believe. I think what is more the case is that we have a need to belong. If this sense of belonging can be instilled in youth, as it was for me as a Catholic student and then as a Jesuit and as it was for Tanya as a student in the schools dedicated to carrying out Steiner's mission, belief becomes as natural as breath.

This psychological fact has to be kept in mind whenever we look at the actual workings of the occultist counterpoint. A person accepts new ideas partly because they are congenial to his own temperament or to his past intellectual framework but even more because they represent the outlook of those with whom he prefers to associate. What we have to consider is the manner in which specific beliefs are incorporated into communities, more or less closed in their structures, which provide a satisfactory alternative to whatever is the social setting of the nonbeliever.

It can happen, of course, that even an imaginary group—the original Brotherhood of the Rosy Cross, for example—can become a spiritual home for the would-be believer. I learned this for myself when, in *The Return of Magic,* I concluded a discussion of the place of magic in contemporary society with a brief description of an entirely fictitious commune located in northern California and dedicated to the study of magic. I soon received letters from across the country in which I was asked for further details on what was necessary in order to join in the activities of my group.

I decided finally not to answer these letters; I was not sure that my correspondents would believe me when I insisted the commune did not exist, nor could I expect them to understand why, for my own part, I would have to decline any active participation in organizing such a group. Perhaps it was better that they simply believed in it and looked more deeply within themselves for the way to realize whatever it was they wanted from exposure to it.

Moreover, if the results of the legend of the traveler to Damcar are any indication, it may just be that such a commune *will* come into existence as still another realization of the occultist counterpoint.

10.

Doing Magic: Astrology and the Tarot

WHEN I FIRST MET Tanya and she told me that she was into witchcraft, occultism seemed slightly ridiculous, a poor excuse for religion that was unworthy of any serious intellectual consideration. Spiritualism, I was convinced, was a fraud, astrology an absurdity, and activities such as divination and spell-casting at best a manipulation of subliminal cues and at worst an outrageous substitute for rational action. I was curious about Tanya and her family solely as representatives of a tradition that I thought had long since disappeared.

That all changed quite quickly. Tanya's presence triggered a certain sensitivity in myself that I had systematically denied all my life, and the events that took place afterward convinced me there was more to the world of magic than fantasy. That, of course, was the beginning of the detective story—my search for the meaning of magic.

An early interest in the history of ideas made it quite natural for me to look at the occult in terms of the individuals and the groups that have provided a kind of counterpoint to the development of our modern linear history. Researching this background was necessary in order for me to appreciate just how it was that contemporary occultists arrived at the ideas they propose.

Yet this was obviously only part of the investigation I would have to make. Tanya's own interests made a natural enough starting point. Besides the spell-casting, which for her was the essence of witchcraft, she engaged in astrology and in divination through the tarot. What does it mean to *do* magic? Not in the time of the Caesars or in the Renaissance but right now?

The descriptions of the Western alchemists of their materials and processes in terms of psychologically provocative metaphors made possible the division of alchemy into two relatively distinct "sciences," one dealing with the transmutation of metals and the other with the transmutation of the soul. The alchemy that was explicitly devoted to the creation of gold has almost completely disappeared, superseded by the modern chemistry that began with the quantitative approach of Robert Boyle. It is easy enough then, although incorrect, to see alchemy solely as a forerunner of today's science.

Until a few years ago astrology was conveniently dumped into the same dustbin of history. It was interpreted by all good rationalists as a primitive astronomy that went beyond its evidence. The penchant for horoscopes was a type of superstition, the consultation of astrologers (in the statutes of a great many American communities) a criminal surrender to fraud. How, after all, was it possible for the patterns of the sky either to influence human events or to function as a celestial tote-board?

Some true believers did, of course, continue to make annoying intrusions into the rationalist thicket. The most famous example is probably that of Evangeline Adams, who was arrested in New York in 1914 on the basis of the usual statutes against fortune-telling. In an amazing courtroom display she interpreted the chart of an unknown male selected by the judge—and presented a devastatingly accurate picture of the judge's somewhat delinquent son. Of course she was acquitted, the judge reasoning that she had raised astrology to the dignity of an exact science.

How did she do it? Many who consider astrology to be a fully occult undertaking on the same plane as the tarot or the I Ching would reason that the proper Mrs. Adams was a belated Massachusetts witch and that her reading was less scientific than it was psychic. Still, whatever the role of "intuition" in an astrological reading, most reputable astrologers themselves reject this Gypsy tearoom image.

In England particularly, where the Astrological Lodge of London (an offshoot of the Theosophical Society) has for a quarter of a century sustained a rigorous training program for apprentice astrologers, the emphasis is on astrology as just what the New York judge said that Evangeline Adams had made it. American astrologers, despite having their own licensing body in the American Federation of Astrologers, are less bookish about it than their British cousins, but they too generally insist that there is an entirely objective validity to the charts they compute.

At one time, before my witchy wife began working on my conversion, I insisted that in the cluster of general characteristics associated with each of the dozen signs of the zodiac (the sun signs) there would be just enough to permit the ordinary person to feel that his horoscope really did apply to him. I argued that this was even more likely if rising and moon signs were taken into account as excuses for whatever mismatching there seemed to be in the sun signs. A basic principle of communication, after all, is that people tend to hear only what they want or expect to hear. Would not this principle of selective attention explain why people were satisfied by their readings? And should not the few extraordinarily accurate readings (such as the chart that Evangeline Adams presented in the New York courtroom) be written off as no more than interesting coincidences?

What is wrong with this theory is that the use of rising and moon signs provide for a greater concreteness in a horoscope rather than for a greater generality. A good horoscope, moreover, takes into account a thing called the midheaven, the location of each planet within the zodiac, and the aspects or angles formed by the sun, moon, and planets.

This impressive number of variables must then be balanced out in order to provide a rather circumstantial portrait in which the likelihood of purely chance correspondences is tremendously reduced. It is here that skill at interpretation comes into play, and, despite the proliferation of computerized horoscopes, there is no substitute for a measure of intuition, although perhaps it is that kind of intuition that marks artists rather than psychics.

There have been a number of attempts to test the validity of astrology through statistical analysis. In general they have concentrated on the sun signs of individuals in particular professions or with various other easily identified characteristics. Results have been mixed, although, in looking at astrologically related characteristics, the French Michel Gauquelin has shown the proclivity of physicians to be born when either Mars or Saturn is rising or at its zenith, and the Czech Eugen Jonas has presented evidence for an association between conception and the phases and positions of the moon. Most astrologers, however, have not felt that they require this type of statistical confirmation. Like the American Grant Lewi, who stated that he engaged in astrology knowing only that it worked but neither knowing nor caring why, they feel that the facts speak for themselves.

Although various how-to-do-it books are available, an amateur such as myself quickly discovers that erecting a horoscope is a complicated, time-consuming business. There is a modest degree of mathematics involved as well as a quite complex shorthand, and, whatever their cavalier attitude toward the astronomical zodiac, astrologers demand a high degree of precision about the location of other celestial bodies.

Getting the facts, however, is only part of the job. Although the code of ethics of the American Federation of Astrologers requires that all interpretations be based on the chart and not on the reader's whimsy (this, I suppose, is as much to avoid legal action on a charge of fortune-telling as to reinforce a certain respect for tradition), neither the A.F.A. nor anyone else can codify *exactly* what a horoscope is to mean. There are sets of key words for the signs and the planets that have become quite conventional, but basically it seems to be each man for himself. Perhaps the best technique, one used quite well by Linda Goodman in her delightful *Sun Signs*, may be to assemble a stock of anecdotes about individuals who are already of a particular sign and then to proceed quasi-empirically.

As a preparation for this chapter I tried my hand at doing my own chart. First off, I am a Cancer with a Leo rising and a Virgo moon. The key, then, to what I'm like is to be found from the sign traditionally associated not just with the sidestepping, hard-shelled crab but also with water and the moon.

Its meaning is tempered by Leo, the fire sign associated with the lion and the sun, and by Virgo, an earth sign linked with the Greek goddess of justice and with the planet Mercury.

Since Leo is my rising sign (the constellation on the eastern horizon at the time of my birth), my more leonine qualities will show up in my appearance and social personality, and that Virgo moon suggests something about my more spontaneous or internal reactions. Putting these three together, I am some-one protective and sensitive, I strike others as creative and powerful, and I have a natural tendency to be critical and analytical. Also, on the basis of my sun sign, I tend to be emo-tional, to have good business sense, and to like old silver; if I have ever been ill, it is likely that it was because of my chest or stomach.

What else? My chart is of the type that astrologer Marc Edmund Jones called "the bucket": I have eight planets, in-cluding the moon, in one hemisphere, a ninth (Saturn) in the other. According to Jones, this means that I am very purpose-ful and especially concerned with self-preservation. I have a Taurus midheaven, which, like my rising sign, indicates some-thing of my outer personality: I am not only leonine but bull-headed.

As for aspects, I have my sun in conjunction with Pluto (suggesting a bit of a power complex) and at a 30-degree angle from Venus, itself in Gemini (I am flirtatious, but things work out). My moon is at a 60-degree angle to Mercury (in-tensifying my tendency to be analytical), but Mercury is at a 90-degree angle to Jupiter (a less good aspect suggesting the possibility of poor judgment). Also, Venus and Jupiter are trined, i.e., at a 120-degree angle (a conjunction that I share with Elizabeth Taylor and one that is supposed to indicate financial success). Finally, since my planets are bunched in the

last and the next to the last divisions made in my chart beginning with my rising sign (i.e., in the eleventh and twelfth
houses), I am somewhat intellectual, with escapist tendencies.

What I have done, of course, is to take only some of the key
phrases that are associated with each of the characteristics of
my chart. This is not itself a reading, only some of the raw
material for one. Still, if a complete stranger were to throw
these things at me, I would be impressed if not amazed by the
accuracy of his perception. A skilled reader, particularly one
who knew me rather well, would be able to weave it all together into a pattern through which I might deepen my self-
knowledge and perhaps gain a better control of my own tendencies. Most contemporary astrologers are quick to point out
that this is all they will attempt. The most I should expect is
information on the tendencies indicated from my chart and
not infallible judgments about what I have done or what I
should do.

This use of astrology as a key to a person's makeup has
largely replaced forecasting for many contemporary devotees.
Carl Jung, for example, used to do his patients' horoscopes;
and Dane Rudhyar, whose *Astrology of Personality* owes much
to Jungian theory, has argued that psychological analysis and
the integration of consciousness are the only legitimate concerns for the twentieth-century astrologer.

Forecasting, though, is still a much practiced profession.
The ordinary daily or monthly horoscope is, for most people,
the only thing that astrology means. Let's admit it. Except for
you and me, who really want to understand ourselves, everyone would rather hear not about who he is but about what's
going to happen to him.

None of this appears particularly occult, except in the sense
that there is no satisfactory explanation of why an astrological

reading should have a better than chance accuracy. But neither is it really "scientific." The correlations that have been
established between biological and even social phenomena and
the positions of the moon or the planets (as in the research of
Gauquelin and Jonas mentioned earlier) do not themselves
vindicate astrology as the complex body of lore that it has become. Even should some causal links be established between
personality and the stars, it would still not justify the mass of
trivia—astrologically correct colors, gems, numbers, and all the
rest—that has been left over from the debris of the Hellenistic
world.

One thing that is curious in the history of occultism is the
manner in which alchemy was remade into mysticism as it
came to center its concerns less on the supposedly hidden powers of nature and more on the mysteries of the human psyche
as revealed through a traditional symbolism. Except for the
work of Dane Rudhyar, the interests of astrology have remained remarkably constant from the days of the Roman Empire down to the present.

I am not too likely to run into someone else with the same
cluster of characteristics as mine, since there are 1728 combinations of these three signs possible. I will, however, meet
many another Cancer with whom I can feel a psychic affinity
even while I recognize our differences, and I do find it reassuring that my wife is a Pisces (a very compatible sign for a Cancer) and that my Aquarian son shares my rising and moon
signs.

Astrology may not itself be magic except in a most extended
sense, but it does form a remarkably colorful bridge leading
away from the strictly linear. For this reason, so long as it is
not used as too much of an escape, I find its resurgence in the
Age of Aquarius a sign of hope that the grayness of Orwell's
1984 can be prevented.

With the return of magic the idea of divination through symbolic correspondences has gained new attention. The reluctance of many law-abiding astrologers to function as soothsayers has meant that other, non-Hellenistic techniques would become popular. Particularly favored by the counterculture have been the tarot and the I Ching, the Chinese *Book of Changes*. Crystal balls, tea leaves, and, of course, dreams are still much in use as prophetic devices, although one of the earliest practices, letting a Bible or some other "book of wisdom" fall open and then reading the first passage one sees, seems to have come on hard times. All of these, however, are the ways of an older generation. To be "with it" requires an excursion into quite different worlds of symbolism.

In the last few years most persons have seen at least a few of the reconstructed illustrations from the tarot, the world's first deck of playing cards. They are, as Colin Wilson points out, a tableau of the social order of the Middle Ages. There are four suits of cards representing the four classes of society: swords for the nobility, cups or chalices for the clergy, coins for the merchants, and rods or staves for the peasants. There are kings and queens and knights and pages for each of these suits. And there are twenty-two suitless cards that depict other positions in society (such as Pope and Emperor and juggler and fool) as well as assorted symbols that would be particularly meaningful to an audience of the late medieval world: fortitude and temperance, death and the Devil, the sun and the moon.

Altogether there are seventy-eight cards, fifty-six of which, except for the loss of the knight and a variation in the pips, correspond to the decks of playing cards still in use. The twenty-two picture or trump cards remaining are now used only for divination, although it is probable that they too were played for points in early games of chance.

The exact history of the tarot is uncertain. It appeared in Western Europe in the fourteenth century and may have been a contribution of the Gypsies. The word "tarot" has been subjected to a fantastic amount of exegesis by occultists. The eighteenth-century Count de Gebelin attempted to reconstruct it from the Egyptian *tar-ro*, supposedly "the royal road." Eliphas Levi saw it as a compound of the four Greek letters making up "the monogram of Christ." Aleister Crowley gave it a numerological interpretation.

All of these proposals obviously depend on there being a necessary correspondence between the letters in a word and the idea that it represents, and this in itself is a clue to the kind of thinking historically associated with the tarot. One fairly plausible but much less romantic explanation is that "tarot" comes from a term for the crossed diagonal lines on the backs of the first cards. Another is that it is derived from the Hungarian Gypsy word *tar* (card), itself related to the Hindustani *taru*.

The designs on early decks were hardly standard, although some cards, such as the one representing the hanged man, did take on their present form at a very early date. Many, such as the cards reproduced in an illustration for Louis MacNeice's *Astrology*, depicted astrological motifs that are missing today. Most of the sets of cards now in use are either reproductions of the so-called Marseilles deck of de Gebelin or variants of the Rider deck designed by Arthur Waite. Less traditional are the quite lovely deck devised by Aleister Crowley, the Egyptian deck of the Los Angeles Brotherhood of Light, and the Theosophical "New Tarot" of John Cooke and Rosalind Sharpe.

Many of the current interpretations of the tarot depend on an acceptance of one major premise: that the tarot, or at least the twenty-two major trumps, reflects the lore of the Cabala, the esoteric teaching of medieval Judaism. Since the first Cabalists appeared in the southern France of the twelfth century, it is possible that the originators of the tarot *could* have intended the major trumps to express the hidden meanings of the twenty-two "paths" of the Tree of Life, the diagram representing the *sefiroth* or emanations of God. Yet it hardly seems likely.

The first historical connection made between the tarot and the Cabala was in the discussion of the eighteenth-century fortune-teller Etiella. His suggestion was taken over by Eliphas Levi in his own effort to trace the "true" history of magic back through the Gnostics to the wisdom of the Jews derived from Egypt. Levi thus attempted an imaginative reconstruction of the entire myth of a Hermetic (or Enochian) wisdom for which the tarot became the symbolic expression.

Arthur Edward Waite, who translated Levi and wrote a commentary of his own on the symbolism of the cards, scoffed at so explicit an association of the tarot with the *sefiroth*; but Aleister Crowley, who considered himself the reincarnation of Levi, just as strenuously defended it. Waite's disclaimer to the contrary, the authority of Levi, Crowley, and the documents of the Golden Dawn seem to have been enough to perpetuate what is at best wishful thinking and at worst an unfortunate distortion of a remarkable mystical tradition.

This is not to say that the tradition of the Cabala was not heavily involved with the practice of magic, or that Western occultism did not accept much of this magic into its lore. But the tarot cannot this easily be assimilated to the Cabalistic teachings, nor is it even necessary that it should be.

Unlike the Chinese I Ching, in which interpretations are fixed by a long tradition, the tarot appears to function best as a device for the intuition of the reader. Although there is still the assumption that the fall of the cards corresponds to the inquirer's situation, the particular set of symbols appearing in the cards is also expected to trigger deeper processes within the one interpreting them.

One of the simplest procedures for a reading is for the questioner (the querent) to shuffle and cut the deck of cards after he has already removed one card (called the significator) that will stand for himself. The reader then deals out the cards in a fixed pattern (the Celtic cross) in which each card represents some one facet of the total situation in which the questioner is involved. The reading may then follow some fixed set of interpretations, but it may also be varied according to the overall feeling gained by the reader.

There are, of course, some rules that any good reader observes—basically the same rules used by responsible astrologers. The querent is never told of his own death, for instance, and the reader always attempts to suggest positive aspects in his situation. Some cards by their appearance are baleful: death, the Devil, the tower blasted by lightning. Their meanings, however, have been traditionally altered to suggest change, fate, and distress.

The tarot has taken us back again into the complex world of the late Middle Ages and to a cosmopolitan situation in Western Europe paralleling the Hellenistic period that first saw the rise of the myth of Hermes Trismegistus. Whatever its origins, this remarkable deck of cards was a pocket-sized initiation into much of the magical symbolism then current.

The standardization of the tarot from Levi on has increased the intensity of this initiation—a fact recognized by the Golden Dawn in its requirement that a specially designed tarot be studied early by the apprentice magician. The symbols for the suits could be taken to represent the implements used in ceremonial magic: the sword (for conjuring the element of air), the chalice (associated with water), the magician's wand (associated with fire), and the coin or pentacle (a disk inscribed with a five-pointed star used in conjurations involving the element of earth).

The major trumps, as they appear in the Rider deck, reinforce this symbolism: the Pope and the "Popess" (a reminder, perhaps of the medieval legend of Pope Joan) are transformed into the hierophant and the priestess, and the gay juggler becomes the omniscient magician. As presented first in the Golden Dawn manuals and then in Crowley's works, the tarot is also linked with astrology and with the alchemy of Paracelsus.

The value of any of this symbolism to divination is clear enough if it is thought of as providing a constant source of images which may trigger the reader's natural capabilities without at the same time effecting a psychic overload. But for the true psychic, such as Jeane Dixon or Peter Hurkos, "the sight" is not a matter of ceremony but of a somewhat unpredictable rush of images. Divination, then, is not a skill but a gift; seers are born, not made.

The very word "divination" suggests the supernatural as well as a type of society in which ritual contact with the spirit world by shamans or by priests is taken for granted. Magic involves this conception of a multidimensional reality, not as a private illusion but as a collective affirmation.

Even the more modern view of the Golden Dawn and Aleister Crowley, drawing on Paracelsus, is that this reality is not one of "gods" but of elemental forces capable of conjuration and personal communication. The natural psychic is reluctant to accept any of this. He is not "divining" as though he is the magician in contact with some alien intelligence. Rather his "knowing" is a matter of an as yet inexplicable but completely natural capability.

Systematic exploration of this capability has been the task set itself by the fledgling science of parapsychology, and already some fascinating hypotheses have appeared. Explanation of how systems of divination such as the tarot could work on any other basis than some type of telepathy are far harder to come by without resorting to the mind-boggling possibility, expressed in Jung's term "synchronicity," that there is a pre-established harmony between the fall of the cards and events in the querent's life.

In the language of the counterculture, which some writers feel is closer to the physics of paranormal events than the young who use it would ever guess, the cards are picking up the questioner's vibrations and responding to them in a pre-determined manner. The skilled tarot reader will be able to interpret the results with remarkable accuracy. There is nothing "spiritual" in this; it is simply a matter of having an efficiently designed program that will permit the questioner's own psychic energy to express itself adequately. The tarot, by this analysis, is no more mysterious than an IBM computer.

A skeptic's approach might be to call for a repeated trial of the divination. The same vibrations should produce the same results, should they not? Any divinatory tradition, however, counters this objection by stating that repetition, or even an initial query done out of the wrong motives, can be said to scramble the vibrations and so make it, if not impossible, at least unlikely for there to be valid results. In other words, magic does not permit statistical confirmation.

It is this catch-22 that has perhaps more than anything irked the person who protests that he would be willing to accept the validity of a technique such as that of the tarot provided it can be *proven* to him. The fact of a highly appropriate reading is, however, dismissed as insufficient proof. The experiment must be replicable, and traditional strictures against casual or repeated interrogation seem designed as a self-serving guard against the nonbeliever. "Heads I win, tails you lose."

I began this chapter by indicating my original skepticism. After my research and experimentation I do have to accept astrology and the tarot as seemingly valid indications of the influences at work within a person's life. Both seem to work within certain limits, but it is difficult to specify just what those limits might be.

Tanya's feelings about this are far stronger than mine. Jung's idea of synchronicity is for me a hypothesis that has become increasingly acceptable. For Tanya, however, both astrology and the tarot bring us into a world of interlocking spiritual forces, a world of magic in its truest sense.

Later we shall have to come back to the question of the reasonableness of such a view. But first, perhaps, we should look at what contemporary occultism itself has to say about the world of spirits—the world within which the magician has traditionally sought the source of his power. We shall do this in two stages, first considering the fairly recent tradition of spiritualism, then looking at the manner in which various occultists have attempted to provide a theoretical base for their own expressions of the reality of a world beyond.

11.

The Rites of Passage

ONE THING ABOUT being married to a witch is that I have been
brought a lot closer to the world of ghosts, demons, and whatever else lurks on the fringes of everyday experience because
she appears to attract them.

I remember quite well the evening, before we were married,
that I received a panicked call from Tanya and a girl friend.
The two had decided to conduct a séance, but seemingly neither was enough prepared for it to be successful. The spirit
that appeared was that of the old family friend who had taken
Tanya to dancing school in England. He had died a suicide
when she was nine, but now he was back for her to call upon.
A completely benevolent ghost, but a ghost regardless. I suggested over the phone that perhaps in the future it would be
better to avoid seeking such experiences if she could not
handle them.

My continuing reservations about séances create a certain

bias in my discussion of spiritualism. From the viewpoint of many occultists this may mark me as somehow too little spiritual (or perhaps too little scientific), but it remains my conviction that the preternatural, whatever it is, is not to be solicited casually.

The trouble is that the preternatural appears too often to show up on its own. Sometimes it is because of the emotional quality of a particular place, sometimes because of a kind of psychic magnetism within a particular person.

As an example of the first I have this rather chilling story from our friend Kathy. Several years ago she attended a college in Munich that was designed primarily for American students interested in earning credits in Europe. The campus dormitory was in a building used by the Gestapo during the Second World War, and if ever a place had a reason to be haunted it was this one.

Most students would have little reason to notice a girl in a white nightgown moving through the halls at night. Unless, of course, the girl did not seem to be from the student body, would carry on totally pointless conversations, and had a habit of turning a corner and disappearing into thin air. Kathy saw her once and attempted to speak with her, only to lose the girl in the shadows. The students who had not encountered her suspected a practical joke; those who had, like Kathy, were sure they had seen a ghost.

Another manifestation at the dormitory was less calm. Every so often students would be wakened by the rumble of trains seemingly coming up from the ground. When the trains stopped, directly underneath the building, the silence would be punctuated by muffled screams and the shouts of individuals denying that they were Jews.

Some of the students began inquiring into the history of the area where they lived. Yes, they were told, there used to be a subway that ran along there. Their building had been directly over it, and the Nazis had probably used the house as a terminal. But the subway had long since been destroyed; it had not been in service since the days when it transported Jews to the nearby camp at Dachau. Were the sounds—and the girl—a practical joke? Or were both echoes of an unspeakable past? Kathy, for one, is convinced that the building was haunted, and I would tend to agree with her.

For an example of the second kind of manifestation I'll go back to Pat, our lady of the black narcissus candle. One day when Tanya and I were over at her home, the kitchen faucet began running full force on its own. That, Pat told us calmly, was her poltergeist. She usually prevented manifestations by talking to the spirit while she worked in the kitchen, but lately he must have been feeling ignored. Before she had learned to do this the manifestations had been far more violent. Materials would be knocked off their shelves or bags of flour and sugar would be opened and their contents thrown over the entire area.

Pat had caught fleeting glimpses of the source of this activity. He was an old man, seemingly very lonely. His presence could at times be felt in the other rooms as well, but Pat had requested him to respect the privacy of her bedroom and bathroom.

Poltergeists ("noisy ghosts") have been distinguished from ghosts in the more usual sense in that they are the invisible sources of mischief that may be as slight as turning a faucet or spilling the contents of a bottle or as violent as a hail of stones or the movement and destruction of heavy furniture. Psychic researchers have noted that typically they appear in the presence of emotionally troubled adolescents, and it is theorized that they are not ghosts at all but storms of psychokinetic activity somehow caused by these adolescents. The view of my witch friends is that they are "discarnate" persons looking for attention.

Gael, another of the witches I met through my classes, even gave a name to her own poltergeist. Ralphie had attached himself to her while she was in Australia, and he stayed until the night of a séance in Los Angeles when he seemingly left with one of her friends. His own specialty was confiscating objects and then replacing them, often with interest. He had done this with Gael's spoons, first leaving her with only one or two that had to be continually rewashed, and then filling her drawer with spoons from only heaven knows where.

This had been endurable, but Ralphie was also getting into her personal papers and this was proving more troublesome. It was then that Gael had asked our advice about how to persuade him not to be so much of a bother.

We had had our own troubles with poltergeists. Usually the manifestations were trivial—a hair brush missing one day, then two of the same kind appearing the next—but still there was the potential for greater mischief. Tanya, like Pat, would talk to her spirits and so keep them on good behavior, but finally we did have to resort to an improvised exorcism when some of the manifestations became more annoying. I suggested that Gael try conversation first, then more ritual means if Ralphie proved uncooperative.

I am not, of course, too sure of the wisdom of having a poltergeist around as a kind of pet ghost. One of my students, a woman who rather desperately wanted some type of psychic adventure, offered to take over our own poltergeist, but the spirit declined the invitation. I advised the lady not to be too disappointed; having such visitors in residence is not my own idea of status.

Still, I am somewhat in sympathy with the English vicar

who engages in a rather unorthodox style of exorcism. On the assumption that ghosts and poltergeists are troubled individuals unable to find rest in the afterlife, he begins by pouring a drink and offering to chat with the "discarnate" on the means to a spiritual peace. Were I a ghost, I think I would appreciate such efforts to be helpful far more than the curses, dares, and hysterical reactions more usually provoked by a manifestation. The last thing I would want is to be treated as something diabolical, and if anything would make me toss around crockery it would be the kind of hostility expressed through the rites of bell, book, and candle.

Nevertheless, being nice to one's local ghost and soliciting such spectral presences are quite different things. I am convinced that there is a logic to spontaneous manifestations, particularly when they take the form of some type of warning. Manifestations achieved through a séance, even provided they are genuine, seem to me to be of a completely different nature, definitely more suspect and possibly more dangerous.

Necromancy, the explicit conjuration of the dead, is quite ancient in Western lore, as the biblical tale of Saul and the "witch" of Endor reminds us. Still, until the nineteenth century, it was regarded as a rather frightening bit of black magic. Ghosts were hardly welcome visitors, and the normal response to spiritual manifestations that did not conform to strict ecclesiastical tests was exorcism. The dead belonged somewhere along the hierarchy described in Dante's *Divine Comedy*, and any other spirits that might pop up were more likely than not to be marauding demons.

The seventeenth century marked the first significant reversal of these old values. In particular it was far more difficult to accept the idea of a personal, transcendent God who utilized the physical universe solely as a testing ground for human frailty. The Platonism revived in the Renaissance suggested instead that all reality was to be seen as a hierarchy of emanations from God; the souls of men, like divine sparks, circulated back and forth between the spiritual and the physical universes seeking an ever greater purification until a complete return to the One who was the Father of Lights would be possible. At the same time Rosicrucianism was familiarizing Western intellectuals, especially the Englishmen known as the Cambridge Platonists, with the idea that the evolution of a man's soul could be accomplished through the process of purification expressed symbolically in the language of the alchemists.

In the early 1700s a young Swedish graduate touring England made contact with the thought of the Cambridge intellectuals, but he returned to a scientific career in his own country with the only indication of mysticism being a concern with uncovering the anatomical link to man's spirituality. Then, in his late middle age, Emanuel Swedenborg abruptly began one of the most remarkable visionary careers of all time.

This prophet of a new revelation first published his visions at his own expense in a ponderous Latin. Heaven and hell were the sites of men and women who carried on much as they had on earth. There were no angels or demons, only the spirits of those who once had been mortals. What is most important is that Swedenborg received his visions while in trance—and these visions were from the souls of the departed. Even though Swedenborg cautioned against anyone else attempting spirit contacts, he both set the example and provided the myth that would allow the spiritualist movement to develop.

The connection between Swedenborg and the later Anglo-American spiritualists was provided by still another movement, that of the so-called magnetists—individuals whom today we would refer to as hypnotists. The roots of hypnotism (a term coined by the English physician James Braid) lie with our old friend Paracelsus and his theory of the spiritual forces contained within all nature.

In the years preceding the French Revolution Anton Mesmer was applying Paracelsian principles through his own curative technique of "animal magnetism," a procedure through which he supposedly "attracted" diseases out of his patients. In 1784 a French lord named Puységur, applying Mesmer's techniques to an ailing servant, induced a trance state in which the boy appeared almost to change personalities. This variation of mesmerism also involved other remarkable characteristics, the most striking of which was clairvoyance.

Today, extrasensory experiences are a rarity in connection with the medical literature on hypnotism, but early in the last century they were so standard as, unbelievably, to be taken for granted. Slater Brown, in *The Heyday of Spiritualism*, suggests two reasons to account for the disappearance of these phenomena. The first is the relative simplicity of contemporary hypnotic techniques in comparison with the lengthy, burdensome procedures used by Mesmer and his imitators. The second is the absence of the myth of "the universal fluid" operated upon by the magnetists. In brief, the mental set involved in today's hypnotism is somehow all wrong for extrasensory experiences, but it was quite right two centuries ago.

It was half a century before magnetism made its way to the United States, but when it did it provoked a riot of private spirit contacts in the style of Swedenborg. The most famous visionary of the period was Andrew Jackson Davis, whose writings strengthened the views, particularly welcome to many liberal churchmen, that the afterlife was also a state of learning and that the quick and the dead were thus united in a common task of enlightenment.

In 1848 the spirit world set up a different communication system that was at first free of the need for a trance state. The first manifestations were in the rural New York farmhouse of the Fox family. Mysterious rappings were heard, and, in answer to a request from one of the children, a code was established according to which the ghostly source of the raps revealed himself to be a peddler murdered by the former owner of the house.

After the family moved away from its home at Hydesville, it developed that the Fox sisters, Kate and Maggie, had taken their spirit contact with them. Their enterprising older sister quickly made the girls a prominent attraction on the lecture circuit, which, a century and a half ago, provided much of the entertainment for American audiences. The ghost obliged by doing a quite remarkable mentalist act. The girls were frequently accused of fraud, and Kate is supposed to have shown a relative how she made the raps by cracking her toes, but all the evidence suggests that most of the phenomena were quite genuine.

The first manifestations at Hydesville were followed by similar phenomena throughout New York. Within a few years the entire country had come under the spell, and séances were rapidly becoming a standard form of family amusement.

Coded raps soon gave way to even more spectacular demonstrations, the most famous of which were the spirit orchestras of the Koons family of Ohio and the Davenport brothers of New York—both of which were headed by a jovial backwoodsy spirit called King Number One by the Koons and Johnny King by the Davenports. Instruments were played raucously by completely invisible musicians in the case of the Koons, who had built a special cabin for their appearances, but ghostly hands were evident in the case of the Davenports. Spirit hands now became a stock item in spiritualistic manifestations, and again the evidence seems to point away from fraud—at least in those first few hectic years.

One of the oddities in the history of spiritualism is the eventual silencing of the raps. The other poltergeist phenomena also quieted down—or perhaps it was that whatever genuine spirit manifestations there may have been were lost in the rising sea of fraud. Remarkable mediums remained, but the money to be had from demonstrations led many of them, such as the Italian Eusapia Palladino, to help out the ghosts by tricks of their own. The rule by which the Society for Psychical Research, organized in England in 1882 to study paranormal phenomena, took a single instance of provable fraud as altogether discrediting a medium may have been somewhat unrealistic in view of this.

The fact of widespread fraud did in time destroy the credibility of spiritualism for most educated persons here and in England. Also, as Slater Brown points out, the tremendous gullibility of many of spiritualism's strongest defenders, such as Sir Arthur Conan Doyle (who charged Houdini with being a genuine medium who just would not admit to it), simply did not help matters.

Nevertheless, even before the Society for Psychical Research, a forerunner of today's parapsychology institutes, there were scientists who subjected many mediums to exhausting tests and were left convinced that the phenomena, however they were to be explained, were quite definitely outside known laws of physical causality.

By the twentieth century spiritualism was limited pretty much to automatic writing (including the use of William Fuld's Ouija board) and to oral communications coming from mediums who were supposedly in a trance state. Little occurred that could not be explained either through telepathy or through wishful thinking. Laws aimed at curbing fraud led to the keeping of activities of spiritualists, genuine and fraudulent alike, within the genteel bounds of organized religion.

Much of the present revival of spiritualism is due to the work of Arthur Ford, a minister who has recently achieved the distinction of having a posthumous writing of his become a best seller—"posthumous" here taken in the most literal sense. Ruth Montgomery's *A World Beyond* is allegedly the report that her old friend has made through automatic writing of conditions in the afterlife.

Arthur Ford's family background was Baptist, but he was finally ordained as a Disciples of Christ minister shortly after the First World War. During the war he had discovered that he possessed psychic abilities, and these were heightened while he was under the tutelage of Paramhansa Yogananda, founder of the Self-Realization Fellowship.

Conan Doyle persuaded Ford to become a professional medium after seeing a demonstration of his abilities, and in 1928 he is claimed to have passed the test that the late Harry Houdini had set up for the validity of any spirit contact with himself. In 1956 Washington columnist Ruth Montgomery (who has also produced a best seller dealing with Jeane Dixon) began research on Ford, and as a result of her work with him she embarked on her own mediumistic career.

In 1966 James Pike, for years the maverick Episcopal Bishop of San Francisco, appeared on Canadian television with Ford in what he took to be a successful effort to contact his dead son. Pike's book *The Other Side*, part of which appeared in *Look* as one of that magazine's most controversial features, made Ford even more of a national celebrity.

The thinking apparent in *A World Beyond* reflects not just

the ideas of Swedenborg but also the heavily Orientalized variant of spiritualism first developed in the United States in the
Theosophical Society. This movement did much to popularize
karma as well as to reinforce the theme of reincarnation already familiar from the Platonists, and both are carefully
worked into the concept of the afterlife as a classroom. In addition there is the recommendation to practice meditation
through the use of a mantra or consecrated sound, a technique
Ford learned through his study with Yogananda.

The dead, as described in A *World Beyond,* experience hell
only as the closure created by their own misdeeds and heaven
only as an opportunity to prepare themselves either for rebirth
as a further stage in their purification or for progression to spiritual planes "closer" to God, the creative energy that is the
source of all the thought forms that we call "reality." Yes, the
dead can maintain contact with the living, although some
spirits may do this rather maliciously. Moreover, all significant
human progress is to be credited to the subconscious inspiration coming from the spirit world, which is obviously quite
concerned with the evolution of mankind.

Ruth Montgomery's book is not just a study, but it is clearly
a phenomenon itself. I have no reason at all to doubt that her
descriptions of the afterlife are a product of automatic writing
(in her case done with a typewriter) and that in some very
real manner they can be credited to Arthur Ford. No matter
how much I am personally put off by its self-congratulatory
tone and by its denunciations of smoking, drinking, and political radicalism, I have to take A *World Beyond* far more seriously than I do the curious works of the English writer who
claims to be the medium for the displaced Tibetan T. Lobsang
Rampa.

First off, it is a remarkable contemporary example of the

genre begun by Swedenborg. For example, like Swedenborg (and also like Madame Blavatsky and the mysterious Gurdjieff), *A World Beyond* describes the planets as inhabited; it perpetuates the myth of Atlantis (due to reappear this decade) as the continent-home of a highly evolved race that existed before the dawn of history; and it continues the Edgar Cayce prediction of the great California earthquake that will, if it comes, make the place where I am writing just another spot in the Pacific Ocean.

How valid is all this? Even granted that Arthur Ford does live on and that the automatic writing is not simply a projection of Mrs. Montgomery's own psyche, is it the case that the great medium is experiencing anything *except what he expected to experience?* One striking thing about the book is the complete lack of surprise—an indication either that Ford had always been correct in his understanding of the afterlife or that the afterlife becomes what we take it to be (a concept familiar enough to the Buddhist interpreters of *The Tibetan Book of the Dead* but almost unthinkable to a non-Buddhist).

Of course, in answer to this there is the fact that Edgar Cayce, coming from a fundamentalist background, was at first horrified when he learned of the similar descriptions of the afterlife that he had presented in trance. Edgar Cayce did not "see" what he expected—although he saw what, by then, other psychics would have agreed that he should see. Telepathy again? Or, possibly, a creation of psychic realities through a collective imagination?

Another possibility is that spirits are real enough, but they play games by pretending to be something they are not. Just as it was fun to rap out codes and play instruments for a few decades, perhaps now it is fun to give modestly pleasant descriptions of a judgment-free heaven—and perhaps in a few more years it will be fun to paint new pictures of inevitable damnation. (Anyone who wishes to call this interpretation the biased verdict of a Catholic sore loser might be able to make a case for it. Arthur Ford, I'm sure, would—perhaps does—smile and say that I'll be able to see for myself soon enough.)

The spiritualist tradition that began in the United States gradually lost the exuberance that had characterized it in the first days of the rambunctious peddler of Hydesville and the band-playing ghosts of the Koons family. The celebrity given the best mediums doubtlessly accounted for much of this.

Well-paying appearances before New York society or European aristocracy already tended to induce a measure of decorum, and the fact that the strongest advocates of spiritualism turned out to be quite proper clergymen did the rest. Elaborate productions, such as the ectoplasmic hands and invisibly played instruments, were soon reserved for the out-and-out frauds, and the genuine mediums became content with a dignified trance and a pious, always optimistic correspondence between the departed and the bereaved.

In time, with the founding of specifically spiritualist churches, séances became as routine as the sermons of a more traditional Protestantism. Their one advantage, apart from the spiritual comfort offered participants, was that they did provide continuing evidence of the reality of paranormal phenomena.

The historians of spiritualism have discussed the connection between the early history of the movement and the popularity of "animal magnetism," but typically they have failed to examine the manner in which poltergeist phenomena that originally occurred without a medium going into trance (as in the case of the Fox sisters) later required the trance as an almost necessary condition.

The trance, in fact, became the characteristic feature of a séance, even though not all psychics enter into such altered states of consciousness. Edgar Cayce did, but Jeane Dixon and Peter Hurkos—to cite only two living seers—do not. Moreover, although Peter Hurkos has discussed his own "sight" as the often unwelcome activity of a second personality that seems to inhabit his brain (a parallel to the idea of the "control" of a spiritualistic medium), Jeane Dixon's "sight" does not require even this much alienation of whatever is her own self.

Spiritualism, it would seem, is a curious social phenomenon whose changing character is more a clue to the possibilities of magical (or religious) experience within a culture—or even an individual—than it is to any objective discussion of the reality of an afterlife. In settings that permit the psychic to function on his own (and Jeane Dixon, as Ruth Montgomery describes her in *A Gift of Prophecy*, grew up in just such a setting), advice and predictions might be given without any recourse to a spirit monitor.

In settings more hostile to this type of "witchery," the trance is a necessary vehicle either for releasing the psychic's own inhibitions (as I think happened with Cayce) or for lowering the threshold of skepticism of his auditors. A medium, after all, would have to be exempted from the normal processes by which we test one another's veracity.

It is through the concept of mediumship that spiritualism assimilates itself to many of the traditions of divination that are more properly part of the world of magic. The great oracles of the ancient world—the priestesses at Delphi and the Sibyl at Cumae, for example—were "possessed" no less than tribal shamans, and anyone who even involuntarily exhibited some of the characteristics of possession—an epileptic, for instance—was granted a deep reverence as a vehicle of the gods. Moreover, as in Plato's theory of poetry, there was a curious parallel to Arthur Ford's presentation of the source of human creativity in the spirit world. Artists, as Plato portrayed them in *The Republic*, were also possessed and must be honored, even if they could not be permitted to remain in a completely rational utopia.

One of the offshoots of Anglo-American spiritualism that has particularly reaffirmed this connection is the upper-class Spiritism of Brazil. With ideas derived from the writings of the French Allan Kardec, whose early acceptance of reincarnation distinguished him from the Swedenborgian approach that dominated spiritualism until the advent of Helena Blavatsky, the Spiritists offer an elite counterpart to the lower-class ceremonies adapted from African practices.

Both the elite and the popular spirit worship stress the phenomenon of possession, and to the less sophisticated adept it would seem only a matter of preference, or prejudice, whether the spirit guide is an Indian princess or an African divinity. The result is that in Brazil the idea of contact with a world of spirits of one kind or another permeates an entire culture.

Contact also suggests "control," referring in spiritualist literature to the personality temporarily replacing the normal consciousness of the medium, but the question is whether this personality, which can so readily be summoned, interrogated, and then dismissed, is commanding or commanded. In the African practices of Brazil and Haiti there is typically an element of barter (which in black magic often assumes the form of pacts borrowed from the European grimoires), but spirits do come to function as servants as well as advisers.

Anglo-American spiritualism has typically avoided such an

outright recourse to magic, although the showmanship of the first generation of spiritualists came very close to it. *A World Beyond,* like the film 2001, makes our present humanity out to be a somewhat impotent creation, and the spiritualism of Arthur Ford urges too ready a surrender of both human joys and human sorrows to purposes that are not quite human.

If whatever we call spirits exist, they are nonetheless outside our ordinary conception of a human world. Are they above it (as Arthur Ford suggests), locked into some odd parity with it (the assumption of Brazilian and Haitian Voodoo), or somehow beneath it (the perspective of Paracelsus that has continued throughout modern ceremonial magic)? Or is it the case that they are just what we make them out to be? I tend to favor this last possibility. If I am right, both conjurations and exorcisms might make more sense than séances.

One question: What is the psychological state of the medium when he is functioning in a séance? The hypnotic trance, unlike the trance states resulting from drugs or from various techniques of meditation, is physiologically indistinguishable from waking consciousness. Moreover, the same effects that can be achieved through trance, such as a change in sensation or an alteration of perception, can be achieved without it.

This has led many psychologists to argue that there is no such thing as hypnotism, only the power of suggestion—but this, I feel, is largely a matter of semantics. The hypnotic subject is not *really* asleep, just as he is not *really* regressed in age, but he does behave according to what he thinks it means to be asleep or to be regressed. In some manner his mode, if not really his state, of consciousness has been altered.

Does this explain the phenomenon of the séance—or for that matter the phenomena that can be noted in the rites of

Voodoo? The ethnologist Alfred Métraux in his study of Haitian practices attempted to penetrate the mystery of possession only to conclude that, despite lapses that would indicate a certain retention of the normal personality, the one "ridden" by a *loa* or god did behave as the spirit was expected to behave —and the spirit's "horse" would afterward bear no conscious recollection of his rather singular behavior.

The African metaphysics underlying Voodoo had no difficulty in accounting for this. Since a man had two souls, one (the *gros bon ange*) was simply displaced by the divinity who had been ritually summoned. A more psychologically oriented explanation would be that the *loa*, whose characteristics were collectively defined, did emerge from the subject's own consciousness as a projection of the self (an archetype, if you will) that at the same time possessed a quasi-objective validity.

The automatic writing by which Arthur Ford dictated posthumous memoirs to Ruth Montgomery would easily fit into this same analysis. Mrs. Montgomery *became* Arthur Ford, a close personal friend, just as Ford, in his own séances, *became* Fletcher, his boyhood companion. By so doing, each quite possibly tapped still other paranormal capabilities that would not be present in an ordinary consciousness. In any séance, telepathic or clairvoyant "hits" serve to confirm the apparent reality of the control—just as in a Voodoo ritual these same phenomena validate the "fact" of spirit possession.

Dedicated spiritualists may find these crosscultural comparisons odious. Ruth Montgomery, I'm sure, would shudder at the manner in which I put her into the same category as a Haitian *mambo*, but it is my contention that the reality of the world of magic becomes apparent only when there is an effort to enter deeply not just into one tradition but into several. The differences, after all, are as revealing as the similarities.

The *mambo*, or priestess, reflects a culture in which the collectivity is more important than the individual—and the spirit manifestations of Voodoo are a communion with the shared guardians of an exiled people. Mrs. Montgomery is very much the conservative individualist, and her spirits are simply other individuals who describe a curiously non-historical world.

I tend to see spiritualism as something of a substitute for magic. There is in it the same desire for a more holistic vision than that offered by modern technology. At the same time, by its stress on human submission rather than human action, its vision blurs the meaning of man except as a prelude to something less objectionable.

12.

Is Anyone Out There?

It MAKES SENSE to talk of occultism as a counterpoint only when there is a contrary rhythm against which it plays itself out. In a tribal society there is not yet the type of differentiation that makes magic the preserve of an intellectual elite. Even in the world's first high civilizations—Sumeria, Egypt, India—the magus is still the priest, not the heresiarch.

Only when the contacts, or conflicts, of cultures promote a certain degree of cosmopolitanism does magic cease to be a more or less natural outlook. When a society's own earlier sense of magic is either obscured or diminished to the level of superstition, then the magic of an alien culture can take on a new importance. Occultism, the legend of a secret wisdom, appears as an effort to elevate a society to a new plateau of spirituality.

This was the story of the Hellenistic world when astrology

and sorcery were brought from the Mideast to Greece and Rome. It is the story of the Middle Ages when contact with Islam sparked European interest in the literature of alchemy attributed to Hermes Trismegistus and the recipes for sorcery alleged to have been handed down from King Solomon. And it is the story of the nineteenth century when the translation of Egyptian hieroglyphics inspired a new look at the Cabala with Eliphas Levi and the Golden Dawn and also when exposure to Hinduism and Buddhism permitted the Theosophical Society, originally a curious offshoot of spiritualism, to become a worldwide organization.

The same process is occurring at present, although now there is not just one source of esoteric wisdom but several. From the Arab world has come Sufism, especially as it appears in the meditation techniques of the Chilean Oscar Ichazo. Out of the Communist world there is the study of new forms of radiant energy (the bioplasma and the phenomena of "pyramid energy"). And, of course, there is the interest in Amerindian sorcery expressed in the works of Carlos Castaneda.

Whether the occultist counterpoint is realized fully through any of these sources depends on the skill—or interest—of their promoters in developing an appropriate organizational form. Castaneda, for instance, states that he has no desire to be a guru, and the teachings of don Juan will probably remain a source of private inspiration rather than the basis of a lasting movement. In contrast, Oscar Ichazo, whose Arica techniques were first presented to the American public in John Lilly's *The Center of the Cyclone,* is now attempting to promote a national movement headquartered in New York.

One perennial difficulty for the occultist is that any outlook that requires an individual exploration of a "separate reality" tends to make itself, almost by definition, exempt from institutional controls. This is part of its attraction for the temperamental heretic, but it remains to haunt his own efforts to develop a movement that may transcend himself. The mystic's charisma may hold his immediate followers, but this is almost on the condition that they develop no real charisma of their own.

Jesus, for example, seemed to appreciate this when he spoke of the necessity of his physical absence for his church to succeed. The martyr paradoxically is a more potent source of an atmosphere of faith than is a living master; the charisma of his followers is no longer a challenge to his authority but rather a continuation of it. But even here the occultist counterpoint becomes muted and in time the esoteric character of a group's origins is rather easily overlooked.

The most potent device for securing institutional continuity while preserving either a mystical or a magical outlook is the postulation of fixed stages of induction into the regions of spiritual experience. Violation of institutional rules can then be held as a sign that the neophyte has wandered off the true path.

As an example, the early Christians, if we are to judge them from the warnings found in Paul's letters to various communities of converts, tended to an anarchistic pursuit of spiritual wonders that made them an easy prey for Gnostic proselytizers. To counter this the church was forced to distinguish the operations of the Holy Ghost from the deceptions of Satan, with the immediate result that any expression of the paranormal not strictly in accord with orthodox expectations was seen as somehow diabolical. The long-term result was a persistent hostility toward magic, even a refusal to consider it as in principle distinguishable from any given theological framework.

In much the same way the various shamanist traditions, such as the lore presented by don Juan, require a minute attention to detail that serves to keep the apprentice sorcerer from an institutionally destructive psychic adventuring. It seems to be the case that, like language itself, the power of any ritual depends on the fact that it can be regarded as transcending the individual.

The idea of fixed stages of induction is paralleled by a conceptualization of the spirit world in terms of fixed orders of beings. It is this that makes the world of magic seem so outlandish to those of us raised in a strictly secular environment. Ghosts or "discarnates" are one thing, but this talk of angels or demons or elementals is something else altogether. Is it really the case that anyone is out there?

Lately a torrent of books have played on the theme that the gods and demons of ancient cults were in fact astronauts from the more highly evolved civilizations of other planets. Erich von Däniken's *Chariots of the Gods?*, the subject of a television documentary narrated by Rod Serling, began this trend by citing technological achievements, such as the construction of the Pyramids, that presumably should have been beyond the capabilities of the early peoples who accomplished them. Illustrations from various cultures are cited as evidence that the ancient world was familiar with the appearance of a spaceship and of an astronaut, and curious archeological remains are reinterpreted as having been built to serve as guideposts for space travelers.

If this argument is valid, both magic and religion are the distorted recollections of a superior technology. The gods and demons of legend were real persons long since forgotten except as the objects of strange cults that converted science into witchcraft. Someone is out there, all right, and the reports of flying saucers may be an indication that the beings who came from the skies to colonize this planet will come again.

A quite opposite picture is that presented by Carl Jung, for whom the images of the occultist arise out of what he calls the collective unconscious, a kind of reservoir of human experience somehow available to the individual who attempts to achieve the full integration of his own personality.

Among the images that arise spontaneously are those that could be construed as representing men in capsules (or in space helmets) or men in flight. On this basis there is no need to postulate beings from outer space as the source of ancient iconography. Moreover, given the resources of human consciousness argued by Jungian theory, even the accomplishments of ancient technology need not be supposed as having an other-worldly origin.

Both approaches, the one looking to the stars and the other to the depths of the human psyche, at first blush appear to be reasonable enough explanations of the complex demonologies of other cultures. There is nothing really supernatural to be taken into consideration.

Or is there? Medieval students of sorcery would have had little difficulty with von Däniken's evidence. A standard theory of the period was that demons possessed an intelligence superior to that of men and consequently had discovered the hidden powers of nature. Even if there was a superior technology involved in the construction of the architectural wonders of the past (such as Solomon's Temple), those who possessed it were still spiritual beings.

Contemporary occultists similarly have found Carl Jung's concepts of synchronicity and the collective unconscious fitting completely into their own frameworks. Israel Regardie, for example, has adopted Jungian terminology in his own presentation of occultism, and in his introduction to a four-volume set of Golden Dawn materials he advocates a program of Jungian analysis as an aid to the serious student of ceremonial magic. Yet for Regardie, if not for Jung himself, the gods, angels, and elementals invoked by the sorcerer remain objectively real; they are spiritual beings whose existence is quite independent of the human imagination.

I have to admit to a certain impatience with science-fiction explanations of human events. Typically they ignore the particular modes of thought expressed through myths and icons in order to concentrate, quite selectively, on a literal reading of isolated elements that would seem to reinforce the space traveler hypothesis. Also, in their emphasis on contact with more highly evolved beings as the source of our first high civilizations, they fail to come to grips with the question of the cultural evolution of these space contacts; either they were contacted themselves, or cultural quantum jumps are possible without the need of such contacts. The first pushes us into the problem of an infinite regress (the domino theory in reverse), the second destroys the need of the hypothesis.

Carl Jung's analysis of the human psyche is far more attractive to me, and my own first attempt to account for the reality of magic in terms of an objectification of human images (the idea of "the flashing mirror" which I proposed in *The Return of Magic*) clearly derives from it. While it comforts those who do acknowledge the supernatural as a reality, it also permits the skeptic to accept the occurrence of paranormal events and still maintain a completely naturalistic framework.

Nevertheless, there is a weakness in Jung's approach also, too much of a tendency to downplay the type of rationality found in myths and folklore in order to stress the spontaneous manifestation of archetypes. Rather than thinking in terms of "hierophanies" (manifestations of the sacred) as does Mircea Eliade, Jung in his own way tends to fall into the reductionist trap of modern science by more or less limiting the scope of mythology to the needs of individual psychology. Eliade is like the occultists in that he stresses the cosmic interests of mythology, and on this point I think he makes the better case.

How do the occultists themselves feel about the supernatural? Most older writers, particularly those raised in a Rosicrucian atmosphere (and this includes the Theosophical Society and esoteric groups such as the Golden Dawn), are entirely comfortable with an emanationist metaphysics; whatever we can mean by reality is a downward filtering of the energy of an ineffable cosmic source. Man may establish an intentional contact with other entities through the practice of magic, here usually understood in terms of theurgy or "white magic" to distinguish it from the selfish exploitation of goetia or "black magic."

Younger occultists, typified by Anton LaVey and Philip Bonewits, are more avowedly materialistic. There are psychic forces, but they represent an extension of known laws of the physical universe rather than any supernatural reality. Elementals can be conjured through the old ceremonials, but these are strictly projections of the human will and imagination rather than independent entities. Later we shall come back to this question of the physics of paranormal events, but for now let's look more closely at how the views of the older occultists have been updated from the time of Agrippa and Paracelsus.

The first significant intrusion of the paranormal into the boxlike universe proposed by Newton's physics came in the eighteenth century with the "animal magnetism" of Anton Mesmer. One of those who theorized about the basis for the phenomenon of paranormal healing associated with Mesmer's work was Baron Karl von Reichenbach. In a series of carefully constructed experiments this German scientist attempted to demonstrate the existence of what he termed "odylic force," a kind of radiant energy that could be perceived by individuals in a trance state in the form of colored flames. Animal magnetism, which itself had been based on the ideas of Paracelsus, was supposedly a manipulation of this force.

Von Reichenbach's research was published in 1845. Not long afterward Eliphas Levi took over the concept of odylic force in his own idea of "the astral light," the occult energy of the universe that was tapped by the magician. Levi himself, however, was already hopelessly out of date in his efforts to restrict occultism to traditional Western sources.

A new enthusiasm for Indian philosophy had been triggered by the discovery that Sanskrit, the sacred language of the Vedas, was a linguistic cousin of the Latin and Greek that had preoccupied classicists since the Renaissance. Writers such as Helena Blavatsky were quick to see the value of integrating the now conventional approach to the occult expressed through the Cabala with the heady metaphysics of Hinduism and Buddhism. Everything Levi meant by the astral light was assumed into the still more complex concept of the *akasha*.

Indian philosophy, particularly the Sankhya and Yoga schools, had already developed an intricate theory of evolution which paralleled the emanationist concepts of the Gnostics and Neoplatonism. One idea that might strike us as a bit strange is that color and sound are understood as vibratory forces existing independently of physical objects and consequently available to the soul's perception without the need of ordinary sense experience. Colored and sounding objects would be only a further embodiment of these vibrations.

Akasha, which is equivalent to the Greek ether as a fifth element to go with earth, air, fire, and water, is to be seen as the medium for these "supersensible" colors and sounds. A soul purified from a dependence on ordinary sensation would have the power to read the *akasha* much as we otherwise perceive the physical world but with the obvious advantage that this supersensible perception would be free of the ordinary limitations of space and time associated with physical objects.

Paranormal phenomena can then be understood as resulting from the use of the *akasha.* Clairvoyance and precognition, for example, would follow from what various occultists, following Madame Blavatsky, have termed a reading of "the akashic records." Manipulation of the *akasha,* as in the occultist system developed by Rudolf Steiner, is also the basis for the conjurations of ceremonial magic.

Besides the idea of the *akasha,* Western occultists were quick to take over several other Indian concepts. One, of course, was the understanding of the law of karma, the renewed existence of the soul in a body in keeping with the state of purity achieved in past incarnations. Another was the division of the world of psychic entities into six levels with the human soul situated midway up a hierarchy that ranged from the denizens of hell to the hosts of heaven.

The Theosophists added their own wrinkles through the idea of root races, stages in the evolution of the human from an elemental form to something more ethereal. It was here too that they worked in the ideas of Lemuria and Atlantis. Steiner's own depiction of this process is even more complicated. In his *Occult Science* he develops a picture of the evolution of the solar system that ties in the "old" Saturn, sun, moon, and earth with the appearance of various types of spiritual beings, all of whom would have an influence on the evolution of human consciousness. Some, the Luciferic, are beneficent, but others, the Ahrimanic, are not. The man who experiences supersensible reality comes into contact with these spirits just as he also sees the subhuman forms of the elementals.

One thing Steiner himself insisted upon was that his "occult science" was the result of direct personal experience. Moreover, allowing for differences in terminology, he argued that his own spiritual vision was no different than that of anyone else able to "see"; his occultism, then, was as objective as physics or chemistry. It could not be experienced without vision, but that vision could be systematically developed and it could be verbalized.

This, to someone as unspiritual as myself, is a remarkable assertion. As a Jesuit scholastic working on my thesis for an M.A. in philosophy I had my first brush with occultism when I researched the career of Proclus Diadochus, the last great heir of Plato's Academy in the fifth century of the Christian era. At that time I attempted something of a psychohistory of this particular Neoplatonist that resulted in my saying that the ultimate justification of his quite complex metaphysics was its aesthetic appeal, the nicety with which his concepts were elaborated into a balanced synthesis. The theurgy Proclus engaged in I tended to dismiss as somehow incidental. At best I saw it as a psychological aberration that was held to confirm the truth of his philosophy after it had been developed on strictly logical grounds.

I continued to hold this outlook in my first study of the Victorian magicians. The systems of Blavatsky and Gurdjieff, with all this seeming nonsense about Atlantis and the characteristics of inhabitants of other planets, did nothing to change it. But with Rudolf Steiner, as with Carlos Castaneda, I have found myself having to reconsider just what it is that does go on in the mind of the occultist. Was there in fact some kind of experience of a "separate reality" that would not just be a curious kind of hallucination? And was this experience something sufficiently free of cultural expectations that it could begin to take on the form of what Rudolf Steiner described it to be—a science?

These, for me, are mind-boggling possibilities. Even as a Jesuit, despite my exposure to the *Spiritual Exercises* of Ignatius Loyola, I had to take the realities of the spiritual life on faith. I did not "know" God or Christ or the Virgin Mary as Loyola himself claimed to know them. I believed in their existence and their presence to me in my prayer, but never did I have the type of experience that would make them any more real to me than as entities to be accepted because it was logical to do so. Given my own background, I find the occultist discussion of spiritual experience puzzling, to say the least.

Obviously I am not in a position to comment personally on the phenomenology of the psychic encounters described by Rudolf Steiner. Does it matter? The dedicated occultist would answer that until I meet my Double, the Guardian of the Threshold (according to Steiner) or my Holy Guardian Angel (according to Crowley and Israel Regardie), I am limited in my self-knowledge and therefore in my spiritual advancement. Nevertheless, once I have crossed this barrier, I find that I am to make my way through a region in which I will be assaulted by demonic powers determined to mire me down in images that are solely of my own making. For this reason I must continue meditative practices that will identify me with the positive forces that guide the universe.

One of the things I find striking in these occultist discussions is the manner in which they are paralleled by descriptions arising out of quite different contexts. Kirlian photography, the Soviet-developed technique of making an exposure by placing an organic object within an electrically charged field, has produced evidence that something very like the aura of the occultists does exist and that it in some manner is involved with paranormal healing. Moreover, researchers investigating astral projection or the out-of-the-body experience (one of the concerns of the emerging field of transpersonal psychology) have reported encountering a figure that corresponds to the Guardian of the Threshold.

Could it be, then, that occultism has anticipated science by discovering both a new type of energy and a peculiarity of the psychology of altered states of consciousness? Or is it the case that science has stumbled upon evidence confirming the "objectivity" of what Steiner called supersensible reality? Whatever the answers, one thing is certain: psychic research has made a full circle to come back to the point where it began with Baron von Reichenbach.

Where does the idea of magic fit into these occultist frameworks? Helena Blavatsky, in her *Isis Unveiled*, stated that "Arcane knowledge, misapplied, is sorcery; beneficently used, true magic or wisdom," but the Theosophists generally were uncomfortable with the term. Steiner, whose own movement was first organized within the structure of the Theosophical Society while it was headed by Annie Besant, similarly played down its usage. But for occultists trained within the Golden Dawn tradition—individuals such as Aleister Crowley, Israel Regardie, and Dion Fortune—the terms "occultism" and "magic" become synonymous.

Crowley himself opted, for numerological reasons, to talk of "Magick" and to define it as "the Science and Art of causing Change to occur in conformity with Will." Regardie, at one time Crowley's secretary and today the editor of much of his material, elaborates on this by discussing magic as "a mnemonic system of psychology." He also goes on to present magic as one branch of mysticism with yoga the other, a usage that may prove somewhat surprising to theologians.

If I may paraphrase all of this, magic is the study of what Dion Fortune has styled "ultra-consciousness." Since consciousness in some manner involves intelligence and whatever we mean by personality, this ultra-consciousness deals not just with unknown forms of energy but with forces that are somehow intelligent, somehow personal, and also somehow beyond man himself.

Are these forces more ancient than man, or are they products of human action? Do they make man's consciousness or are they made by it? In the particular doing of magic that is represented by astrology and the tarot there is little reason to be concerned with such questions. But in the more sophisticated practices of ceremonial magic, dealing with these forces, either reverently or rudely, as beings whose existence is quite independent of man himself is what the practice of occultism is said to be about.

Is it necessary to believe in them in order to perform the old ceremonials? No, not really; the "words of power" are presumed to be efficacious regardless. Still, for the classical magician if not for younger practitioners, not to believe in "the gods" after an experience of their power would have to be not just stupid but quite possibly suicidal.

Do I believe in them—or does Tanya? My wife, of course, grew up with their presence a menacing part of her inner world. I did not. Nor have I attempted the kind of involvement with magic that would bring me into Tanya's particular atmosphere of faith.

I admit that I find it a great deal easier to keep with the hypothesis that magic can be explained in terms of the psychic potential (the capability for effecting paranormal phenomena) of the individuals who engage in it, intentionally or otherwise, rather than to think in terms of noncorporeal entities. The obvious difficulty with such an outlook is that it eliminates much of the poetry that makes magic a thing of value even if there were no paranormal effects whatsoever. At least in theory it is enough to act *as if* the world is permeated with spiritual forces, but I tend to doubt that such a calculated conjuration would take the apprentice sorcerer very far. Either he will come to believe in these forces as somehow personal or he will become rather bored with the whole thing.

The trouble with a more explicitly supernatural outlook is not just that it goes beyond the sense evidence available but that it threatens to tangle the magician in some quite complex religious questions. Much of the theological hostility toward the world of magic stems from the fact that Western occultism has typically attempted to substitute itself for the institutional church. Certainly this was true of the Neoplatonists who saw theurgy as an answer to the cults, Gnostic and Christian alike, that were sweeping through the late Hellenistic world. It was also true, I think, of those who delighted in the ferocious anti-Catholicism of the Rosicrucian legend, a bias that carried over into the work of Eliphas Levi and Helena Blavatsky.

It is one thing to point out that occultism in theory is something quite apart from theology and another to avoid being caught in the webs of theosophical propositions spun by ancient and modern occultists. Consequently, as soon as one talks of spirits it is taken as an open invitation to religious commentary. If the rhythm of secularization makes divinity more and more remote from the everyday world, the occultist counterpoint functions by exaggerating the manner in which divinity is present.

Elsewhere, particularly in a chapter of *The Return of Magic*, I have attempted to note points that might be brought up in any future dialogue between the theologian and the occultist. For the purposes of this book I will restrict myself to saying only that in my own view magic and religion represent separate spheres of human concern. Precisely how they are interrelated is a bit more than I feel I can answer, but the question is clearly important for the believer who must reconcile two somewhat distinct senses of this term "supernatural." My own plea is simply that theological preconceptions not be used to prejudge the truth of magic—and, just as important, that occultist preconceptions not be used to prejudge the truth of religion.

My reason for this plea will be made somewhat clearer in the next chapter. After all, what is a book on magic without some discussion of the Devil—and yet how do we talk of the Devil without also talking of God?

13.

Speak of the Devil

IF A SENSE of the holy and a desire for purity are the basis of religion, and if a sense of wonder and the desire for justice are the basis of philosophy, perhaps we may say that it is the kind of experience which Dion Fortune labeled ultra-consciousness coupled with a desire for power that is the basis of magic. The occultist counterpoint, which appears most strongly in periods when religion and philosophy alike are in a decline, typically involves an appeal to the magician to substitute for lax priests and suborned intellectuals. If purity and justice seem unavailable in the everyday world, why not look to the "separate reality" of the magus?

The problem is that, since it is usually a disordered world that brings about occultism, its proponents feel themselves obligated to present a new metaphysics and a new theology to account for this disorder. Sometimes this can be done by adapting an earlier outlook and stressing its more negative aspects.

Neoplatonism, for example, took over Plato's theory that the physical world was like a cave of shadows in order to concentrate on a life of withdrawal. In movements emerging within a later Hinduism and Buddhism the concept of *maya* (illusion) led to a similar outlook. In both cases the novice was exhorted to pursue a life of inner experience directed to bringing about the submission of spiritual entities. The goal of these exercises might, of course, be the transcending of the ego that marks true mysticism, but at the same time it made possible the desire for power as an end in itself. For both Greeks and Indians there was now the concept of sorcery as something evil, a misuse of power that could be interpreted as one reason for the world's disorder.

A more obvious way of accounting for disorder is to postulate a dualism, the existence of counterweighted principles of good and evil. In Iranian thought, the basis for Gnosticism, these were personified as Ahura-Mazda, the source of light and of order, and Ahriman, the source of darkness and chaos.

The Gnostics elaborated this concept through a number of systems, many of which transformed the Jahweh of Hebrew scripture into a malicious cosmic sorcerer and Jesus into a messenger from the unknown God beyond the cosmos. The purpose of magic was to gain a mastery of the cosmic forces that would otherwise prevent the soul, the divine spark, from completing its ascent to its true source. Those who had the knowledge (gnosis) of their real nature were forever exempt from ordinary standards of conduct. In theory this meant that the one illumined by a true faith was an other-worldly ascetic, in practice it often meant that he was free to follow a life of unbridled licentiousness.

In the early passages of the Bible the original reason for disorder in the world (the original sin) was Adam's disobedience.

As time went on, a more sophisticated concept appeared. In the story of Job the angel Satan ("the adversary") is presented as a skeptical lieutenant of the Lord who is granted permission to harass a just man as a test of his faith. By the time of the New Testament, a period when Babylonian demonology and Persian dualism had completely infiltrated the Judaic outlook, Satan had been advanced to the role of an opposing general. He was now also identified with Lucifer, the angel of the morning star, and thus indirectly with the erotic goddess Ishtar.

For the Christians who encountered the old gods of Europe it was an easy enough matter to personify Satan (or the Devil, using the Greek *diabolos* as an equivalent for the Hebrew *satan*) with the animal-like figure of Cernunnos. Instead of being simply a source of affliction, the Devil assumed the form of a lusty goat offering the promise of every physical satisfaction in return for a betrayal of the vows of baptism.

The Gnostic outlook continually reasserted itself in the Middle Ages, and it could be manifested in the opposite extremes of total asceticism or total license. It also led to the appearance of sects in which the Devil was worshiped as the true lord of the world, although this typically required an exchange of concepts in which the austere Christian God was made the adversary of mankind and Satan became its protector. The existence of such sects was one factor in the witchcraft trials that increased in intensity throughout the Middle Ages.

In the popular view, which differed considerably from the theories of intellectuals exposed to Islamic and Jewish influences, whatever was magic had to follow from a bargain made with the Devil. This idea, which was a natural outgrowth of the commercial atmosphere of the Hellenistic world, first appeared in Christian literature in a life of Saint Basil and represented a type of compromise between the conjurations of Greco-Egyptian sorcery and the straightforward worship of the true diabolist. Since the only thing that could be of value to Satan would be the Christian's damnation, the pact, implicit in any act of sorcery but explicit in the case of the true witch, had to be an exchange of the soul for worldly pleasure or power. As such, it was an act of treason deserving of the most extraordinary measures for its detection and prosecution.

The procedures for the explicit pact varied with the imaginations of the medieval writers describing them. Some depicted a full ceremonial that parodied Catholic practices, others demanded a document, drawn up in blood, that presumably would be honored both in this world and in the next. In the sixteenth century the career of a wandering sorcerer named Johannes Faustus provided the basis for a number of cautionary tales linking the idea of a pact with the rising anti-intellectualism of many of the Protestant reformers. Embodied in the plays by Marlowe and Goethe, this legend has provided the basis for most modern versions of the Devil as an exquisitely polite negotiator offering to satisfy a man's wildest dreams and—in contrast to the medieval version of Satan as a cheat—keeping his promise until his victim discovers some loophole in the contract.

During the Middle Ages the Devil was pictured either as the center of obscene revelries or as a horrific apparition whom only a witch could love. I have followed modern usage in speaking of the Devil in the singular, but the medieval writers typically considered diabolical activities to be shared by literally hordes of demons, only some of whom could be identified with the proper names (Asmodeus, Beelzebub, etc.) handed down from antiquity. In the fourteenth century the demon lover of Dame Alice Kyteler, an Irish lady accused of murdering her first three husbands by poison and then attempting to take the life of a fourth, was named Robin, son of Art. Isabel Gowdie, a seventeenth-century Scots woman, in her voluntary confession told of how a devil named Black John punished coven members guilty of one or another infraction. (Both these cases from the British Isles are cited by modern covenists as examples of the persecution of the "Old Religion." Robin Artisson and Black John are presumed to have been actual persons, the secret heads of local covens.) Satan, after all, was too majestic a personage to be concerned with routine witchery, particularly since, as it was argued, there were witches everywhere.

As we saw earlier, there is no evidence that there was any degree of organization among those who did engage in witchcraft. Even in its actual practice there was little that we might recognize as unabashed diabolism. The ordinary witch or sorcerer was not out to bargain with demons, and even the grimoires did not at first acknowledge the practice.

The same must be said of at least one of the other staples of modern occultist fiction. The Black Mass, the worship of Satan through an indecent parody of the holiest of Catholic rituals, forms no part of the lore either of the trials or of the reconstructed coven tradition. It first appears in connection with the confessions obtained between 1680 and 1682 in the prosecution of a murder ring operating within the highest circles of the French aristocracy. The center of the ring was a woman nicknamed La Voisin, and in an investigation conducted in utmost secrecy (through what came to be called the *Chambre ardente*) evidence was heard of how priests had performed various sacrilegious actions in connection with Masses said to promote the love affairs of noble ladies.

Louis XIV attempted to suppress all records of these investigations when it developed that his former mistress, Madame de Montespan, was deeply involved, but the story leaked out and continued to spark the interest of writers from the Marquis de Sade to J. K. Huysmans. And, as so often in the history of occultism, fiction became fact as actual diabolists came along to try out the dark experiments of their legendary predecessors. Their rituals, if Huysmans's *Là-Bas* is any clue, were more absurd than evil—perhaps another indication that the Devil's best works are reserved for those who feel they are acting in the name of God.

The rather strange legend of the Knights Templar should also be considered. The Templars, who might be remembered as the heavies in *Ivanhoe*, were organized as a Catholic religious group in Palestine early in the twelfth century. As military men who lived like monks, the Templars soon became a too-powerful force in the countries of western Europe. Two centuries after the order's founding, the King of France attempted to destroy it by charging its members with heresy and sorcery. Jacques de Molay, the last Grand Master of the Knights Templar, was executed in front of the cathedral of Notre Dame, and the order was suppressed by the Pope. From that time on, its memory was stained with forced confessions to sodomy, blasphemy, and diabolism.

Later occultists attempted to link the Templars with the Gnostics before them and the Rosicrucians afterward, but there is no solid historical basis for this. Were any of their members actual diabolists? The Templars, it seems, did have a peculiar symbolism, but I would tend to agree with occultist Lewis Spence's judgment that they were simply "the victims of their own arrogance, their commercial success, and the superstitious ignorance of their contemporaries." What their trials did leave to the legacy of occultism, besides another legend of a secret wisdom, was a new name for the Devil: Baphomet, perhaps a corruption of the name of Muhammad.

Belief in the Devil, it would seem, can survive even when a belief in God cannot. Perhaps there is a cause-and-effect relationship involved. To the extent that religion provides not just an image of order in society but also a rationale for that order, the decay of religion demands an appropriate image of disorder. Satan, after all, is perhaps the perfect expression of man's ambivalence toward his own condition. He is at once the exciting Prince of Darkness—the proud rebel of *Paradise Lost* and the one to whom Shaw gave the best lines in *Don Juan in Hell*—and a defiling fiend who assaults the innocent.

It is in his first capacity that Satan can be romanticized by Anton LaVey as the symbol of a liberated humanity. In his second he is the loathsome antagonist of William Peter Blatty's *The Exorcist*. The connection between the two is often provided by the element of sexuality, the reason perhaps that the early Christians found the animal-like Cernunnos such an appropriate image in which to visualize the Devil.

One of the early influences of the occultist counterpoint on Christianity was in compelling a strict asceticism more in keeping with the logic of the Gnostics than with the tone of Judaism. Repression, however, has the curious effect of intensifying desire rather than extinguishing it. The Buddha recognized this phenomenon in his proposal of the "Middle Way" between total asceticism and complete self-indulgence, and Freud set out to explain its mechanism twenty-four centuries later.

The Egyptian Fathers of the Desert, the early Christian anchorites whose lives were proposed in the daily spiritual reading of the Jesuit novitiate, were living examples of the problems involved in a direct assault on the life of the senses. Throughout their biographies there are accounts of demonic temptations, including the appearance of luscious succubi, as well as records of spectacular ascetic failures. As a novice I found the casual references to rape and murder on the part of fallen monks merely absurd. Today I find them chilling reminders of the dangers of a precipitous spiritual adventuring. It would almost seem that the surest way to invoke the Devil's attention is by pretending that something of one's own nature is in fact an alien thing to be beaten and starved into submission.

This may explain why, despite the stories told in the course of the witchcraft trials, almost the only overt diabolism of the Middle Ages appeared in connection with offshoots of the ascetic Catharist movement, not with a self-indulgent or corrupt Catholic clergy. When the Black Mass does come into existence, it is in the France of Louis XIV, the era in which Jesuits and Jansenists battled the theological question of human sinfulness.

The Jansenists, whose mood is best represented by the *Pensées* of Blaise Pascal, argued the evil of man's nature and the need of religious strictness against what was seen as a sinister permissiveness on the part of the Jesuit casuists and confessors. At the time of the *Chambre ardente* affair they were a powerful force in France, and it is my guess that the priests who engaged in the obscenities described in the hearings were acting out the reverse side of Jansenism, just as the diabolists of an earlier era were acting out the reverse side of Catharism. An enemy who was feared so greatly as was the Devil was also an enemy to be cajoled by those not quite able or willing to live up to almost superhuman ideals.

What is the status of Satanism today? Anton LaVey is no more a genuine diabolist than was Aleister Crowley. Charles

Manson may have acted diabolically, but he and his group appear to have had only passing contact with the occultism of Southern California. There is a cult, the Church of the Process of the Final Judgment, which does include Satan and Lucifer together with Jehovah as "gods of the universe," but again this is not diabolism in any ordinary sense. The point is that to be a true diabolist one must accept evil as something more than a metaphor, then deliberately choose this vision of evil on the risk that the forces of the Devil can still defeat the forces of God in some future Armageddon. There is little evidence that diabolism exists on any organized basis.

There have, of course, been groups that have adopted the view that good and evil, God and the Devil are ultimately identical. Conventional morality, accordingly, is to be transcended through a life style that defies social norms in a test of the adept's enlightenment. This was the outlook expressed by Charles Manson, and in his case it led from simple larceny to the chilling Tate-LaBianca murders. It is also the outlook that has permitted the existence of sects such as the Thugs, the ritual assassins who terrorized India until their suppression by British colonial administrators. But this is not evil for its own sake. Rather it is the translation of what is defined as evil by conventional standards either into something insignificant or into something that is right and holy according to a higher code.

But if diabolism is something of a rarity except as the expression of an individual aberration, black magic is not. Israel Regardie, in his classic study of ritual magic in the 1930s, found it difficult to imagine anyone attempting to gather the ingredients (eye of newt, tail of toad, wing of bat, etc.) called for by the old rituals. Today there are wholesalers, perhaps inspired by *Bell, Book and Candle*, who have packaged almost everything that would be needed to try out the formulas of medieval magic. Despite the admonitions on the packages that their contents are only curios, one must presume that most of the customers for bits of the anatomy of black cats, bats, scorpions, and various other creatures are quite serious about having authentic materials for authentic spells.

The distinction drawn here between black magic and white is not so much in terms of their purposes as in terms of the types of powers being solicited. The principle of sympathetic magic that like attracts like demands that anyone drawing on the universal powers involved in death and decay must use fitting symbols. A really serious vengeance spell, for example, might well require the desecration of a grave in order to obtain appropriate materials. On the basis too of the traditional association of the spirits of the underworld with the wealth contained in the earth, there might be a demand for a blood sacrifice of a black cat or a black cock in connection with an appeal for prosperity. Some individuals may improvise on the old grimoires by also including elements from a largely fictional diabolism—the use, for instance, of the desecrated hosts stolen from the tabernacle in a Catholic church—but this is considered by most purists to be rather poor form in that it totally confuses the symbolism.

For many writers any further distinction between black and white magic is quite irrelevant. Paul Huson in *Mastering Witchcraft* blithely advises the beginner to recite the Lord's Prayer backwards as a symbolic rejection of old hang-ups, and Anton LaVey feels no scruple in encouraging the use of forms from the grimoires for psychic seduction and psychic attack. Of course, neither man considers the Devil to be a metaphysical entity in the style of *Rosemary's Baby*. Black magic is simply applied psychic science in the service of the libido. White magic, the spiritual alchemy of Dion Fortune and Israel Regardie, is seen as a gutless substitute for religion.

To the outsider the invocation of demonic forces, particularly through blood sacrifices, might seem indistinguishable from devil worship or diabolism in the classical sense, but this is a misreading of the entire tradition of ceremonial magic. This is true also of Voodoo. The gods of the underworld, the *petro loa* in Haitian usage, are not symbols of evil but rather expressions of forces as necessary to the totality of reality as the forces of life and growth. The one who would deal with them, however, must be prepared for merciless retribution should bargains not be kept, and the true Voodooist would never solicit them quite as casually as might the tourist who does not take their powers seriously.

Unfortunately this distinction between black magic and a genuine diabolism, while true enough for the classical occultist, may be more academic than real when we are talking about the free-lance sorcery that has appeared in recent years. In 1971, for instance, *Newsweek* carried the story of a New Jersey youth who had two friends bind him and throw him into a lake so that, by means of his violent death, he might be reincarnated as a captain in the legions of Satan. An investigation of the teenage subculture of the small city in which he lived turned up evidence that indicated perhaps a dozen youths were active Satanists and upwards of a hundred had attended the rites. Hamsters, fortunately, were the only blood sacrifices made to the powers of darkness, but the story is still a disturbing sign of how one or another individual can attempt to turn his occultist reading into gruesome reality.

In California, particularly in the area around Santa Cruz, there have been reports of small groups that have similarly experimented with diabolism, allegedly even to the point of murder and cannibalism. What is unknown is the motivation present in these situations. Given the atmosphere of unrestrained sex and drugs within which these groups would have developed, they may represent nothing more than a counterculture variant of the frivolous blasphemy of the Hell Fire Club of the eighteenth-century Sir Francis Dashwood. Or they might be something far more sinister, actual efforts to realize the world of *Rosemary's Baby*.

One problem in attempting to survey the exact status of Satanism is that a reputation for evil tends to become magnified in direct proportion to the distance of the reporter from that which he reports on. When there is also the psychological distance created by a contrary belief system, it is not too difficult to see the Devil incarnate in persons or activities that may be offensive but are otherwise relatively harmless. Many devout Protestants, for instance, read diabolism into the activities of the Catholic Church, and many devout Catholics see it present in the secret lodges that have sprung out of the Rosicrucian legend. Occultists themselves are hardly exempt from this tendency. Israel Regardie, for example, was able to damn hypnotism as "one of the most loathsome forms of Black Magic" and spiritualism as "an abomination against the entire trend of Nature's processes."

For the Christian the essence of diabolism is deliberate blasphemy. Anton LaVey comments on the therapeutic value of ceremonies such as the Black Mass for unlearning the Christian attitude of self-denial as well as for paying back centuries of Christian oppression, but the point is that one would have to be bothered enough by orthodox Christianity to feel such blasphemy worth the trouble. Western occultists, despite the fulminations of centuries of churchmen, have generally considered themselves faithful if heterodox Christians and, consequently, would have little need for such therapy or such retribution.

Occultists who profess themselves to have rediscovered the "Old Religion" have redefined the Devil as the Horned God, hardly a principle of evil, and thus would fail to see their own rites as in the least blasphemous. The same must be said of those who belong to the Church of the Process of the Final Judgment. In none of these cases, then, is there the slightest reason to act contrary to one's own conscience or to coerce others to do so.

Tanya and I have had some experience with individuals who do accept Satanism on a more serious basis. Our friend Pat finally married a man ten years her junior who combined a fascination with guns and attempts to draw on the darker forces of the occult. One of his first enterprises after their marriage was to dig out a cellar in their yard in which he might conduct his experiments somewhat closer to the powers of the underworld. We asked him about his interest in Satanism and were told that he thought of it solely as a type of countermagic, a protection for his psychic wife that might prove as effective in the spiritual world as his guns were in the physical.

Despite such contacts, my own conclusion is still that most of the scattered incidents so often cited have only a superficial relation to the world of the true occultist. Whether, for example, a psychotic murderer attributes his actions to God or to the Devil is a matter of individual pathology. I am, of course, disturbed by the ease with which the most obnoxious features of the old grimories and lingering descriptions of the Black Mass (which legendarily requires a nude virgin as the altar) presume to represent what the world of magic is all about. Individuals eager to experience a bit of magic for themselves may be quite tempted to try out recipes for calling up the

Devil—and they may get results beyond what they are prepared to handle. Nevertheless, such experiments no more
make anyone an occultist in any meaningful sense than a tour
of the Vatican makes someone a Catholic.

Even if a literal diabolism is far more the stuff of fiction
than it is fact, the question remains of how much of the
world of magic plays into the Devil's hands. Christian writers,
one recalls, have traditionally damned all the works of the
magician as involving at least an implicit pact with Satan.
Since the revival of widespread occultist interests with the
counterculture, fundamentalist writers have had a field day
citing scriptural references to the rule of the Anti-Christ.

More liberal theologians, especially those caught up with
the effort to "demythologize" Christianity, were far more inclined to dismiss the Devil as an outmoded allegory. Even a
Dominican priest, Richard Woods, was able to write a basically sympathetic account of the world of magic in *The Occult Revolution: A Christian Meditation.*

Then, on November 15, 1972, Pope Paul VI made international headlines with a rather remarkable public address that
was taken to reflect a certain concern with the significance of
revived occultist interests. The highest Catholic authority as-
serted bluntly that not only was Satan a malevolent spiritual
being whose existence could not be denied except by stepping
outside the pale of biblical and ecclesiastical teaching, but he
was on the rampage in the modern world. This was language
that American Christians were used to hearing from Billy Gra-
ham, but coming from the institution that had pioneered in
witch hunts it could be regarded somewhat ambivalently.

A blanket condemnation of occultism by the church is
hardly reasonable, even if it might seem a fair response to

the anti-clerical tirades of the occultists themselves. Certainly the magic presented by Rudolf Steiner or Israel Regardie, whatever the theological objections to an implicit Gnosticism, cannot be faulted as leading to moral corruption, and I would say the same about the coven witchcraft of people like Sybil Leek.

Even Voodoo, despite its totally unfair description by Dennis Wheatley as "one of the vilest, cruelest, and most debased forms of worship ever devised by man," should not be thought of as somehow intrinsically evil. Perhaps its characteristic blood sacrifices may be disturbing to Western sensibilities, but only a dedicated vegetarian should have the right to object to their appearance in connection with either religion or magic. As for the tales of the sacrifice of "hornless goats" (infants) or the culmination of rituals in forced group sex, we have to recognize again, when we are not just dealing with fiction, that the basis for such stories can be found in sects that have the same relationship to the mainstream of Voodoo as the Thugs do to the mainstream of Hinduism.

The one area in both witchcraft and in certain schools of ceremonial magic that does prove more troublesome in any moral evaluation of occultism is the emphasis on sex magic. There is a modest amount of this in the coven tradition reconstructed by Gerald Gardner, but it is hardly the group orgy an outsider might be led to expect. In the O.T.O. (the Order of the Temple of the Orient, a German equivalent of the Golden Dawn organized at the turn of the century) sex rituals played a far more important role. Once again a legend was created. This time it was the supposed sex magic of Sufism transmitted to the elite of the Knights Templar and by them handed down through various secret groups. The actual origin of these practices appears to be a fascination with the

Tantric practices of India, particularly with the so-called left-handed path.

Tantrism itself appeared in both Hinduism and Buddhism in the early centuries of the Christian era. It differed from the classical Yoga of writers such as Patanjali primarily in that it chose to work out the process of enlightenment through the use of the imagination rather than through its suppression. As developed by the monks of Tibet, Tantrism in its advanced stages was recognized as the potentially dangerous effort to rise above emotional responses through the visualization of disturbing situations—including imaginary participation in rape and murder. Indian Tantrism was more closely identified with the feeling for the sexuality of the cosmos, and intercourse, either real or imaginary, was seen as a reasonable approach to a mystical union with cosmic reality. In both traditions the room for misunderstanding was great. It was too easy, as in the case of the Thugs, to adopt an outlook that would make moral evil appear to be something holy.

In left-handed Tantrism, intercourse was real, not imaginary, and according to one explanation, the term "left-handed" originated from the fact that the female partner was positioned at the male's left during meditative exercises. But since this particular path might include other activities that were extremely offensive to more orthodox Hindus and Buddhists (the consumption of meat and alcohol, for instance), "left-handed" was also a strong expression of disapproval.

For the O.T.O., sex magic was institutionalized into an elaborate set of practices coded in the mysterious terminology of the alchemists. Aleister Crowley moved into the circle of the O.T.O. after his own break with the Golden Dawn; and through Crowley the sex magic of the O.T.O., which came to include homosexuality, became part of the underworld of twentieth-century occultism. The O.T.O., or a group that claims to be derived from the original German order, is also part of the California scene, and its activities have contributed to the somewhat seamy image the world of magic has gained in the state.

The object of sex magic is the achievement of an altered state of consciousness through sexual ecstasy. This is not the "high" of orgasm itself but the excitement that precedes it. The techniques of sex magic, which begin with an effort to depersonalize the partner in order to see him or her as an expression of one's own "daemon lover" (an equivalent of the Holy Guardian Angel), are directed to the suppression of climax in order to attain, through a protracted period of intercourse, the state of consciousness that exists when one is not quite awake but still not completely asleep.

So far so good. Were this the whole of sex magic it would hardly lead to a feeling that the Devil lurks in the corner of the bedroom. The trouble begins when the search for a magical partner is made to outweigh all normal considerations of fidelity or propriety. Since magic is made the highest possible good, the practitioner is to disdain any concern for the age, sex, or previous commitments of the partner. The same argument can also be used to sanctify the use of drugs or of sadomasochistic practices in the pursuit of sexual ecstasy.

At this point, of course, we have already crossed the boundary between a healthy sexual outlook and something pathological. Why, in the mind of the modestly fanatic practitioner, should rape be any less permissible than seduction, and why should murder be any less right than sadomasochistic torture? Push the logic of this and we are into the terrifying world of vampirism, as in the career of Gilles de Rais, the magic-oriented nobleman who went from being the bodyguard for

Joan of Arc to a reign of terror that, if the trial accounts are credible, in an eight year period caused the deaths of at least seven hundred children. Whether the Devil is ever deliberately invoked in this type of occultist thrill-seeking is by now completely irrelevant. Evil of such proportions is present that one would rather acknowledge a demonic origin than accept that man himself is capable of such horrors.

The reader should not take this to be a total repudiation of sexual activity as a legitimate pursuit of the kind of awareness that is one part of what is meant when we use the word "magic." Given consenting adults and the sense of restraint that does not reduce a person to an object, it *might* accomplish something of what the Tantrists and writers like Crowley have hoped for from it.

The point, as Hindu and Buddhist traditions have recognized in their basic hostility toward the left-handed path, is that sex magic is extraordinarily risky. By its nature it attracts the type of unstable personality who might do better to avoid the occult altogether. It is not easy to control the psychological forces it unleashes, and advising the novice occultist to get into it is rather like telling the child just learning to walk to try his luck on the flying trapeze.

Is there really a Devil, a malevolent spiritual being capable of affecting human events? Or is the Devil simply the other side of what we mean by God, a rhythm of death to balance out the rhythm of birth? These clearly are theological questions that do, I think, matter in the final judgment of what really happens when we move from white to black magic or from a right-handed path to a left-handed one. In my own mind I have no ready answer for them.

Still, perhaps I should provide the account Tanya has given

me of a rather strange dream she had at the time the question of her own religious commitment was pulsing in her unconscious.

"The dream began with my seeing myself seated with a very large pad of drawing paper that was very thick, a black charcoal pencil, and an artist eraser, and I seemed to be waiting. I heard a voice speak, although I didn't see anyone. It was the voice of a man, and from the way his voice sounded it seemed as if he must be very old. The voice requested that I draw him. Now although I couldn't see him, there was something about the voice that touched my senses more than just hearing. It made me aware on a different level of what this person must look like. And I knew what he looked like and I drew him.

"After I finished the drawing, he requested that I draw what was behind his eyes. Although ordinarily I wouldn't understand what he meant by this, I instinctively seemed to be able to go ahead with it. I turned the pages and began to make different drawings. One drawing was of an infant crying, another drawing was of a child in sort of an old-fashioned schoolroom looking very intent. Another drawing was of a man in an army uniform, and I also made a drawing of a woman.

"When I had finished this series of drawings, he said, 'Yes, that's my life, but what is behind my eyes?' I then began another drawing that was different from all the others and was different from anything that I would ever have expected from an ordinary sort of drawing. It was a cloud, and in the cloud there were faces of many people. And all the people, all the faces seemed to have distinct personalities. They were almost like caricatures, although they were still realistic drawings.

"Around the cloud there was smoke, and around that there was something I can't quite describe. It looked like waves of energy. At least this is what I felt I had drawn. The closest thing I can describe it as would be bolts of lightning. It made the whole drawing extremely intense, and it seemed to give it a kind of life that was different from anything I had ever seen.

"I was fascinated by what I had drawn and I continued to look at it. As I looked at it, although the drawing I had done was with a black pencil, the forms began to take on color. There was something very different about the color. Although the faces were the ordinary flesh tones and the color of the hair was blond or brown or black and everything else was its expected color, there seemed to be an undertone of color beneath the faces and everything else in the drawing that glowed through and was barely detectible but yet was very startling at the same time. For instance, there might be a lavender undertone to the skin of one person's face and a green undertone to the skin of another's, and it caused an almost luminescent quality. I can't remember ever seeing anything quite like it before.

"I was even more fascinated by this, and I continued to stare at it. After a period of time the drawing began to move in a circular motion and it picked up speed. It began to whirl until everything merged into a smoky, whirling mass, almost like a tornado on the page. At that point it began to fade and a gigantic number '1' appeared on the pad of paper. There was something very funny about it, and after looking at it for some time I realized that where the '1' was there was empty space— there was no paper behind it. Although the paper remained around the '1,' the '1' itself was hollow. From inside the '1' there came a hand, a very old hand, and it's the kind of hand I would have imagined to have belonged to the face I had drawn at the very beginning of the series of drawings.

"In this hand there was a small snake, about the size of an ordinary garden snake, and the snake could speak. It said sim-

ply that it had something to show me. A door appeared somewhere above the middle of its body and opened, and out of the
door there came a very tiny, very plain brown wooden box.
The snake did not have any hands; the box simply floated out
of the door, the door shut in the snake's body, and the box
levitated at the same point where it had come from. The door
opened on its own, and out stepped a little man that you
could barely see.

"I got very, very close to be able to see it clearly as a man at
all, and its voice was almost inaudible. Although it seemed to
be trying to shout to me, its sound was barely a whisper. He
said that he was God and the reason that I could never get behind the idea of God and that I could never believe in God
was because I had always thought of God as being very, very
large and I thought of it in the wrong way. Actually he was
the smallest thing there was, and he had made himself as
large as possible in order to be seen, but that he was really the
smallest thing in the universe. Then he told me that the greatest amount of energy lay in the things that were the smallest
rather than in the things that were the largest.

"He also said that his servant, the voice that I heard in the
beginning before I started the drawings, knew this better than
anyone. I asked him who the servant was, and he said, 'the
Devil.' And that's the end of the dream."

Tanya's dreams have always fascinated me because of their
striking imagery. Usually when the Devil has appeared in
them, it has been in the classic forms of medieval demonology.
Still, hanging in our living room there is a pen and ink sketch
of an old man whose dark eyes appear to be probing some
deep inner horizon. Tanya had drawn it while her conscious
attention was concentrated on the demands of our child on
the one hand and on an ongoing conversation with her mother

on the other. Later she found the sketch strangely disturbing until she realized that, to her, the old man was the image of death. In his eyes was all the knowledge of the world, the type of knowledge that Adam was to learn when he ate of the forbidden fruit.

This, Tanya told me, was also the face in the drawing in her dream—the face of Satan not as some horrendous fiend but as the proud and weary servant of the Lord who challenged man's desire to make sense of evil. An image hardly spectacular enough for either the diabolist or the witch hunter, but it is as reasonable as any that I have found.

14.

Doing Magic: Sorcery

A COUPLE OF YEARS ago Tanya and I paid our first visit to an occult shop quartered in Ports O'Call, a quaint shopping area located on the pier in San Pedro. There, along with vials of aromatic oils for each sign of the zodiac, decks of tarot cards, and crystal balls (made of resin), we also found jars of herbs, reproductions of the classical amulets, and little packets containing zoological oddments such as withered newts and dried bat's blood. There was anything a witch could want and a great deal more besides.

There are now a number of such shops in the Los Angeles area. Most are updated versions of the "religious goods stores" that for years have dealt in the oils, powders, and candles of an Americanized Voodoo. At least one that I know of stocks the tricks and novelties of parlor magic at the front and the "curios" of occultism in the back. But none, at least as far as I know, is a cover for the dark occultist conspiracies that are the stuff of fiction. Contrary to the themes of many stories, magic does not come packaged in cellophane. The would-be witch needs more than the right herbs, and the apprentice sorcerer is not any further advanced by purchasing all the amulets ever made.

Witchcraft and sorcery both require a certain innate potential which, if Colin Wilson's concept of a "dominant minority" is valid, is not that particularly rare. But even more than natural ability they call for a systematic training, an immersion into the atmosphere of faith that makes the idea of "a separate reality" more than a hypothesis. Books are not enough; even "tell-all" volumes such as Paul Huson's *Mastering Witchcraft* or Robert W. Pelton's *The Complete Book of Voodoo* can only scratch the surface, and they fail completely to develop the sense of discipline essential if the world of magic is to be anything more than a potentially dangerous pastime.

A young friend of ours did embark on this type of training several years ago when he was a student at a private college in Oregon. Through a sorcerer acquaintance he began with simple forms of divination, but, as he told me, his appetite was whetted for more elaborate ventures. He incautiously attempted hexes that quite literally backfired; he found his dormitory room scorched with tiny fires for which he had no natural explanation. He was disturbed both by this and by the fact that he was achieving close to a 90 per cent accuracy in his divination. Knowing the future, he found, could be somewhat uncomfortable. Finally, after four months of apprenticeship, he broke off his lessons.

Another friend became quite deeply and even more dangerously involved with the occult with at first just his own reading to guide him. Patrick had originally been a student of

mine whom I had encouraged to help with forming a chapter
of the S.D.S. on our campus. He did become one of the organizers for this particular radical group and then went on to
an activist career that brought him into close association with
student revolutionaries throughout California.

If Patrick was set on proving himself more of a rebel than
I was, my own developing interest in the occult inspired him
to surpass me in this also. With a fair measure of awe Tanya
and I followed his experiments in classical sorcery. Then, just
as Patrick had begun playing somewhat out of his league with
rebellion, he began moving into an occultist circle that it
would have been better for him to avoid.

This particular adventure began when a girl, the sister of
one of his close friends, came to be solicited by a coven that
was being organized in the San Diego area. Patrick, together
with his own witchy girl friend, visited the coven on the night
that it celebrated the spring equinox. His rather meager acquaintance with the old rituals permitted him, as he admits,
to bluff his way through a ceremony that was used to test ap-
plicants for the coven. Afterward, in conversation with its
members, Patrick encouraged several of them, including the
girl who was being trained to be the group's high priestess, to
break away from the almost hypnotic hold of the coven's organizer.

At the time Tanya and I had not known of his visit to the
coven nor of what had happened afterward. On the day following, however, I felt that Tanya was unusually tense. I had
an evening class, and while driving to it I attributed my own
feelings of almost suicidal depression to my concern for my
wife. The feelings did not let up until, part of the way through
the class, I realized that I must be under psychic attack. The
depression lifted the moment I engaged in an exercise to coun-

ter this attack. I phoned Tanya from the college during the coffee break and learned that her own tension had been a reflection of something that she felt was troubling me. A short while later the receptionist sent word that I had an emergency call from my wife. I again called home to find that the force I had repelled had manifested itself in our apartment. I broke off my class and rushed home to stage an impromptu exorcism.

Shortly before midnight I called Patrick to find out if he was somehow involved in what was happening to us. I learned that he and his girl friend had also come under psychic attack. It was probable, he thought, that our San Diego covenist was attempting a death spell on all four of us—on Pat and his girl friend for interfering in his work and on Tanya and myself as people from whom Patrick was drawing energy.

The early hours of the morning were hellish for Tanya and for Patrick's girl friend, the two "sensitives" among us. Tanya saw the face of a man bent on her destruction, and both of us had to struggle against an unseen wave of hatred that was threatening to engulf her. Patrick similarly was forced to draw on all his knowledge of ritual countermagic to keep his girl friend from being submerged by the same dark torrent.

The next day Patrick phoned the would-be high priestess, a girl whom I'll call Jane, in San Diego. She too was experiencing the same attacks and confirmed their source. Patrick learned also that the covenist, whom we had all tended to regard as limited in his knowledge, considered himself to be possessed by the soul of the dead jazz musician Jimi Hendrix. Jane insisted that even the color of the man's eyes was changing as his personality took on the characteristics of Hendrix himself.

The attacks continued but with diminishing force. Some weeks later Jane came up to Los Angeles and visited us. She was a charming, sensitive girl who was steeling herself for the confrontation in which she would have to make her final break with the coven. She and Tanya found themselves in an instant rapport, and we agreed to help out in any way we could. At the same time all of us advised Patrick to slow down on his sorcery. We did not particularly appreciate being made the targets in this type of magical warfare.

Patrick did continue his experiments, however. Finally we had a call from him shortly after his girl friend had found him sprawled half-conscious inside the magic circle he had inscribed in his bedroom. He had, as he explained, succeeded in conjuring a spirit who had shown him a scene of widespread devastation in Latin America within the next decade. Patrick had seen that this was the result of a brutal conflict to which he had contributed through his own earlier association with gun-running student revolutionaries.

Weighed down by the horror of this vision and by an overwhelming sense of guilt, Patrick at last agreed to suspend his conjurations. Like our friend who had been a sorcerer's apprentice in Oregon, he decided, somewhat to our relief, that the perils of magic were more than anything he was willing to cope with at this stage of his development. The last time that we talked with him, Patrick argued that his interest in magic remained, but he would express it only in his writing and perhaps by opening an occult shop of his own.

Can people really affect each other through such intangible means as spells? I had stopped being a doubter the Halloween weekend that a presence made itself felt in my home, and the experiences I had shared because of Patrick's interference in the San Diego coven only confirmed me in my belief that the invisible forces described by occultists were quite real.

In the Middle Ages it was simple enough to identify these forces as demons. Most modern magicians, following Paracelsus, talk instead of elementals, soulless beings that embody the powers of earth, air, fire, and water. These elementals appear also to correspond to the allies that Carlos Castaneda was taught to find within the plants of the Mexican desert.

But what are they? And how does someone control them?

For a start let's begin with something quite simple. One of the old superstitions by which one can determine the sex of an unborn child is to suspend the mother's wedding ring on a string above her stomach. If the ring begins to revolve clockwise, the child will be a son; if counterclockwise, a daughter. Tanya and I conducted this experiment early in her pregnancy; the ring revolved clockwise, and some months later our son Michael was born. At the time I thought it was curious that the ring revolved at all, but then I learned that a similar practice is used by the Japanese to determine the sex of unborn chicks. A bead is used in place of the gold ring, but the technique is the same.

The technical term for this peculiar behavior of a ring or a bead is radiaesthesia, the perception of radiation. Its most common practical application is in dowsing, the discovery of water or of minerals through the use of an extension of one's outstretched arms that can be as simple as a forked twig or a twisted coat hanger. It is known to work, but so far there is no adequate explanation of why it should. The possibility of ordinary electrical or magnetic activity has to be ruled out, and the reason that we talk about radiation at all is that this is the only model for physical interaction without direct mechanical contact that we have.

For the medieval intellectuals, who regarded Pliny as a standard for scientific reporting, it was easy enough to talk of the occult or hidden powers of nature. Albert the Great earned his own undeserved reputation as a sorcerer because of his curiosity about the mysterious properties of stones and plants and beasts. Writers such as Cornelius Agrippa attempted to systematize this knowledge by linking it together with the traditional lore of angels and stars in order to create the modern tradition of ceremonial magic, but even in his time the man-centered pride of the Renaissance was breeding a quite different outlook that would make the occult a synonym for superstition.

By the turn of the eighteenth century experimental science had developed sufficiently to create a new myth of secular progress to replace both Christian eschatology and the alchemists' visions of spiritual transformation. Two hundred years later there were new mysteries. Light, that curious manifestation of energy that could act as either a wave or a particle depending on one's experiments, refused to behave according to the predictions of scientists who thought it should appear to be traveling either faster or slower depending on whether the observer was moving toward its source or away from it. The speed of light turned out to be a constant, according to Einstein the only constant in a strange new universe in which space and time were relative. And then there was the effect of the element radium on the sealed photographic plates of the husband and wife team of the Curies.

Radium, its very name a symbol for a brand new physics, became the substance that permitted science to discover that the alchemists were right on one crucial point: elements could be transmuted. Moreover, the dogma about the conservation of mass and the conservation of energy no longer held. As Einstein, who tied together the loose ends of light and radioactivity into a single mathematical knot, was to express it, a standard amount of energy was equivalent to its corresponding amount of mass multiplied by a number that was the same as the speed of light used twice: $E = MC^2$.

Isaac Newton himself had welcomed the failure of his own theory to account for all the observations of astronomy. It meant that there was still evidence of the necessity of a God to keep the clockwork going. Einstein, the man whose physics displaced the Newtonian machine, could still talk of God, but he had no room for a discussion of cosmic irregularity. "I cannot believe," he remarked once, "that God plays dice with the universe." That same mood has driven scientists to expand their knowledge of the order of the universe, but it has also acted to inhibit any talk of phenomena that, like light and radioactivity in the days before Einstein, refuse to fit prevailing physical models.

Dowsing clearly does not fit, nor do other even more peculiar phenomena. Nevertheless, the existence of telepathy and psychokinesis has been sufficiently well established—particularly through the extensive statistical testing developed by J. B. Rhine at Duke University—for these paranormal activities to be recognized as legitimate subjects for scientific research (in 1969 the Parapsychology Association was finally accepted as an affiliate of the American Association for the Advancement of Science). Some Soviet scientists have attempted to relate these phenomena to the electromagnetic spectrum by seeing them as effects of long-length radio waves for which the human body acts as a natural transmitter and receiver, but almost the only justification for this hypothesis is the fact that the "radiation" from a talented subject appears to follow the physical law of exponential decay. Again, we know that things happen, but we have no solid theory about how.

The rediscovery of acupuncture by Western medicine is another case in point. Physiologists now feel more certain that it functions as a successful anesthetic because it creates neurological blocks at the gateways for pain impulses to the brain, but the other properties attributed to acupuncture still remain unexplained. The Soviet discovery that the hundreds of anatomical points recognized by Chinese acupuncturists correspond to "flare points" in Kirlian photographs of the human body has only deepened the mystery.

Soviet science now postulates the existence within any living organism of a plasmic or energy body that is a counterpart to the strictly physical body. This plasmic body, which corresponds quite closely to Rudolf Steiner's occultist descriptions of an "etheric body," can survive the loss of parts of the physical body (as in striking photographs of torn or perforated leaves), and the intensity of the radiation captured in the Kirlian photographs turns out to be a reliable indicator of the organism's general health. Still more remarkable, Kirlian photographs of the hands of so-called faith healers show an unusually strong radiation that diminishes after the laying on of hands that forms part of the ritual for this form of paranormal medicine.

What would be quite useful would be for all these phenomena to be manifested under conditions sufficiently similar for a few easy generalizations. Unfortunately this doesn't happen. Telepathy (mind reading) and psychokinesis (the movement of objects by the mind alone) are correlated with different types of brain waves—alpha for telepathy and theta for psychokinesis. Faith healing, which is also coming in for more serious scientific consideration, appears to be an equally specialized ability that draws on a still distinct form of energy.

One of the problems for researchers is that there is no sharp line between strictly physical phenomena and whatever can be meant when we speak of altered states of consciousness. A laboratory connected with Maimonides Medical Center in New York has established that telepathic communication improves when the intended receiver is asleep. In Kansas the Menninger Institute has been at work documenting the control of the autonomic nervous system—and thus of the more "occult" capabilities of the human body—by individuals skilled in achieving a state of yogic trance.

Hypnotism, still a source of debate among psychologists in that there are no measurable physiological cues by which to discriminate between the trance and the waking states, has also been shown to affect the performance of telepathic receivers. Subjects have, for example, been able to respond to telepathic commands to enter and come out of trance, even when they are shielded against any normal means of electronic communication. The rapport between the hypnotist and his subject, like the rapport between two individuals linked by strong emotional ties, appears to be enough to establish a means of communication that otherwise defies scientific explanation.

Paranormal events, altered states of consciousness, emotional rapport creating some type of psychic link—how far can all of this be taken in order to develop a science of the psyche? The obvious difficulty for empirical research in these gray areas is that the presumed emotional barrier between the observer and his subject must be breached if significant results are to be obtained. For some types of research, as in the consideration of the out-of-the-body experience (what occultists refer to as astral projection), the observer *is* the subject, a procedure that plays havoc with the traditional canons of scientific method.

Normally the purpose of any experiment is to confirm the

educated guesswork by which the scientist bets that, given the right conditions, he will be able to make something happen on cue. Any competent observer should be able to duplicate the experiment with the same results. When we are dealing with the paranormal, however, things do not usually happen on cue.

Why should these phenomena occur at all? In an older age they were clearly the stuff of witchcraft, an indication of demonic intervention. For the nineteenth-century intellectuals who remembered Paracelsus, magnetism went a long way toward explaining all these mysteries. Updated in Reichenbach's concept of odylic force, this was a curious anticipation of more recent attempts to explain the paranormal in terms of vibrating force fields.

The most elaborately developed theory is that of the neurologist Andrija Puharich that postulates what he terms a psi-plasma field whose waves travel at speeds *greater* than the speed of light. Within man there is a "nuclear psi entity," a "mobile center of consciousness," which is responsive to the vibrations of this field. These vibrations provide the communication between minds that occurs in telepathy. Presuming an interaction between material fields and plasma fields, this theory would also account for the apparent "memory" of objects involved in psychometry. It might also account for precognition on the basis that the plasma field would create the changes in the material environment that it would seem to be recording in advance.

The link between physiology and the phenomena of parapsychology is provided, according to Puharich, by "cholinergia," an activation of the parasympathetic nervous system created by the presence of the chemical acetylcholine, and "adrenergia," the activation of the sympathetic nervous system through the release of adrenaline. The cholinergic person is the telepathic receiver, the adrenergic is the sender. The use of drugs such as one or another variant of hallucinogenic mushrooms in shamanist rituals is explained as a tribal recognition of the means to achieve this cholinergic state.

Arthur Koestler, in *The Roots of Coincidence*, prefers a different theory. Noting the concept of "seriality" of biologist Paul Kammerer as well as Carl Jung's "synchronicity," Koestler argues for a law of integration in the universe that balances the law of entropy, the principle that energy tends to become more diffused rather than more concentrated. He then cites the concept, proposed by English mathematician Adrian Dobbs, of a second time dimension in which "objective probabilities" correspond to the causality of our normal physics.

The vehicles for information regarding these objective probabilities would be "psitrons," particles with (mathematically) imaginary mass traveling faster than light and operating directly on the brain. Psychics, then, would be individuals who were especially well endowed as natural receivers for these "vibrations." This theory is only somewhat less "occult" from a commonsense viewpoint than the concept of positrons as particles moving backwards in time that was proposed by Nobel Prize winner Richard Feynman.

None of these theories is ultimately satisfying. But what they do suggest is that scientists are at least taking the world of the occult seriously. It may be that out of their research we will come to understand better the reality of this elusive thing we know as consciousness.

Already there have been tantalizing clues indicating that we humans may be far less unique in our sense of personality than we thought. In the mid-1960s John Lilly, a physician who was to go on to engage in a remarkable set of voyages into the "inner space" of his own consciousness, believed that he had established that dolphins were a species as intelligent as man. At about the same time polygraph expert Clevel Baxter discovered, quite accidentally, that his plants displayed a telepathic consciousness that permitted them to react both to unexpressed volitions on his part and to the entirely automated destruction of organisms in their vicinity.

Neither discovery would particularly surprise the followers of Indian philosophy. For Hinduism every living thing possesses a soul and all souls are ultimately equivalent, even if they are at different stages of evolution. But to a Westerner, trained to think of man as unique in his universe, they are startling—and disturbing.

As yet there is no established theory that links all these observations together. Any talk of new energy fields—much less of a type of consciousness, an intelligence and a will—that could exist apart from the physical body or be manifested not in a single individual but in a group is still entirely speculative. Nevertheless, in the work of Lilly and Baxter as well as in the study of the alphabet soup of what have come to be called psi phenomena—ESP, PK (psychokinesis), RSPK (repeated spontaneous psychokinesis, otherwise known as a poltergeist), OOBE (the out-of-the-body experience)—there is some confirmation of the lore of the occultist. The universe increasingly appears to be a living whole in which all events are somehow interdependent and somehow accessible through the symbolic connections that make up the varied traditions of magic.

We are, it would seem, caught in interlacing webs of vibrations that affect us more profoundly than we would ever have thought possible. The sun, the moon, and the planets all bombard us with radiation, and the known responsiveness of earth's organisms to these varied waves of energy begins to give astrology a new respectability. The discovery that man in turn is able to affect his environment by his mind alone, as in psychokinesis, also makes the world of the sorcerer much more than a superstition.

And this, of course, leads us back to our original question of the objective reality of the forces solicited by sorcerers as different in their backgrounds as Aleister Crowley and Castaneda's don Juan. The occultist answer is that these forces, despite the cultural variations in the manner in which they are conceptualized, do pre-exist man, perhaps as beings whose evolution is not as complete as his, perhaps as beings more evolved, perhaps both. The answer of an emerging parapsychology is that they are vibrations set up by the mind itself, perhaps in the manner of a plasmic videotape capable of being played many times over.

My own sympathies are entirely with this second account, providing it be kept in mind that we are dealing with a most peculiar videotape—one that seems to be open to renewed audience participation. The "plasmic vibrations," if that is what they are, that we know as ghosts or as demons or as elementals are not just sequences of intrinsically static images following a predetermined course until the show is over. They definitely appear to interact with human consciousness, particularly when it is functioning in a mode distinct from a normal waking awareness. They might provide information, or execute a request, or even frighten a person to death. The knowledge of how to deal with them effectively, not just as blind forces but as somehow personal, is what witchcraft, sorcery, or magic is all about.

It is with good reason that this knowledge is considered something secret. There is an objective reality to the strictures against an indiscriminate presentation of the lore of magic. In part it is the question of scrambling the vibrations and so weakening their effectiveness, but it is also the recognition that the effort to become receptive to these vibrations makes the apprentice sorcerer overly vulnerable to forces that he does not as yet know how to control.

Magic, I would insist, is one sphere of human reality that has no room for the dilettante. Some individuals are born with striking natural capabilities, which means they will be immersed in magic whether they consciously will it or not. Tanya is one, our friends Pat and Kathy are others. When I advised Greg, my student who had come to recognize his own hostility as having been a factor in several deaths and injuries, that he too was a genetic witch with an obligation to channel his powers constructively, I was not at all giving way to a sensationalist "witch hunting" of my own. I was simply spelling out what I hope will soon be recognized as a basic principle in the counseling of those caught up in parapsychological experiences.

Patrick, my intellectual radical turned sorcerer, is in a somewhat different category. His capabilities, I feel, are quite real, but because of their latency there was no necessity for him to attempt to control them. I feel that I am in this same category, and were it not for the fact that in a sense I live with magic because of Tanya, I would quite readily let my own interest in magic remain purely academic.

And then there are the individuals who for one or another reason crave psychic experience and are somewhat reckless in soliciting it. The lady who once attempted to lure away our poltergeist is a perfect example. Another is the young student of mine who asked if he might set up an interview with Tanya in order to learn more about witchcraft. Curious, I asked him why he felt it so important to meet a real live witch since there is already so much available about witchcraft in print—far more, really, than Tanya would ever have to say for herself.

His reply surprised me. He said that he was earnestly seeking enlightenment and he desperately needed to meet with someone who held the key to it.

But Tanya makes no claims to being a mystic. She has no shortcut to enlightenment, no more than does anyone who happens to have been born with some ability out of the ordinary.

My young friend was confusing power and what, as a born Catholic, I would call grace. The wisdom of so-called primitive societies lies in their recognition that all power, but especially the power of magic, must be integrated into a moral context. Despite its lack of historical validity, the coven tradition's assimilation of the "Old Religion" is beneficial insofar as it does permit the apprentice witch to find just such a context. Anyone else who chooses to enter the world of magic—or, like Tanya, is already born within it—must find this for himself.

Through his search the magician may, like Castaneda's don Juan, also cross whatever shadowy line separates magic from mysticism, but the skilled sorcerer is not by the fact of his skill alone any closer to whatever can be meant by enlightenment than is the trained scientist or the accomplished artist. It is just that, perhaps like the scientist and the artist, it is far more important that he be looking.

It perhaps goes without saying that I tried to steer my young friend away from witchcraft, suggesting that he try meditation instead.

The lack of any moral context for sorcery, apart from a crude hedonism, has been one of the points troubling me in many contemporary discussions of magic. To talk of a morally neutral magic strikes me as being rather like speaking of a morally neutral medicine. It is possible but it is also terribly disturbing.

Permit me yet another story, this an incident from his child-hood recounted by a Hawaiian friend of mine. His grand-mother was a *kahuna* or witch who continued the old practices that Christian missionaries had attempted to destroy, but his parents were devout Catholics who lamented the paganism that remained in their own family. One day on the way home from school he and some young friends were helping them-selves to the mangos that grew in the yard of another old woman who, like his grandmother, was known as a *kahuna*. The irate witch tried to halt their depredations, but the boys laughingly ignored her. My friend never forgot the ominous look he was given as he ran off.

That evening the boy became violently ill and for a week re-mained unable to hold down food. Doctors called in by his parents were unable either to diagnose what was wrong with him or to improve his condition. His grandmother meanwhile pleaded with his parents to permit her to engage in the sorcery that she insisted was necessary if the boy was to live.

At last, in desperation over his weakened state, they re-lented, and my friend recalls the manner in which his grand-mother performed one of her ancient rituals over his body. He was told that he would be well enough to go to school in a few days, and on the way back he was to be sure to catch sight of the mango tree from which he had stolen the fruit. He did re-cover, and on the way home from school he looked up at the tree. All the fruit upon it was inexplicably rotted.

A baleful witchcraft—and the magic that alone could reverse it. How does this contest of sorceries fit into any moral per-spective? It would at first seem to be a clear example of the moral neutrality of magic argued by writers like Anton LaVey.

I would interpret it differently. The witch who hexed my friend had been wronged, and the boy's sickness was hardly a gratuitous exhibition of her power. It was, however, a retaliation out of proportion to the offense, and this itself required appropriate countermagic. The boy was healed, but the mango tree was blighted as well in order to create a kind of psychic balance within the situation.

Both *kahunas* might have been said to be engaging in "black" magic, in that a type of destruction was intended through their sorceries. Nevertheless, there was a crucial difference in the manner in which power was used. In the one case it was out of personal pique and in the other out of a need to protect a loved one and to punish an excess. The boy's grandmother had no reason to fear that she was provoking a witchly vendetta. The vindictive neighbor had been appropriately warned, and further malice would only invite a more fearful reply.

In all the traditions with which I am familiar there is a similar emphasis on the limits to be observed by the magician. Induction, unlike the quick course in ceremonial magic available through some local occult shops, is very gradual and is accompanied by the lessons in restraint needed if magic is not to be an almost suicidal adventure. Moreover, there is a clear repudiation by the community of sorcerers of the one who would violate a more or less explicit code of ethics.

In Haiti, for example, there is a great contempt for the Voodooist who would "work with both hands" (engage in malicious sorcery) and a strong suspicion of the person who too eagerly solicits the *petro loa*, the more malevolent spirits within the Voodoo pantheon. The way of the black magician, either the one who seeks assistance from the more baleful powers of the world or the one who uses magic in a way to harm others for his selfish advantage, is always dangerous.

Sorcery, in sort, is most definitely not for the dabbler. The results can be disturbing if not disastrous, as the cautionary tales of occult literature point out. There are, of course, objections to a casual sorcery of any kind. The most obvious is the possibility of inducing quite undesirable hallucinatory experiences—"bad trips." Also, just as the techniques of astral projection and Kundalini Yoga, or even ordinary hypnosis for that matter, can upset the normal sense of balance by which we regulate our conscious lives, the intense concentration required by ceremonial magic may easily provoke powerful psychological reactions.

Magic, I feel, is just not an area in which we should "let it all hang out." Approached respectfully, it can be something extraordinarily beautiful, a glimpse into unsuspected dimensions of human potential. Treated less seriously, it can be a shortcut to madness—or worse.

15.

This Way Madness?

IN THE COURSE of preparing this book I asked our friend Kathy to review for me her story of the haunted dormitory in which she had lived while in Munich. A few days later I received a phone call, which I thought was from her, in which Tanya and I were invited to meet her for coffee at a restaurant near her house. We waited for nearly an hour, then went on to Kathy's home only to learn from her parents that she was out somewhere else. Tanya and I left rather puzzled. At times we had received inexplicable phone calls that we were tempted to attribute to some type of poltergeist activity, and it seemed that our message from Kathy might fall into this same mysterious category.

Back in our apartment we seemed to have a visitor. Both of us felt the prickling sensation that we had grown used to in the presence of spirits. Using first a Ouija board and then automatic writing we learned that our guest was a girl named Katha, the ghost that had walked the halls in Munich. She was the oldest of three sisters, Polish Jews, who had been slated for Dachau. To save herself, Katha had in some manner betrayed the others. They had died and been reborn, one as Tanya and the other as Kathy. Katha had died as well, but for her there was no rest and no rebirth.

What did she want? She had first begun to spell out the Polish word for "advice," then she had called for exorcism. Finally she stated that she wanted Tanya to rejoin her in death. At last, when Tanya acknowledged that she had forgiven her for this offense in a past life, Katha left us.

The evening was not yet over for Tanya. She had told me before of a recurrent dream in which she had seen herself as a prisoner at Dachau, and now I attempted to regress her through hypnosis back to what Katha had said was her previous lifetime. The memories came back, and Tanya collapsed in horror. She had, it seemed, died while serving as a human guinea pig for Nazi experiments.

The next day I learned that we had kept another friend of ours waiting at a different restaurant. It was one of those strange coincidences that always seem to be something more than just coincidence. But there was still more. Kathy herself was now experiencing the sensation of an unseen presence. Tanya's mother also confirmed that from the time her daughter was quite small she had somehow associated her with the tragic history of her people in the days of the Third Reich.

At present I am hardly willing to rule out reincarnation as a hypothesis, but I would not submit this story as any kind of proof. The thought of Dachau was clearly locked in Tanya's unconscious, perhaps on early suggestions from her mother, and her "memory" under hypnosis as well as the story told by Katha through automatic writing both fit into the category of unusual but not necessarily paranormal phenomena.

But at the same time we may very well have been contacted by a troubled spirit, and the type of simple exorcism we performed through Tanya accepting and forgiving its actions in a past life may have proven effective. At least this is the manner I have chosen to treat sequences of events which, while they may have routine psychological explanations, may also be part of the curious interaction between this world and some other. I am willing to act on a possibility of the spiritual without attempting to prove either that what is there is only natural or that it must be supernatural.

This attitude of a suspension of both belief and doubt is the best that I can do when dealing with the occult. Were I immersed in the atmosphere of faith of the complete skeptic (forgive the paradox), I would be testing and retesting occult manifestations with all the open-mindedness of a hanging judge. Yet were I fully an occultist, I fear that I might too readily fail to recognize the limits of the world of magic. I might attempt to make it either into a religion or into a religiously oriented "science."

Hypnotic regression to past lives is a standard technique for many occultist investigators. The classic case in recent years was the investigation of a lady named Virginia Burns Tighe, who under hypnosis began speaking in a brogue and identified herself as Bridey Murphy, born in Ireland just before the beginning of the nineteenth century. *The Search for Bridey Murphy* by Morey Bernstein appeared in 1956 and was a best seller. Despite the claim of the *Chicago American* to have discovered the means by which Mrs. Tighe could have known the details of life in Ireland a century before her birth, it remains one of the more challenging indications that the occultists may have something going for them after all.

Yet what is it that happens when a person is functioning in

an altered state of consciousness, whether that state is produced through hypnosis, meditation, drugs, or some other means? One way of answering this is by saying that in some manner the soul ("the mobile center of consciousness") is simply in another place—or in another space, to use a phrase now popular. A rather different answer, coming from the work of Carl Jung, is that the mind is experiencing the rush of images out of an "objective psyche."

For Jung, it is as though nothing uncovered by man as a symbolic expression of the truths of his being is ever really lost. A child might dream in images that reflect details from some ancient mythology to which the child could not have had access by any normal means. In fact, it was an incident of just this kind that led Jung to formulate his unique theory of archetypes.

Despite the drawbacks I feel are in Jung's approach (its failure to recognize the rationality of the "primitive" mind and its emphasis on the psychological rather than on the cosmic interests of most mythic systems), it has the advantage of being able to account for some of the odd features in the stories told by travelers into "inner space." Descriptions of the out-of-the-body experience or astral projection typically include an exposure to a world that replicates that of ordinary reality and yet differs substantially from it. For example, Robert A. Monroe, a businessman whose work with Charles Tart has provided much of the impetus for the new field of transpersonal psychology, found a world in which there were automobiles but no internal combustion engines, buses but no fares, a modern society but no electricity. In this strange universe it is as though he had stepped through Alice's looking glass to find everything the same yet also oddly reversed.

Jungian theory might be used to explain why this should be

so. Collective human experience creates differing pictures of the way things are, yet this "objective psyche," like the world of dreams, allows for odd permutations of familiar elements. It is not, then, solely a world of one's own imagination. To use an occultist phrase, it represents the construction of a "Group Mind" into which anyone attuned to the group may enter. If, as many sociologists now insist, our ordinary reality is not simply the world "out there" but instead is the world as we have learned to interpret it, why should not the same laws of consciousness apply to any "separate reality"?

I have already suggested that the examples of the afterlife presented from Swedenborg to Arthur Ford may very well represent "objective" experiences and yet at the same time be no more than products of a strictly human consciousness functioning in a non-ordinary manner. They too would be cases of a "Group Mind" at work. So also would be all the descriptions of Atlantis to be found in Helena Blavatsky, Rudolf Steiner, and Edgar Cayce. They are real and unreal at the same time, imaginary and yet not just subjective. The contemporary Western occultist, exposed to the "vibrations" initiated by modern magicians, perhaps has no choice but to discover a "separate reality" of the type described by his immediate predecessors.

For Mrs. Tighe as well as for Tanya, the vibrations would include the simulation of past lives according to scripts that would have only a limited basis in each woman's personal experience. Both Bridey Murphy and the tragic Katha would then be no more than projections, yet they would not be entirely fictitious. In a very real sense they would have lives of their own, even if the details of these lives would be as inaccessible to the ordinary biographer as Atlantis is inaccessible to the ordinary archeologist.

Immersion within an alternate tradition would create a quite distinct set of occult experiences. For someone entering the world of the Yaqui sorcerer there would be the encounters with the allies described by Carlos Castaneda. For the initiate into the Buddhist tradition represented by *The Tibetan Book of the Dead* there would be the visions of the limbo state that occurs between incarnations.

The idea of such cultural pluralism might seem bothersome, to say the least, for most dedicated occultists. The occultist counterpoint functions largely to provide an escape from history, and yet on this basis history appears as a crucial determinant of the "separate reality" in which the occultist finds himself. The world of magic, rather than being an embarrassment to the secular historian, becomes a clue to the deepest thoughts of a people.

In order to understand this better, we might consider the rich traditions of Amerindian magic, especially as represented in the careers of two extraordinary shamans, the Juan Matus described by Carlos Castaneda and Black Elk, an Oglala Sioux who in his youth had taken part in the conflicts that ended in the destruction of Indian hopes at Wounded Knee.

Castaneda's *The Teachings of Don Juan* is a fascinating book that quickly became a classic for the counterculture after its appearance in 1968. As a piece of anthropological research it marks a significant effort to apply the phenomenologically oriented techniques of ethnomethodology pioneered by UCLA sociologist Harold Garfinkel. As a description of an Indian way of life maintained despite (or because of?) the repression of white society it corrects the picture we tend to have of the medicine man as a tribal fraud taking advantage of savage credulity. As a personal document it is a moving piece of autobiography, particularly since the eager but frightened student does not hesitate to show the ways in which he must have proved a great disappointment to his Yaqui guru.

As Castaneda points out in *The Teachings of Don Juan* and its two sequels, his Indian master will use the Spanish *brujo* to describe himself and his companions in magic, but he prefers to think of himself as "a man of knowledge." His emphasis is on "seeing," a manner of vision that permits the sorcerer to perceive directly the qualities of a man as what others might term a psychic energy system. The outcome of such vision is not to be a continued rapture but an intensity of living in keeping with what don Juan calls "a controlled folly," a sense of the ultimate insignificance of any human purpose that combines with a relentless determination to act purposefully regardless.

Other aspects of don Juan's intricate cosmology parallel themes we have already taken up in earlier chapters. The role of the allies, the forces associated with substances such as jimson weed and a variety of hallucinogenic mushrooms (the stuff of the "little smoke" utilized by don Juan), is similar to that of the elementals solicited by the Victorian magicians in the rituals of the Golden Dawn. Mescalito, the personified power associated with peyote, functions much like the mysterious Guardian indicated by other occultists as the source of a pervading personal wisdom.

Other bits of sorcery, such as the use of lizards for divination, similarly correspond to techniques appearing elsewhere, but there is more emphasis on the use of hallucinogenic materials in reaching the altered states of consciousness in which either clairvoyance or a kind of astral projection would become possible. Of special interest, perhaps, is the same idea of shape-shifting or the transmutation of forms (as in flying like a crow) that played such a large role in the witch lore of the Middle Ages.

Particularly relevant is the manner in which don Juan deals with the moral significance of magic. Throughout his teachings there is the idea that the transition from an ordinary perspective to the solicitation of the hidden forces of the world creates a vulnerability that can easily result in death—from sheer terror if nothing else. The true sorcerer must be the warrior who closes the gaps within himself by following "a path with a heart," a manner of life that brings spiritual peace. Castaneda's difficulty, as don Juan saw it, was that he insisted on reducing the mysteries with which he was confronted to a type of intellectual puzzle. Once a man had embarked on a career of sorcery, his failure to achieve a more intuitive harmony with the world in all its dimensions could only be a source of disaster.

We know of Black Elk, don Juan's spiritual cousin, through the immensely moving *Black Elk Speaks*, the narrative recorded by John G. Neihardt. As a boy Black Elk had become gravely ill and fallen into a coma. During this period he experienced a vision of "the Six Grandfathers," the presiding spirits of the world, and through them he came to believe that he was to play a major role in the salvation of his people from the depredations of the greedy Wasichus (white men). Later, in a ritual patterned after the content of his vision, he began his career as a powerful medicine man.

Following the submission of the Sioux after Custer's defeat at the Little Big Horn, Black Elk permitted himself to be caught up in the messianic craze of the Ghost Dance religion that had swept eastward from Nevada. The white man's alarm at the sight of bands of Indians dancing in expectation of a new era of freedom and plenty precipitated the final conflict at Wounded Knee. Afterward Black Elk, like the rest of his people, lived meagerly as a dependent of the government with only memories of his visions to sustain him.

The cosmology of Black Elk, while less complex than that which Castaneda records for don Juan, is nonetheless impressive. Again there is an emphasis on the fraternity of man with nature, in particular with the animals that were the basis of an Indian economy. Also there is the acceptance of an inter-penetration of spirit and human worlds, although Black Elk's categories do not include the purely demonic presences that caused Castaneda some of his worst moments.

It might be possible, of course, to write off Black Elk's childhood visions as simple hallucinations brought on by the illness that nearly claimed his life. For the person unwilling to abandon a strictly linear conception of reality, anything dealing with the world of magic must be interpreted this way. The difficulty is that such a facile analysis fails to recognize the qualitative differences between the type of vision that marks the man acceptable as a true psychic and the delusions of the psychotic. In the case of Black Elk, which parallels the rules of very many shamanist societies, what mattered was his very reluctance to acknowledge his vision and the overpowering dread that compelled him at last to discuss it with the medicine man called in by his anxious parents.

From the time that his tribe participated in the Horse Dance that re-created his vision, Black Elk would be a respected shaman, but the point is that his vision—and his own powers—would be seen as a literal gift of the spirit world, not as a device for self-gratification or even a pious fraud coinciding with a group need to believe in miracles. Ultimately, of course, the hopes expressed in the Horse Dance were defeated. Black Elk himself, who later felt that by his acceptance of the visions he experienced through participation in the Ghost Dance he had somehow compromised his first great vision, lacked don Juan's more individualistic conception of magic. Consequently, he regarded himself as a spiritual failure.

Black Elk's recounting of his vision to Neihardt, a Wasichu scholar, was meant in some manner to perpetuate the deeper truths of how man was meant to live together with nature even if the specific promise of Indian freedom had not been fulfilled. The popularity, particularly among college students, of *Black Elk Speaks* is an indication that it is not just some drug-oriented version of the shamanist tradition which appeals to a new generation.

Too often, of course, this appreciation of the Indian experience tends to be superficial, and efforts to assimilate to an Indian life style (as in the experiments of students affiliating with the so-called Sun Bear Tribe in Northern California) underestimate the degree of asceticism required to live peacefully with the earth. But what is understood, even if dimly, is that the world of Black Elk, like that of don Juan, above all involves levels of psychic experience that Western society generally has come to write off as either fraudulent or indicative of mental disorder.

It is this same concern with varied psychological states that has led some apprentice sorcerers whom I have known to explore the Kahuna magic of Hawaii, and at the California State University at Sonoma (also the site of much of the work of the Sun Bear Tribe) there have been efforts to develop a communal life style applying the principles of the Malayan dream analysis described in research included in Charles Tart's *Altered States of Consciousness.*

In both cases, as in the interest in don Juan and Black Elk, there is an acknowledgment that magic involves a particular development of the world of the mind—and, conversely, that any experience of the world of the mind beyond the commonplace perspectives of a workaday existence leads to the para-

278 : *Living with Magic*

normal events familiar to the sorcerer. Moreover, there is a badly needed recognition that the reality of the world of magic involves a harmony between man and man and between man and nature.

The popular image of the witch is of someone at least a little bit crazy. In European folklore, the source of our fairy-tale conceptions, the witch is a woman, old and ugly, who prefers darkness and the moon to the light of day. She can know someone's thoughts as well as his future, and she possesses powers, either to cure or to harm, that are beyond those of ordinary men.

From our enlightened modern perspective we no longer think of those who were the first victims of the witch hunts as having been evil, but we do tend to think of them as demented. They had no supernatural powers except within their own imaginations and in the minds of the simple folk who consulted them in good times and burned them in bad.

A reconsideration of the history of medieval witchcraft suggests that we are not entitled to this convenient a dismissal of the world of magic. The witches may not have been the priestesses that they were made out to be by Margaret Murray, but they were the heirs of practices that reached back to a time before Europe had learned to think in the sober lines of a Latin syllogism. Yet even more than this, they were people who were psychologically different, able because of their differences to accomplish seeming miracles.

With our present understanding of paranormal phenomena we no longer have a reason to attribute precognition or psychic healing to a pact with the Devil—or even to some peculiar rustic sanctity. We know that there are types of energy that some individuals appear able to control, even if not always at will. The physics behind these types of energy still remains a mystery, but curiously we seem to be in a somewhat better position when we discuss the physiology of the individuals who operate with them.

Recent research has indicated that the traditional associations of magic with femininity and darkness have a basis in the anatomy of the brain itself. As Robert E. Ornstein has pointed out in his recent summary of the relevant research into the psychology of consciousness, apparently unique to man is a lateral specialization in which, for most persons, each hemisphere of the brain is responsible for distinct psychological functions.

The left hemisphere, controlling the right half of the body, permits the type of linear functioning associated with analytic thought of any kind. The right hemisphere, controlling the left half of the body, appears to dictate the sense of spatial relationships and with it the capacity for aesthetic expression. In a manner we possess not just one type of consciousness but two. Our right-handed self reads, writes, calculates. Our left-handed self grasps the world more holistically. With it we are poets, artisans—and, I think, witches. Almost instinctively we regard our right-handed self as masculine, our left-handed self as feminine. (With about 5 per cent of the population these left and right relationships are reversed.)

Our modern world encourages only one mode of consciousness. Within our culture to be rational is to be scientific. Intuition, precisely because it is not amenable to logical programming, comes to be identified with the irrational. Dreams, feelings, the wisdom of the body—all three are set apart in an odd cultural limbo. When they intrude into the world of light and reason as the sources of paranormal phenomena we find ourselves fearing for our sanity.

This opposition of two modes of awareness has been proposed by many writers in many different manners. In China it is the distinction between the way of Yang and the way of Yin (with Taoism stressing the Yin, or the dark and the feminine). In ancient Persia the contest was between light and darkness, between the spirit and the flesh. For Nietzsche, using Greek myths as his source, there is the contrast between the Apollonian and the Dionysian. For Robert Graves and Colin Wilson it is the difference between solar and lunar knowledge.

In any society that has failed to achieve or to maintain a full integration of all its parts, it is almost to be expected, I think, that the dominant group within the society will express a right-handed sense of order while those who cannot feel they belong to the same universe as their masters will opt for the chaos, creative or destructive, of a left-handed vision. Earth-centered cults will be opposed to a dominant cosmic religion, women will be priests, old taboos will fall and new ones appear. In such a situation the magus and the bureaucrat will cease to be allies, the shaman will be an outlaw, the seer will be reduced to the level of a prostitute.

This is the setting for what have been called "the religions of the oppressed." Intellectualized by a disenchanted elite, the same mood expressed by cults can appear in "heresies" such as Catharism, Rosicrucianism, and the costumed occultism of esoteric groups such as the Golden Dawn and the reconstructed covens of Gerald Gardner.

From a sociologist's perspective it appears that an opposition to established values will often, as in the counterculture that appeared in the United States in the mid-1960s, find a somewhat natural expression in the modes of a left-handed consciousness—and this obviously includes a feeling for magic. The fact that in the days of the French Revolution those who favored change preferred to sit on the left side of the Assembly and those who wished a restoration of established values opted for the right (the origin of our continuing metaphors of a political left and right) is, I think, more than just a coincidence.

There was in this civil millennialism, which at first seems so opposed to all that can be called occult, the same demand for ecstasy—for release from physical bonds—that marks the religious millennialism of the dancers at Wounded Knee. Whether the occult as such plays any great part in the movements that appear will depend on other factors, but we can see here an extension of the argument of Mary Douglas that the language of the human body provides natural symbols for our vision of society.

A feeling for magic is only part of the totality of a left-handed consciousness. Another is the type of perception involved in the arts. One thing that I have noted repeatedly since I first began my own excursion into the world of magic is the manner in which the one type of sensitivity tends to shade over into the other. Tanya, for instance, was a trained dancer and actress when I met her, and at present she is a promising painter. Most genetic witches will, I have found, show similar talents and interests. And by the same token I have noted a tendency for artists to be drawn to the occult. One of Tanya's art instructors, for instance, quietly acknowledged that she too had been involved in witchcraft, and artist friends of ours have shown remarkable proclivities for paranormal experiences.

Rebels, artists, psychics—all are deviants by the norms of a linear (or right-handed) consciousness. Depending on the social climate, such deviance may be defined as criminal—or as a mark of insanity. The dreamer already walks a thin line between what is real and what is solely imaginary; it is not surprising, then, that a prejudgment of mental imbalance will often come to be a self-fulfilling prophecy. (Was this, I wonder, what happened to Gilles de Rais? Did the tragic end of the remarkable woman for whom he had served as a bodyguard lead him to believe that the world of the visionary was madness after all? And did he then proceed to act in a thoroughly insane manner as a perverted tribute to the martyred Joan of Arc?) "Think me mad and I'll prove you right."

Given the cultural barriers against a free development of the aesthetic and the intuitive, it is also understandable that the esoteric techniques utilized to break down an all too linear outlook might themselves precipitate a violent reaction. One thinks of the drastic procedures made use of by don Juan to balance out Castaneda's tendency to accept as real only that which he could verbalize; the sorcerer, as Castaneda came to appreciate, at the least risked his sanity and at the most his life. One thinks too of the cautions given by Tibetan monks advancing along the path of Tantric practices.

Yet even without the difficulties created by a more or less linear culture, the evolutionary direction of the human mind appears to move toward a suppression of left-handed consciousness. As research on sleep indicates, all of us must dream in order to remain sane. But it is also known that the more analytic a person, the less likely he will be to recall the content of his dreams. It seems as though an increased capacity to function in terms of linear symbols cancels out the type of attention required for this other type of awareness to manifest itself.

There are, however, paradoxes in what we know of how the brain functions. The more verbal a person, the more pronounced the particular type of electrical activity termed the alpha rhythm (eight to twelve cycles a second). But we also know that in the quite non-verbal process of meditation the alpha rhythm (associated as well with the capacity for telepathic reception) tends to increase in amplitude and duration. Curious.

More curious still is the fact known from research done with Zen monks that the theta rhythm (four to seven cycles a second) tends to appear in the later stages of meditation. Theta waves originate in the area of the thalamus and normally are associated with emotional excitability. (These are the brain waves associated with individuals capable of telepathic transmission. They appear also in the production of psychokinesis, and it is theorized that this "mind over matter" may represent the effect of bottling up rage—permitting it, perhaps, to fly off by means of plasmic vibrations.) Why is it that experienced monks should exhibit the same brain waves as temperamental children or frustrated adults?

One answer may be that not only do the two hemispheres of the brain make it seem as though we have two minds—one the rational self and the other some dark counterpart that we acknowledge only with reluctance—but the distinction between the cortex and parts of the brain older in evolution adds still another duality of consciousness.

This is a point raised by Andrew Weil in *The Natural Mind*. For Weil, a physician who has come to reject conventional medical theory, disease comes from "unnatural restraints placed on the unconscious mind"—from the blockage, in other words, of the limbic area of the brain (the region of the thalamus), which appears to be the seat of memory and of emotion, of the desire for food and for sex, and of pleasure and pain. To take Weil's discussion a step further, it might well be the case that the reason for the theta rhythm appearing in the EEG's of meditating Zen monks is that the full relaxation of the conscious mind (signaled by alpha waves) permits the unconscious mind to act without interference. Rather than being an electrical indicator of frustration, it could be a sign of total harmony.

The predominance of the alpha rhythm in meditation may also be an expression of harmony. Although normally only a sign that a subject is relaxed, in the case of the monk or the yogi it may mark a type of superconsciousness. Through biofeedback (the use of machinery that converts brain waves into light or into audible sound in order for a subject to monitor his own internal rhythms) it is possible to increase the output of alpha waves, but the individuals who engage in this fail to report any particular progress toward what the Asian mystic understands as enlightenment. The verbal person—one who thinks more in words than in pictures—also shuts down internal imagery, but the alpha rhythm that appears in his EEG would have an entirely different significance than it would in the case of the monk.

Research into brain waves and their correlation with distinct modes of consciousness is still in its infancy, but it is here, I think, that the study of paranormal phenomena will make its greatest breakthroughs. Already, as we have seen, there are a number of intriguing discoveries that as yet do not fit together. When we know more we may be on our way to identifying the true physical underpinnings of the world of the magus and the shaman. We may then also be in a position to distinguish more adequately between psychiatric disturbances and phenomena that are of a different order altogether. Until that time we are left with the problem of interpreting the accounts of those who claim in some manner to deal with a spiritual world beyond the ken of the ordinary man.

A few years back the newspapers carried the story of a man who had been confined for most of his adult life in a state mental institution. He had been diagnosed as mad, and the gibberish that he continually poured out in protest to the psychiatrists was regarded as a sign that his madness was incurable. Finally someone came to the institution who recognized the "gibberish" as one of the lesser-known languages of Eastern Europe. Lost in this country after the death of the relative who had brought him here, the bewildered man had attempted to explain himself in the only language he knew. No one thought to ask whether his failure to use English was attributable to anything but a mental disorder, and since he could not communicate in English there was no way to treat his disorder. He had been ignored, prevented then from learning English because no one tried to teach him.

The genetic witch may often experience something quite similar. According to one study, as many as three out of four small children may be capable of some type of paranormal activity. One consequence is that, by whatever laws govern the manifestation of this capability, the child reports personal encounters either in a half-sleep or while awake that the adult must dismiss as imaginary. They didn't, couldn't happen. And most children learn to turn off an activity that may already prove frightening to themselves and will certainly bring punishment from adults. Some for one reason or another (their own physiology? their environment?) sustain it into their adult lives even at the risk of being judged insane. They learn simply not to talk about it.

Tanya was a child like this, yet she was fortunate in that through her mother and grandmother her accounts of prophetic dreams and astral projection were accepted as evidence not of madness but of a psychic inheritance. Later, of course, she did break down, but even in her schizophrenia I wonder how much was madness and how much a frightening excursion into another dimension. (R. D. Laing is one psychiatrist who argues that what has been called schizophrenia may in fact be a psychic journey that has been mislabeled and mishandled. Rather than attempting to medicate the symptoms of schizophrenia, Laing has permitted his patients to complete their voyages within an entirely supportive atmosphere.)

Castaneda, in an interview for *Harper's*, has described the psychology of the sorcerer in language that is strongly reminiscent of Tanya's description of her own state while undergoing her breakdown. "Ordinary people," he remarks, "appear to you as phantoms." The sorcerer in some manner ceases to be a human being. As in Castaneda's tale of don Gennaro, there is no return to Ixtlan, no going home again.

Tanya was never permitted to complete her own internal voyage. Perhaps it would have been endless, perhaps it would have brought her to some remarkable new plateau that would have made her not less sane but far more so. Fortunately, her exposure to the spiritual reinforcement provided by Steiner's system of education did not allow her to continue her magical journey even if in a diminished manner. At some time in the future she may yet be able to follow it to its end.

Hans Holzer, himself a participant-observer in many of the rites he describes in *The New Pagans*, comments that most of the individuals who have consulted him for referrals to one or another coven or esoteric fraternity are psychologically quite stable. My own experience is that witches are individuals who must undergo exceptional stress, most of it from the need to reconcile distinct dimensions of their experience. Tanya, Kathy, and Greg have all received psychiatric attention; most of the other witches I have known would, I feel, benefit from it. Not that they are crazy. They do, however, live in a world of contradictions, the effect of which can only be intensified by the further contradictions they find within themselves.

It is for this reason that I am quite reluctant to encourage the pursuit of magic without proper guidance. I remain unconvinced that the various esoteric groups in existence generally are competent to provide the spiritual guidance required if magic is not to become either a travesty of the ancient mystery religions or a potentially hazardous psychological adventuring.

I have a quite different feeling about the study of magic. To understand it is, I believe, to understand somewhat better the potential man holds within himself for expanding the horizons of his existence.

16.

Living With Magic

WE'VE COME TO THE END of a detective story. The time has come for us to see the meaning of the clues presented. What is the reality of the world of magic—and what does this say for the people I know who so readily accept this world for their own?

When I met Tanya, I thought of magic as a rather peculiar belief in the impossible, and yet before we were married I came to accept the reality of psychic forces despite my inability to define them. Finally, with a strong debt to the thought of William James and Carl Jung, I advanced a theory of my own that interpreted magic as the result of the projections of human imagination and will. The born witch was a person with a more developed capacity for achieving these projections.

I still find this theory attractive but hardly compelling. There are three other interpretations of the world of magic that I could put in its place. The first is that the forces dealt with by the witch or the sorcerer are definitely supernatural, and they are to be understood in terms of one or another theology (or theosophy). The second is that magic is solely a matter of the effects studied by parapsychology and therefore a question of as yet unknown physical laws. The third is that, while there are phenomena at present beyond scientific explanation, magic itself is nothing but poetry, a romantic effort to achieve a sense of transcendence through identification with ancient symbols. Let's consider what might be said for each approach in turn.

Through these pages I have used the word "supernatural," as I have the word "spiritual," much more loosely than would the theologian. This has been in keeping with conventional English usage and is hardly meant to prejudge the theological questions raised by any discussion of ghosts, astral projection, spirit intervention, and the like.

The contemporary return of magic is most definitely a religious phenomenon, but that hardly makes magic itself a religion. As Mary Douglas, the anthropologist whose discussions I have found so valuable in formulating my own ideas, points out, religious millennialism and the use of magic for private advantage are paired phenomena. What I have called the occultist counterpoint seems to thrive most strongly in the same social situation that permits the appearance of messianic or revivalist movements. As manners of relating to the mystery of existence beyond the strictly visible, magic and religion definitely interact in any such period, but I would insist on maintaining the distinction between these two spheres of human action.

One of the problems in reconciling magic and religion at present is that occultists are in the habit of proposing themselves as rivals to the institutional church. Churchmen in their turn have an unfortunate tendency to see all occultists as either open or covert devotees of the Devil. Conspiracy theories, especially when they are raised to cosmic dimensions, are fascinating, but the trouble is that they are almost always the result of imagination rather than honest reporting. There are true diabolists, but they represent an extreme that is odious to most other occultists. To judge all occultists by the few who might take *Rosemary's Baby* seriously makes no more sense than to judge all churches by the extremism to be found in sects such as the snake handlers of the Tennessee hills.

Exactly what one makes of the religious significance of the occult is rather obviously a question of his openness to the supernatural. The proponents of witchcraft as a distinct religion (Alex Sanders, for instance) are quite impatient with an other-worldly vision, and the "Old Religion" is touted as a more than adequate replacement. Yet others, such as Philip Bonewits, feel no need to discuss magic in these terms. This is also the outlook I have found with Tanya (who is Jewish but with a strong exposure to Catholicism in her upbringing) and with most of the other witches I have known. For them witchcraft and religion are quite distinct, even if for most outsiders both appear to be nothing more than arbitrary beliefs serving the same purpose.

Could the devout believer also be a witch? Given the classical theological interpretation of the occult as intrinsically diabolical, there would be certain problems of conscience involved in any practice of cult witchcraft. Yet to the extent that the type of person I've called the genetic witch may have been born into a strong religious tradition, there will still be a certain internal demand to find a spiritual home somewhere within the world of magic.

In an age of ecumenical awareness that has permitted dialogues between Christians and Marxists as well as a new Christian openness to Asian spirituality, is it too much to ask that the theologian and the occultist attempt a similar dialogue for themselves? It may still seem an outrageous proposal, but such a dialogue is centuries overdue.

Is magic just another name for parapsychology? The difficulty with this lab-coat approach to magic is that it tends to rob it of its personal and cultural significance. Perhaps a quite important distinction ought to be made here. There are phenomena often labeled occult—dowsing or water-witching, for example—which have little to do with the state of mind of the one effecting them. Yet there are others for which a highly personal sensitivity seems to be of the essence, as would be the case with any technique of divination. The first type is not any more magical than flipping a light switch, yet the second, precisely because it involves culturally developed symbolic connections, will always be something lying just outside the ken of laboratory science. Parapsychology has generally shied away from a study of techniques such as the tarot and the I Ching, and the result has been that to the layman magic too easily comes to be just a matter of ESP. The witch knows better, although he may not himself be in a position to explain how he works with such techniques without seeming to engage in the pathetic fallacy of attributing human feelings to non-human objects.

Aleister Crowley, the P. T. Barnum of occultism, presented magic as involving the operations of imagination and will, and in his quite serious discussion he emphasized the discipline required in order for these operations to be effective. This is the tone to be found in the Rosicrucian-inspired Hermetic Order of the Golden Dawn. Even with all their penchant for antiquarian charades, the adepts of the Golden Dawn did, I feel, grasp the nature of magic as something quite distinct from science just as it is also distinct from religion, and the serious student of magic would do well to look at their work.

No, magic is more than parapsychology just as art is more than aesthetics. It too is something creative, and while it may and should be studied scientifically, its value is that, like art, it is an expression of human imagination.

Is magic anything more than art? Fantasy is, of course, at the heart of the witch's outlook, but it is fantasy of a quite special kind. In spell-casting, for instance, a fantasy is meant to create an actual effect. To the extent that there are just such effects and their production is somehow dependent on the witch's unique capabilities, magic is quite definitely something that goes beyond art itself.

Again, just as magic is something more than science, I will stress my conviction that it is far more than a special kind of poetry. Nevertheless, all the values to be found within the world of art are, I feel, also present within the world of magic.

To the man who prizes his rationality, the meaning of something is established when he has determined the functional dependence of one part of a whole upon every other part. The great difficulty with this mode of understanding is that it does not permit the mind to grasp the meaning of something as a whole that is *more* than the sum of its parts; consequently, it often prevents the comprehension of the whole for just what it is. But there are other modes of knowledge—or of consciousness. The experience of the self as a robust ego is such a mode, for example, as is the experience in which this ego is transcended and a deeper "self" is found.

What is the best mode for dealing with the "booming,

buzzing confusion" of what we call the world? Rational analysis treats it as a problem, but then the self, the observer, is set in a frustrating opposition to it. Mysticism simply transcends all distinctions in order to grasp a unity that, in effect, makes the world go away, but then the self can be lost as well. But there is also the mode of consciousness, shared by artists and by magicians, by which the self becomes a play-er; the world is a mystery play, rich in symbols that themselves take on life in a sacramental dance.

This has been the means, as Johan Huizinga argued a generation back in his *Homo Ludens*, by which primitive man has acknowledged the mystery of his existence. Man plays, therefore he exists. Through his play he peoples the world with friends and with enemies and, curiously, the primitive one comes to know the world with an adequacy that continues to amaze his cousins who look at the world only with the cold light of scientific logic. In particular, it is through his sorcery, which is no more than a special type of play, that he achieves a mode of knowledge that permits both psychic satisfaction and physical accomplishment.

The tribal shaman, however, does not see the altered state of consciousness achieved through his play as an end in itself. This is precisely what has led the thoroughgoing mystic to reject the magician even when the latter's sorcery is intended for the benefit of mankind rather than for its harm. Patanjali, the great master of the school of Yoga, quite correctly noted the occurrence of paranormal capabilities in connection with the pursuit of *samadhi*, and he just as correctly, given the goal of Yoga as liberation from whatever is the world of nature, cautioned against them. Magic, as has been noted by anthropologists in the effort to distinguish it from religion, is instrumental in its character; it is not just a matter of utilizing symbols for the sake of contemplation but of seeing them as a source of power.

The dislocation of power of any kind from a moral context has been one of the characteristics of any advanced culture. Differentiation in society tends to involve a loss of the sense of interdependence, and the mystic comes to appear as the adversary of all that is purely utilitarian precisely because power has become such a threat. Magic, always a matter of power, is made out to be religion's unholy rival because it does tempt man to look back to the world even as the mystic is trying to draw his vision away from it. And, given the divorce of power and vision in an increasingly secular culture, it is perhaps true enough that sorcery becomes a psychic technology available to the highest bidder, a prostitution of the spirit completely counter to the demands of any honest religion.

Nevertheless, sorcery can also be a source, albeit a risky one, of a secular redemption. Magic, because it calls for a new play of both imagination and will, creates openings in the description of the familiar. To use don Juan's phrase, it permits a man to "stop the world"—to free himself from the routines that hold him to a single vision of his own possibilities. This itself makes a man something of an outlaw, one who has shaken himself free of the definitions by which he knows his role in society. And, to paraphrase Tolstoy, the man who would stay an outlaw must learn to be honest, to be moral in the best sense of the word.

The successful magician, in other words, must accept responsibility for all his acts even though the entire thrust of civilized society is in the direction of surrendering this responsibility to "the system." The sorcerer who would not be destroyed by the forces with which he works is compelled to complete the process of integration he began by his first choice of a magical perspective.

But if the magician must at length learn some of the lessons of the mystic, why not, in the manner of writers from Patanjali to Colin Wilson, regard sorcery as a dangerous bypath? My point is that the mystic begins by withdrawing from the world and, consequently, tends to dismiss its problems as beneath his consideration. The magician, who must see the world more acutely in order to utilize its powers, does risk becoming mired in a completely selfish outlook, but he also holds the possibility of bringing not only himself but anyone with whom he comes in contact to an entirely new vision of the way things can be.

At the risk of tremendously oversimplifying the issue, it might be said that the mystic dispels the illusion of power and so finds peace, while the magician dispels the illusion of impotence and so provokes change. The mystic who seeks change must be something of a magician, just as the magician who seeks peace must be something of a mystic. An era, like our own, that has lost its sense of mystery most definitely needs the mystic, but it is my feeling that it needs the magician even more.

Of course, the forces conjured by a shaman like don Juan—his various allies and, above all, the mysterious Mescalito—are solely imaginary, are they not? It may be possible to explain all the phenomena encountered by Carlos Castaneda in terms of some type of ESP (hypnotic projection, perhaps?), but the point is that the effectiveness of don Juan's magic is bound up with the acceptance of symbols such as Mescalito. These are the symbols he plays with (albeit most respectfully) and which, in turn, play with him in order to allow a remarkable mastery of his world. And on that basis they are real.

It is on the same basis that we can say that the *loa* that ride Voodoo worshipers are real. And, to push the logic of this, God and the Devil are real as well—not for the reasons familiar to a theologian but because they are objects of belief through which the world of the believer, and possibly the world of the nonbeliever who comes into contact with him, is made different.

What is, for purposes of argument, one is willing to accept the idea that magic works? There is still the question of whether or not this makes a primitive mode of response to the world any better (whatever that can mean!) than the mode of consciousness developed by the men of the Renaissance who fathered modern science. The scientist at least does not create fantasies in which beings from other dimensions can come as enemies as well as friends. He knows no demons; in fact, his world is entirely amoral. All that remains to be demonic is science itself.

Again, that is just the point. The world of magic is intensely personal—a projection of human personality, perhaps, but personal nonetheless.

We know that fantasy is intensely functional within human consciousness (presumably we dream—and daydream—for a reason), but at present we live in a culture that restricts fantasy either to the elitist world of the artist or to the realm of escapist entertainment or, in a diminishing degree, to the sphere of the religious. It is not just that we pragmatically eliminate the personal, including considerations of feeling of whatever type, from the sphere of science and then look elsewhere for its release. The difficulty is that by a certain law of convergence a methodology that prizes psychic neutrality carries over from science to everything else. We do not feel in science, we do not feel in life. The imagination and will are stifled, and human potential is diminished as a result. We become truly "one-dimensional."

It is not that science is an inappropriate way to view the

world, or even that science might not succeed in reducing the phenomena we now label paranormal to more manageable categories within physics, physiology, or psychology. My argument is, quite simply, that we need the whole as well as the parts. We require humility—and reverence. It is not necessary, and probably not desirable, that we ourselves become magicians, but we must reorient ourselves to the realities of the world of magic as a most earnest form of play. We must learn to stand again at the frontiers of fantasy and walk once more in visions.

Just how is this to be done? In all honesty I do not know. Through these pages I have been quite critical of the grand schemes of those moderns who have already entered the world of magic, and a too facile reconstruction of the past may not be the answer. Similarly, the differences in cultural complexity might make the paths of Black Elk and don Juan rather inappropriate.

I do disagree with mythologist Joseph Campbell's idea that strictly private myths can supply the outlook accomplished through the collective myths of the past. Magical communities, despite their historical tendency to become islands of the past holding out against the waves of the present, still remain a necessity. But, because I am neither a magician nor an organizer, I have no suggestion for the strategies by which new communities can be established beyond the fictitious setting I proposed at the end of *The Return of Magic*.

A first step, however, is the recognition of the role that fantasy plays in the life of both the individual and the community, and a second is a reappraisal of the significance of past efforts to achieve entry into the world of magic. The work of both psychiatrists and parapsychologists is, I think, particularly important in defining the types of phenomena that can occur through purely natural causes. At some point there must also be the type of analysis proper to the theologian, particularly when it is a question of the religious significance that can be attached to occultist propositions. And at all stages the philosopher, the expert in the analysis of complex ideational structures, has a role to play in explaining the manner in which new ideas are developed to serve as frameworks for the interpretation of various types of experience.

This last has been the manner in which I have understood my own job. Various bits of my life, in particular my original training as a Jesuit and my marriage to a lovely young woman who called herself a witch, brought me to take seriously phenomena that intellectuals are generally supposed to dismiss as beneath consideration. My exposure to the world of magic has not always been reassuring, but I have found it, to say the least, fantastically absorbing. My hope is that at the close of these discussions something of my own interest proves contagious.

A Selected
Bibliography

THE PURPOSE of this bibliography is twofold: to acknowledge some of my own intellectual debts and to provide a guide for further reading. In the interest of brevity I have, with a few exceptions, omitted works by or about older occultists in order to concentrate on more contemporary discussions.

A. *General Discussions*

Cavendish, Richard. *The Black Arts*. New York: G. P. Putnam's Sons, 1967.
Farren, David. *The Return of Magic*. New York: Harper & Row, 1972.
Freedland, Nat. *The Occult Explosion*. New York: G. P. Putnam's Sons, 1972.
Godwin, John. *Occult America*. Garden City, N.Y.: Doubleday, 1972.
MacNeice, Louis. *Astrology*. Garden City, N.Y.: Doubleday, 1964.
Parker, Derek and Julia. *The Compleat Astrologer*. New York: Mc-Graw-Hill, 1971.
Wheatley, Dennis. *The Devil and All His Works*. New York: American Heritage Press, 1971.

Wilson, Colin. *The Occult: A History*. New York: Random House, 1971.

Woods, Richard. *The Occult Revolution: A Christian Meditation*. New York: Herder and Herder, 1971.

B. *The Occultist Legends*

Allen, Paul M., ed. *A Christian Rosenkreutz Anthology*. Blauvelt, N.Y.: Rudolf Steiner Publications, 1968.

Bonewits, Philip E. I. *Real Magic*. New York: Coward, McCann & Geoghegan, 1971.

Buckland, Raymond. *Witchcraft from the Inside*. St. Paul, Minn.: Llewellyn Publications, 1971.

Burckhardt, Titus. *Alchemy: Science of the Cosmos, Science of the Soul*. Baltimore: Penguin Books, 1971.

Culling, Louis T. *A Manual of Sex Magick*. St. Paul, Minn.: Llewellyn Publications, 1971.

Däniken, Erich von. *Chariots of the Gods?* New York: G. P. Putnam's Sons, 1970.

Farrar, Stewart. *What Witches Do: The Modern Coven Revealed*. New York: Coward, McCann & Geoghegan, 1971.

Gardner, Gerald B. *Witchcraft Today*. New York: The Citadel Press, 1970.

Graves, Robert. *The White Goddess: A Historical Grammar of Poetic Myth*. New York: Farrar, Straus & Giroux, 1966.

Haining, Peter, *The Anatomy of Witchcraft*. New York: Taplinger, 1972.

Holzer, Hans. *The Truth About Witchcraft*. Garden City, N.Y.: Doubleday, 1969.

―――. *The New Pagans*. Garden City, N.Y.: Doubleday, 1972.

Huebner, Louise. *Power Through Witchcraft*. Los Angeles: Nash Publishing, 1969.

Huson, Paul. *Mastering Witchcraft: A Practical Guide for Witches, Warlocks, and Covens*. New York: G. P. Putnam's Sons, 1970.

Idries Shah, Sayyid. *The Sufis*. Garden City, N.Y.: Doubleday, 1964.

Johns, June. *King of the Witches: The World of Alex Sanders*. New York: Coward, McCann, 1969.

Lady Sheba. *The Book of Shadows*. St. Paul, Minn.: Llewellyn Publications, 1971.

LaVey, Anton Szandor. *The Satanic Bible*. New York: Avon Books, 1970.

———. *The Compleat Witch: Or What to Do When Virtue Fails*. New York: Dodd, Mead, 1970.

———. *The Satanic Rituals*. New York: Avon Books, 1972.

Leek, Sybil. *Diary of a Witch*. Englewood Cliffs, N.J.: Prentice-Hall, 1968.

———. *The Complete Art of Witchcraft*. New York: World, 1971.

Lethbridge, Thomas C. *Witches*. New York: The Citadel Press, 1968.

Montgomery, Ruth. *A World Beyond*. New York: Coward, McCann & Geoghegan, 1972.

Murray, Margaret Alice. *The Witch-Cult in Western Europe*. Oxford: The Clarendon Press, 1962.

———. *The God of the Witches*. London: Oxford University Press, 1970.

Pelton, Robert W. *The Complete Book of Vodoo*. New York: G. P. Putnam's Sons, 1972.

Regardie, Israel. *The Tree of Life: A Study in Magic*. New York: Samuel Weiser, 1971.

Sadoul, Jacques. *Alchemists and Gold*. New York: G. P. Putnam's Sons, 1972.

Spence, Lewis. *An Encyclopedia of Occultism*. New Hyde Park, N.Y.: University Books, 1960.

Steiner, Rudolf. *Theosophy: An Introduction to the Supersensible Knowledge of the World and the Destination of Man*. New York: Anthroposophic Press, 1971.

———. *Occult Science: An Outline*. London: Rudolf Steiner Press, 1969.

Summers, Montagu. *The History of Witchcraft and Demonology*. New York: The Citadel Press, 1970.

Valiente, Doreen. *An ABC of Witchcraft Past and Present*. New York: St. Martin's Press, 1973.

c. *Historical Background*

Brown, Slater, *The Heyday of Spiritualism.* New York: Hawthorn Books, 1970.

Butler, E. M. *Ritual Magic.* Newcastle Publishing Company, 1971.

Eliade, Mircea. *The Forge and the Crucible: The Origins and Structures of Alchemy.* New York: Harper Torchbooks, 1971.

Hansen, Chadwick. *Witchcraft at Salem.* New York: George Braziller, 1969.

Holmyard, E. J. *Alchemy.* Baltimore: Penguin Books, 1957.

Huxley, Aldous. *The Devils of Loudun.* New York: Harper Colophon Books, 1965.

Jonas, Hans. *The Gnostic Religion: The Message of the Alien God and the Beginnings of Christianity,* 2nd ed. Boston: Beacon Press, 1963.

King, Francis. *The Rites of Modern Occult Magic.* New York: The Macmillan Company, 1971.

———. *Sexuality, Magic and Perversion.* Secaucus, N.J.: The Citadel Press, 1972.

Lewis, I. M. *Ecstatic Religion: An Anthropological Study of Spirit Possession and Shamanism.* Baltimore: Penguin Books, 1971.

Macfarlane, Alan. *Witchcraft in Tudor and Stuart England: A Regional and Comparative Study.* New York: Harper Torchbooks, 1970.

Métraux, Alfred. *Voodoo in Haiti.* New York: Schocken Books, 1972.

Midelfort, H. C. Erik. *Witch Hunting in Southwestern Germany, 1562–1684: The Social and Intellectual Foundations.* Stanford: Stanford University Press, 1972.

Robbins, Rossell Hope. *The Encyclopedia of Witchcraft and Demonology.* New York: Crown, 1959.

Ronay, Gabriel. *The Truth About Dracula.* New York: Stein and Day, 1972.

Ross, Anne. *Pagan Celtic Britain: Studies in Iconography and Tradition.* New York: Columbia University Press, 1967.

Russell, Jeffrey Burton. *Witchcraft in the Middle Ages.* Ithaca: Cornell University Press, 1972.

Shumaker, Wayne. *The Occult Sciences in the Renaissance: A Study in Intellectual Patterns.* Berkeley: University of California Press, 1972.

Somerlott, Robert. *"Here, Mr. Splitfoot": An Informal Exploration into Modern Occultism.* New York: The Viking Press, 1971.

Thomas, Keith. *Religion and the Decline of Magic.* New York: Charles Scribner's Sons, 1971.

Thorndike, Lynn. *A History of Magic and Experimental Science*, 8 volumes. New York: Columbia University Press, 1923–1958.

Trevor-Roper, H. R. *The European Witch-Craze of the Sixteenth and Seventeenth Centuries and Other Essays.* New York: Harper Torchbooks, 1969.

D. *Normal and Paranormal Experience*

Berger, Peter L., and Thomas Luckmann. *The Social Construction of Reality.* Garden City, N.Y.: Doubleday, 1966.

Castaneda, Carlos. *The Teachings of Don Juan: A Yaqui Way of Knowledge.* Berkeley: University of California Press, 1968.

———. *A Separate Reality: Further Conversations with Don Juan.* New York: Simon and Schuster, 1971.

———. *Journey to Ixtlan: The Lessons of Don Juan.* New York: Simon and Schuster, 1972.

Douglas, Mary. *Natural Symbols: Explorations in Cosmology.* New York: Pantheon Books, 1970.

Eliade, Mircea. *Patterns in Comparative Religion.* New York: Meridian Books, 1963.

Jung, Carl G., ed. *Man and His Symbols.* Garden City, N.Y.: Doubleday, 1964.

———. *Mysterium Coniunctionis: An Inquiry into the Separation and Synthesis of Psychic Opposites in Alchemy*, 2nd ed. Princeton: Princeton University Press, 1970.

Koestler, Arthur. *The Roots of Coincidence.* New York: Random House, 1972.

Laing, R. D. *The Politics of Experience.* New York: Pantheon Books, 1967.

Leonard, George B. *The Transformation: A Guide to the Inevitable Changes in Humankind*. New York: Delacorte Press, 1972.

Lilly, John C. *The Center of the Cyclone: An Autobiography of Inner Space*. New York: The Julian Press, 1972.

Monroe, Robert A. *Journeys Out of the Body*. Garden City, N.Y.: Doubleday, 1971.

Neihardt, John G. *Black Elk Speaks: Being the Life Story of a Holy Man of the Oglala Sioux*. Lincoln: University of Nebraska Press, 1961.

Ornstein, Robert E. *The Psychology of Consciousness*. New York: The Viking Press, 1972.

Ostrander, Sheila, and Lynn Schroeder. *Psychic Discoveries Behind the Iron Curtain*. Englewood Cliffs, N.J.: Prentice-Hall, 1970.

Puharich, Andrija. *Beyond Telepathy*. Garden City, N.Y.: Doubleday, 1962.

Roll, William G. *The Poltergeist*. Garden City, N.Y.: Doubleday, 1972.

Roszak, Theodore. *Where the Wasteland Ends: Politics and Transcendence in Industrial Society*. Garden City, N.Y.: Doubleday, 1972.

Tart, Charles T., ed. *Altered States of Consciousness: A Book of Readings*. New York: John Wiley & Sons, 1969.

Watson, Lyall. *Supernature*. Garden City, N.Y.: Doubleday Anchor, 1973.

Weil, Andrew. *The Natural Mind: A New Way of Looking at Drugs and the Higher Consciousness*. Boston: Houghton Mifflin, 1973.

Index

9210B